AS THE CROW FLIES:
My Bushman Experience with 31 Battalion

AS THE CROW FLIES

My Bushman Experience with 31 Battalion

Founding Commander Delville Linford SM, MMM
with Al J. Venter

PROTEA BOOK HOUSE
PRETORIA
2015

As the Crow Flies: My Bushman Experience with 31 Battalion – Delville Linford with Al J. Venter

First edition, first impression in 2015 by Protea Book House

PO Box 35110, Menlopark, 0102
1067 Burnett Street, Hatfield, Pretoria
8 Minni Street, Clydesdale, Pretoria
protea@intekom.co.za
www.proteaboekhuis.com

Editor: Danél Hanekom
Proofreader: Carmen Hansen-Kruger
Cover design by Hanli Deysel
Cover images supplied by SANDF, Petrus Roux, Ziggy Hentze and Al Venter
Set in 10.75 on 14 pt Palatino Linotype by Ada Radford
Printed and bound by CTP Printers, Cape Town

© 2015 Delville Linford/Al J. Venter

ISBN: 978-1-4853-0268-1 (printed book)
ISBN: 978-1-4853-0269-8 (e-book)
ISBN: 978-1-4853-0270-4 (ePub)

No part of this book may be reproduced or transmitted in any form or by any electronic or mechanical means, including photocopying and recording or by any other information storage or retrieval system, without written permission from the publisher.

I am glad that I could have been part of the history of the Bushmen. Many stories are told of these people – many are true and many are not, but these stories told here I know are true. I have many fond memories and will always treasure their loyalty, their uncanny skills and their ability to rise to the occasion when called upon.

– Delville Linford

Contents

Author's Notes 9
Preface by General Constand Viljoen 11
Introduction by Al Venter 13

1. A Litany of Betrayal 22
2. Task Force Zulu – First Battles 26
3. How It All Started 38
4. New Experiences in Kavango 46
5. 'As the Crow Flies' 57
6. My Bushman Experience 64
7. 'Masters of the Unpredictable' – *Al Venter* 71
8. In Search of the Promised Land 77
9. Locating Our Promised Land 89
10. Alpha's Irrepressibles 96
11. Expanding the Operational Profile 109
12. Some of the Ways of Bushman Society 119
13. Operation Savannah 125
14. Group Bravo in Benguela 139
15. Alpha's Battle for Benguela Airport 146
16. The Military Approach in Central Angola 156
17. Ultimate Destination – Luanda? 171
18. North into Angola 181
19. The Pink House 191
20. The Cuban Role in Angola – *Al Venter* 198
21. Nova Redondo Adventures 205
22. Personality Clashes with Our So-called 'Allies' 215
23. Unconventional Warfare 224
24. The Grand Plan 230
25. The Lord Takes Care of His Own 241
26. From Alpha to Omega 251
27. Life After Savannah 257
28. Post-Savannah Tracker Operations 265
29. Exit Alpha 273
30. Back to the Future – *Al Venter* 275

Epilogue by Lieutenant Colonel Scholtz van Wyk 283
Acknowledgements 285
Bibliography 288

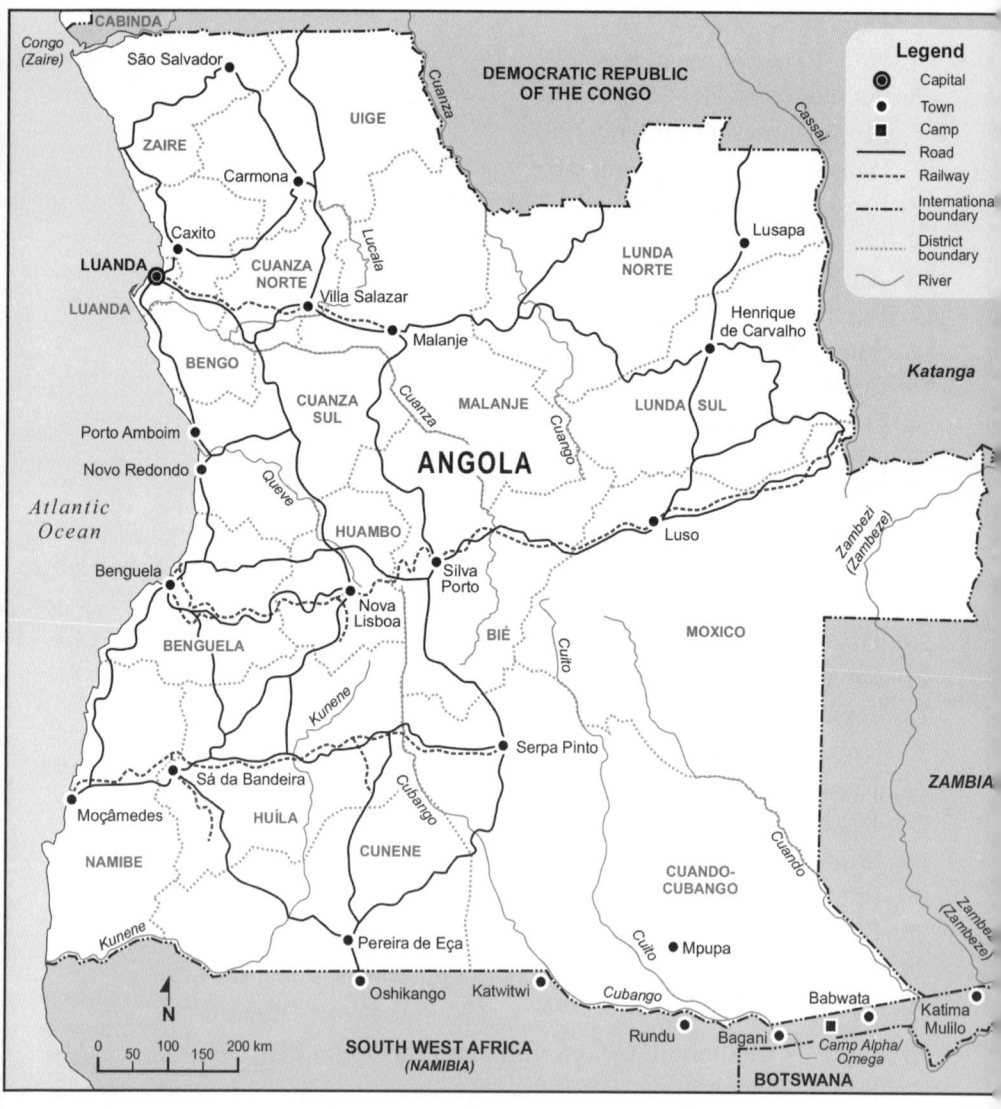

Angola, 1975

Author's Notes

Working on Delville Linford's original manuscript – handwritten over several years by the man himself and retyped by his lovely wife Nelle – the reader will appreciate that I was enormously privileged to be allowed an insight into a chapter of fairly recent South African military history that had only cursorily been made public before.

His diaries not only record events that took place during Operation Savannah, but he allowed me – and now you, the reader – to appreciate and understand what it was like to work with the Bushmen about whom much has been written over the past century, but whom very few people really understand. Delville got to know them well, for the simple reason that he took the trouble to involve himself in the everyday life of a community which, though seemingly quite basic, is also incredibly complex. Also, he listened to what they had to say. His descriptions of them along the front line are unique, as are many of their personality traits.

What emerges is something of a 'touchstone' that is every bit as remarkable as Laurens van der Post's original work *Bushmen of the Kalahari,* or some of the observations made by my friend Professor Phillip Tobias, who played a significant role in opening windows on the San people – in his case, those living in Botswana: same society, different location…

In a sense, the story that Delville relates is almost bigger than the sum of all its parts because the consequences of his efforts are still around, the children and grandchildren of the men with whom he went to war included, and of course, Platfontein, as well as those who stayed behind to live as they have always done, in the bush.

When I was given the opportunity to fill in a few gaps and add some of the sidelights that were quite eventful, I did not hesitate. The illustrious and engaging Delville Linford had a great story to tell and, clearly, I was eager to handle the task.

The result is a broad compendium of his experiences – together with a few of mine which are more explanatory than much else, all done with a view to highlight important incidents that were taking place in Angola in late-1975, like clandestine Cuban involvement in Angola's slowly unravelling catastrophe. At the same time, just about everything centres on Combat Group Alpha, the thrust around which quite a lot was taking place at the time.

In effect, my role has been more of a facilitator than of an author in 'setting the scene'. And what a pleasure it has been. My only wish is that I might have done better justice to the role played by one of the most forceful combat leaders to emerge in South Africa in recent years.

In that we will let the reader be the judge...

Al J. Venter
Downe, England

Preface

The nuclear bombs that signalled the end of World War II in 1945 were a terrifying deterrent to major wars. But, as we all know, conflict has always been a part of history and around the 1960s, Africa's struggle for freedom began. Because of a lack of proper military capacity, terror wars originated – a kind of military campaign aimed at avoiding classic military encounters, but with the intention of achieving ideological objectives with political, psychological and propaganda pressure.

Detrimental to the southern African region, the insurgency struggle that arose lead to a schism between the Western democratic ideology and the Eastern Block's communist ideology. The task of the erstwhile South African Defence Force was to uphold the sophisticated civilised state and government. Similarly, it was strategically essential to gain time for politicians to settle their differences, not only within South Africa but also in the neighbouring countries where ideological conflict was starting to rear its ugly and mostly brutal head.

As a result, the SADF had to rethink its conventional strategy and doctrine as a matter of urgency. To combat insurgency one needs a unique approach because terrorist groups are not countered by conventional brigades and divisions, as was the case in past conventional world wars. This would be uneconomic and inappropriate. As the saying goes: You do not try to kill a fly with a sledgehammer!

In the early days the Bush War was characterised by hit-and-run, cross-border terror attacks on the Namibian and local defenceless population, and it soon became evident that there was a need to adjust the SADF's armament. It was this additional requisite of counter-insurgency warfare that triggered the interest in the potential of the Bushmen, who, unbeknown to the public at large, were already operating as Flechas in Angola, building a formidable reputation in the fight against terror.

These very same Bushman soldiers ultimately became an indispensable addition to the capacity of the SADF. Most servicemen, and even permanent members, did not have the bush skills to match the insurgents. Soldiers who grew up in cities, unlike the Bushmen, were not familiar with living off the land and tracking insurgents. They had to acquire a new set of 'survival skills' necessary to locate enemy groups and, where necessary, to track their progress through the bush to protect the local population.

The Bushman people is a minority group on the African continent, but one of the oldest cultural groups. They used to live close to nature. With their extraordinary skills in tracking, pursuing, hunting, and their knack to survive in any condition, they were the ideal people to be trained in the use of weapons in order to become specialists in our Bush War.

The story of the Bushmen of 31 Battalion at Omega, as told by its founder Delville Linford, is an epic tale and deserves a worthy place in the annals of South African warfare accomplishments, which should never be forgotten. This book gives due credit to the many officers who gave a home to these exceptional soldiers and their families within the fold of the former SADF since 1974. They did not only find refuge after their Flecha days in Angola, but also received excellent military training by the SADF. The fact that they were pushed aside by some people then and had to be relocated did not diminish their place in Africa.

The Linford military 'family' can justly feel proud that they not only fulfilled their mission in shaping these soldiers into a true combat unit, but also succeeded in building relationships between the different cultures at Omega and preparing the Bushmen for life in a modern society.

Even today, the last serving commander of 31 Battalion, Scholtz van Wyk, is still (duty bound) promoting the cause of the Bushmen at Platfontein. This is a commendable effort to give a place and voice to these people who were not politically accepted in Angola, Namibia and even locally, thereby denying them the right to establish their culture within their rightful place in Africa. As veterans of the Bush War, they surely also have a claim to State benefits, and as the people who once fought so closely with this group of soldiers, we, as ex-military men still feel an honorary obligation towards them.

Apart from the emphasis of the book being on Delville Linford's mission in establishing 31 Battalion, the content also offers a nostalgic glimpse of the Border War that gained enough time in Namibia between the conflicting parties to bring about a lasting peace.

This book is a valuable human narrative about a struggle that raged over a period of thirty years, sometimes behind a smokescreen. It will certainly not disappoint.

General Constand Viljoen

Introduction

A few minutes' drive out of the Boland village of Wolseley, on the winding road through the Drakenstein foothills towards Tulbagh, lies a modest country home that would be easy to miss if you did not know what you were looking for ...

Pull off the main road and stop at a large steel gate and the world erupts. Six dogs – large and small and as aggressive as hell – come running. Their antics do not bode well for new arrivals because the feral cacophony has already forced hundreds of birds, that had been feeding in seed trays on both sides of the house, to flee.

Moments later the man himself appears, stepping briskly with his wife Nelle to answer the call. Their efforts to silence the hounds are fruitless, but he opens the gate nonetheless and leads the way back to the house.

A tall, imposing individual in his eighties, you cannot miss the mischievous glint in his eyes, or the smile on his weathered face, which is how he likes to assess new arrivals. This is a trait he picked up in his early years when he battled his way up life's multifarious ladders. His handshake is firm and the gesture that points toward the house is welcoming.

To some, the Linford greeting might initially be a bit guarded, for these are two people who, though comfortable in their rural retreat, are wary of strangers. With coffee and muffins and an array of logs burning in the fire bowl in the lounge, things ease quickly and even first-timers are treated like old friends by the time they are ready to leave.

I'd arrived at the Linford home to talk about his life, but that didn't start until all the usual social pleasantries were over, including the fact that they'd lost one of their dogs to a cobra strike several months before. There are a lot of cobras in the area, Nelle confided, adding that in summer they sometimes had three or four of these reptiles passing right in front of the house or on the stoep.

'Having killed one of our dogs, we don't tolerate their presence anymore.' She didn't elaborate.

While Nelle's roots stem from Natal – something that this 'Zululand gal' is inordinately proud of – the first Linford to emigrate to the southern tip of Africa – Spargo Wood-Linford – arrived in the Eastern Cape from Lincolnshire, England with the 1820 Settlers, where he settled before the family moved north, across the Orange and Vaal rivers.

Ties with the 'Old Country' were always strong, his uncle having volunteered to fight in Europe rather than battle the brilliant German guerrilla specialist General Von Lettow-Vorbeck in German East Africa. The uncle was killed at Delville Wood, one of the great battles of the Kaiser's War that claimed hundreds of South African lives.

Thus, the name of that historic 19-day series of engagements, as part of the Battle of the Somme, was accorded to his nephew, who was born in Potchefstroom on 23 July 1930.

It is worth mentioning that Delville's father, having subsequently joined the army and fought in World War II, went through training as a member of the same gun crew as the man we know today as the legendary General Dan Pienaar who led 1 South African Division at El Alamein in October 1942.[1]

Delville's early years – together with two brothers and two sisters – was the kind of childhood that many kids today can only dream about. Much of it was spent on a farm along the Mooi River in the Potchefstroom area, which meant they were bussed to school and back again and had few opportunities for organised sport. There was a lot to do at home, one of the reasons why he quickly developed physically and was sometimes able to take on youngsters much older than himself.

He also became an accomplished horseman, learned to drive a tractor by the time he was 12, ploughed the fields while his dad was in town working on the railways, and with his brothers became a handyman about the house.

His other preoccupation was with military things. By the time he reached his teens, World War II had been ongoing for several years and he would constantly make believe that he was a soldier-in-training, fashioning himself a rifle from a chunk of wood which he'd use, to the amusement of all, to march up and down. At that stage he had no idea what he was aiming at, but as the saying goes: 'Be careful what you wish for ...'

It is also interesting that though his home language was Afrikaans, it was his mother who stepped into the breach and insisted that the boys go to an English-medium school, which was why he and his *broers* soon found themselves at Potchefstroom Boys High, from where he matriculated. As he says today, it was symptomatic of the way his mother ran the show: she had a good understanding of the way things were going in the world and that ultimately English would be more useful in the world outside than Afrikaans. How right she was…

The military bogey raised its head again for Delville in 1947 when, at the ripe old age of 17, he asked his parents to allow him to join the South African Army. With many of the ravages of Hitler's war emerging after hostilities against Germany and Japan had ended, his mom and dad were totally opposed to him taking up arms, never mind joining the military full time.

But they could not stop him, even while at school, from volunteering to join the local Citizen Force unit for training, which is when he was attached to Regiment De La Rey. He was a fully fledged soldier-in-training at the age of 18 and, concurrently, Potchefstroom Boys High's cadet force sergeant major, the only youngster in South Africa at the time to have served in a reserve army unit while still at school, his Saturdays having been spent at the local military base. Delville's fortitude, even at an early age, it was said by others, was remarkable.

So, having finished school and without enough money in the bank to send him to university, teenager Linford looked about for a job: his first choice was to become a train driver, for which he applied. But, said the South African Railways employment office, he had his matric – and a good pass mark with it – so becoming a driver was a no-go. He should start as a railway clerk, it was determined by some faceless SAR&H functionary, which resulted in him ignominiously selling tickets at Germiston Station.

'It was a mess,' he admits today. 'I hated it! Boring, boring, boring! After a while I left, and then got an equally boring job at Volkskas Bank, first in Durban and later on the Witwatersrand.' When that became too much he returned home and started making bricks on the farm, first in small numbers and later on an almost industrial scale. He admits that this was probably his most successful venture of all as a 'civvie'.

'I went at that hammer and tongs as well and soon we were selling bricks to everybody in Potch that wanted them. Even today I remember some of the homes that were being built with our bricks … and many of them are still standing.'

That was 1951, and the Korean War was in full swing, not that what was going on in East Asia at that stage directly affected him. But it did coincide with him turning 21 and no longer needing his parents' permission to join the army.

'This I did early in 1952 and I was immediately posted to the Army Gymnasium in Pretoria where, like my father and with Constand Viljoen, future head of the South African Defence Force in the year ahead of me, I focused mainly on artillery. It was one of the great experiences of my life and I was able to prove my mettle when I came top of my class.'

The following year saw him as an instructor at 4 Field Regiment in the Transvaal, with mostly Citizen Force troops in his ranks. Soon afterwards he was chosen to attend Stellenbosch University where he graduated with a Bachelor of Military Studies degree and the rank of Second Lieutenant three years later. The School of Artillery where he was an instructor followed.

It should be noted that the youthful Delville Linford went on many staff and technical courses both in South Africa and abroad; and with a single exception, he always made top student. That omission was in 1964/65 when, as a young lieutenant, he attended the British Army School of Artillery at Larkhill in England. And then only because British and Commonwealth officers involved in the course were not performance or academically graded.

Following his return from England, he was posted to the Army College as a specialist in artillery.

A year later, having returned to what, by then, had become the Republic of South Africa, he was chosen to attend an instructor's course at the Army College at Pretoria's Voortrekkerhoogte. SA Infantry Course 274R lasted eight months, and at the end of it he was presented the sheath that went to the top student, something he still treasures more than 60 years on.

By now, the still youthful Major Linford was garnering a reputation for his pragmatic approach to handling difficult issues. He was invariably outspoken and not afraid to tackle impediments head-on. Totally in character, it was nonetheless an unusual trait for a junior officer, and though he made a few enemies along the way, his approach was invariably respected by those above, especially staff officers with whom he shared a common purpose.

By then, Jan Breytenbach, another of Linford's fellow-officers and a good friend, was also starting to make his mark. Almost simultaneously the two men had developed distinctive no-nonsense reputations and it was thought by some – including Generals Malan and Viljoen as well as another officer moving rapidly through the ranks, then Brigadier Jannie Geldenhuys – that if push came to shove along South Africa's frontiers, the two would make a good team.

Though the country's politicians thought otherwise, South Africa's military hierarchy was under no illusions that with the Portuguese guerrilla wars in Mozambique and Angola gathering pace and hostilities in Rhodesia already a reality, it would only be a matter of time before southern Africa's security was seriously threatened.

It was about then that Major Linford was posted to Western Province Command. His commanding officer, in the room next door to him in Cape Town Castle, was Colonel Magnus Malan. Unlike previous appointments, this one was strictly administrative and as he says, even today 'it was, if anything, bloody tedious'.

Fortunately, that didn't last too long. He'd married in the Cape and two children followed. After being promoted to Commandant in 1971, he was transferred to Port Elizabeth where he helped write a book on artillery training in the event of war. As ordered, he handed over the completed manuscript, but the book was never published. Soon afterwards, he and his growing family were again transferred, this time to Pretoria.

Speaking about all these events many decades later, Delville Linford regards April 1973 as one of the defining moments of his life. Because of the heavy security blanket that had enveloped much of southern Africa, there was no ceremony at all when he was sent as the senior liaison officer attached to the headquarters of the Portuguese Army in Serpa Pinto (Menongue today) in southern Angola. A large Portuguese colonial town, it was at the heart of all counter-insurgent activity in a region that was probably three or four times the size of the Metropolis.

His role, attached to the local military headquarters, was to be a none-too-discreet set of eyes and ears for Pretoria as to how the

Portuguese were faring militarily in an extended struggle that had already been on the go for a dozen years.

As he recalls, it was a posting that was both interesting and difficult. The Portuguese shared a lot, but not everything and, essentially, his job was to look beyond the obvious and report back. Unlike Portuguese Guinea and Mozambique, things were going pretty well for Lisbon in his sector of the insurgent war.

From there Lisbon's military commanders focused on trying to stem the flow of black guerrillas coming through from Zambia and the Congo in their bid to create a second front. Until then, the war in Angola had been largely restricted to the jungle or Dembos regions north of Luanda, the capital, and involved the two largest rebel groups – Soviet-backed MPLA and the pro-West FNLA, which received the bulk of its support from Washington.

The only real differences between the two strategic areas was that the northern regions where the war was being fought was tropical and heavily foliaged, all the way up to and beyond the Congo River. The south, in rather stark contrast, was vast, arid, lightly populated and often referred to as *Terras do Fim do Mundo* (Land at the End of the Earth).

It was also where UNITA, the third rebel force headed by Dr Jonas Savimbi lent its weight in a bid to oust Portugal from Africa. This guerrilla group, primitive at first but learning from the mistakes of its adversaries all the time, rapidly gathered its own momentum among the Ovimbundu tribal locals who provided much of its muscle power.

Linford spent a year in Serpa Pinto and learned to speak a passable Portuguese. He also became friends with José Rosa de Oliveira, the local head of the DGS or *Direcção-Geral de Segurança* which, a few years before, had supplanted PIDE, the International and State Police. Like PIDE, the DGS was a controversial and highly secret intelligence-gathering body, both notorious for disrespecting many of the tenets of the Geneva Convention.

While based in Serpa Pinto, Linford was soon made aware of the valuable counter-insurgent role of Angola's fighting Bushmen. Numbering about 2000, they were organised into combat groups called Flechas or 'arrows' and one of his observations reported back to Pretoria was the incredible tracking abilities and intelligence work of these little people in the bush, always a useful adjunct in support of the regular army and Portuguese Special Forces.

General W.S. (Kaas) van der Waals described the Bushman fighters as 'formidable, because of their particular aggressiveness, their ability to cover large distances on foot and without regular resupply.'[2]

Linford goes on: 'It was the 1970s and towards the end of that "liberation struggle" as the insurgents like to call it, when the wheels started to come off what had been a fairly efficient military machine. Almost overnight, everybody around me was faced with the reality of an army mutiny which had taken place in Lisbon on 25 April 1974.'

Termed the *Revolução dos Cravos* or 'Carnation Revolution', it resulted in an abrupt halt to all Portuguese military activity in Africa and it wasn't long before almost all of Lisbon's army, air force, naval as well as marine units in the country began a concerted pull-back to Europe.

For Portugal, it was the end of five centuries of African domination: for the majority of Angola's black people, that couldn't happen soon enough, though obviously, some troops were left on the ground in Angola to oversee the transition. As he says, 'obviously, I was obliged to return to my side of the demarcation line. To my dismay, I was pulled back from the front to man a desk at Army Headquarters in Pretoria where I was kept busy with a series of "odd jobs" that aren't even worth mentioning.'

That, in broad outline, covers some of the earlier years. Right now, many subsequent events have come into focus, in part because the man who commanded Combat Group Alpha has, for almost half a century, been unusually complacent about his role in Operation Savannah.

In the interim, quite a few books have emerged about that remarkable military operation, but hardly a word from Delville Linford. Yet, he enjoys wide acceptance by the majority of cognoscenti who are familiar with what took place in South Angola in the mid-1970s.

In the broader picture – considering the odds that were ranged against his unit by a much better supported, equipped and supplied enemy – he and his men achieved much more than was initially expected of them. Any lesser man might have dragged his heels long before his unit reached Novo Redondo, never mind set sights on possibly marching towards the gates of Luanda.

All this was underscored when it was made public that his book would be published. I and many others associated with the venture received good support for the project, with the parting comment usually along the lines that it was 'the best news yet' ...

Indeed, when I first announced I would be helping Delville bring his book to fruition – it happened one quiet Saturday afternoon at Killarney, the Cape's 'Cuca' MOTH Shellhole – there was jubilation among many of the 31 Battalion veterans present. Some of the unit members were actually quite emotional. Only afterwards was I to discover what an enormously admired and respected man Delville Linford is.

While everybody has their views about their former commanding officers or section leaders, I have yet to hear a word of condemnation about the way he went about his business. This was somebody – strict, scrupulously fair and demanding of his troops – who was always admired by those who served under him, a rare trait in modern armies and something rarely observed in modern society. It is a quality that he shares with his close friend and colleague Colonel Jan Breytenbach who partnered him in Operation Savannah by leading Combat Group Bravo.

The only other military leader I have met who had that distinctive ability was former Selous Scout Founder Commander Ron Reid-Daily. It is interesting that all three men founded and commanded units that excelled, especially when sometimes tasked with impossible objectives. Those involved covered themselves in glory for the simple reason that they had implicit trust in their leaders: they put their lives in the hands of the men who made the decisions and were rarely disappointed.

More salient, all three senior officers were never afraid to speak their minds if someone in the upper echelons of command issued an order that appeared to be based on bad intelligence or, in Jan Breytenbach's words, 'seemed stupid'. Commandant Delville – as he then was – would most times ignore these instructions if he felt they placed the lives of his men unnecessarily at risk. Also, he was never afraid to explain his actions afterwards and was rarely taken to task for doing so for the simple reason that his reasoning invariably made good military sense.

At the same time, everybody who knew Delville was aware that he had more than a few unconventional traits. For a start, he was never shy to kick up his heels. In camp afterwards or on leave back home, many stories emerged of the uproarious events that would usually circulate on Monday mornings. He was that sort of individual and he wasn't shy to admit it.

There is another side to this colonel that is rarely mentioned and which emerges in this book. Delville Linford was blessed with an acute sensitivity for the needs of others – his men especially – but also those people he would encounter during the course of the war and who were not directly opposed to his presence. He would always help where he could, and in the process saved many innocent lives.

An interesting feature of this book is that it reflects the writings of somebody who comes across as pretty well read. Though no academic, Delville Linford's comments reflect a solid grasp of military history in all its spheres. In truth, had he joined the Fourth Estate instead of the military, he would almost certainly have become a very competent scribe.

In the field, in contrast, he was masterful at employing unconventional tactics, all of which suggest an incredibly well-informed mind and the unfailing ability to grasp circumstances that, in quick order, would quite often make the best of a bad situation, which, basically, is the story of Delville Linford's life ...

---

1 This was the same Dan Pienaar who was complimented by British General Bernard Montgomery after El Alamein with the words: 'General Pienaar, tell your South African Division they have done well.' He was killed shortly afterwards on his way back to South Africa in an air crash at Kisumu on Lake Victoria.
2 W.S. (Kaas) van der Waals: *Portugal's War in Angola*, Protea Book House, Pretoria, 2011, p. 222.

CHAPTER 1

A Litany of Betrayal

It is difficult to write about the contemporary southern African Bushman community without some reference to their role in the Border Wars adjacent to and within Angola. It is almost impossible to comprehend the quandary in which this tiny society nowadays finds itself: unconscionably abandoned by their old allies and all but ignored by the Pretoria Government.

The Bushmen are certainly the oldest inhabitants of southern Africa and there is evidence that they have lived there for 20 000 years. In the view of some scientists, the San is the longest surviving 'relatively intact' community on the continent. Traditionally, as far as today's world is concerned, their home stretches north out of the Kalahari across much of Africa. Indeed, there is evidence (together with representative San rock paintings) that suggests historical settlements are to be found much further south and also way north into the far reaches of north-east Africa.

In the southern African context, their first European contacts were made with early Portuguese arrivals who settled in Angola more than five centuries ago. They are almost certain to have met with some of the Chinese explorers who rounded the Cape seven or eight centuries ago and whose peregrinations are documented in a variety of Chinese and Western journals.

Ultimately it took the South Africans, and specifically 31 Battalion, the unit commanded by Colonel Delville Linford, to hone these combatants into the finely tuned group of fighters they eventually became.

Things might have been quite different had their potential been recognised sooner by the Portuguese, because by the time Operation Savannah came along, they had already proved their worth to their new South African masters several times in ongoing operations along the Angolan frontier.

Indeed, Oscar Cardoso, who was operational as a PIDE intelligence officer in the south-eastern parts of Angola, is recorded as

CHAPTER 1: A LITANY OF BETRAYAL 23

having declared that [the Bushmen soldiers] 'didn't need logistical support. Gatherers since kids, they could live out of nothing, with special ability to find food and water. We really had good operational results with them ... we never had a desertion from the Flechas' ranks.'

It was Cardoso who transformed them into a series of true combat units, exploiting the cultural distance between these small men of Khoisan origin and the African populations of the remaining areas.

The experiment was so successful in operational terms that the concept soon spread to other areas, particularly Luso (Luena) and Luanda-Caxito, where the Flechas unit was almost entirely composed of ex-MPLA guerrillas.

Consequently, when Lisbon's soldiers needed trackers to guide them through the African bush in the Angolan War, they found willing participants in the San, as did the South African Army, subsequently.

Bushman soldiers, usually moving about innocuously but always with their ears close to the ground, were able to spot who was enemy Fifth Column or not: a most invaluable role as hostilities progressed, both in Angola and what was later to become Namibia.

This age-old Palaeolithic society, known as San (or Saan) people, refer to themselves as Bushmen or Basarwa. Issues are further complicated by the names they give their various clans or subsections: some prefer to be identified by the names of their individual nations, for example the *!Xun, Xam, ǂKhomani, Nusan (Nu), Khwe (Khoi, Kxoe), Naro, Hailom, Tsoa, Auen, Kua, G!ui* and *G!ana*.

That said, all are Khoisan members of various indigenous hunter-gatherer peoples of southern Africa, whose domain spans Namibia, Angola, Botswana, Zambia, Zimbabwe and South Africa.

Some of these people were fighters, something they did remarkably well when the need arose and which comes readily to the fore. More salient, they fought fearlessly when they had to.

Which begs the question: Why was this miniscule community placed in such invidious circumstances? Also, how did their unit, 31 Battalion, come into existence?

In this regard, the focus is on 13 years of guerrilla warfare in Portuguese Angola which started with an armed insurrection in 1961. Three liberation groups, MPLA, UNITA and the FNLA, were involved in what was termed 'a liberation struggle' and it wasn't long before Lisbon's secret police – then known as PIDE or *Polícia Internacional e de Defesa do Estado* – started recruiting Bushmen as trackers.

It wasn't long before this San community proved remarkably resourceful, one of the reasons why, after the Portuguese Army had left for healthier climes in Europe, their black fellow-countrymen launched a particularly brutal version of 'Payback Time'. Within months, most of the Bushmen communities that survived this ethnic purge sought and were given sanctuary across the border in South West Africa (Namibia today).

Pretoria took the initiative in November 1974 to move the first group of Bushman combatants (traditionally referred to by the Portuguese as Flechas) – with Commandant Delville Linford in command – to Camp Alpha in West Caprivi.

Almost a year later, on 14 October 1975, two companies of Bushman fighters (from both the Vasekela and Barakwena tribal clans and now termed Combat Group Alpha) crossed the frontier into southern Angola and went to war. That, in a nutshell, was the start of Operation Savannah.

The Angolan operation was a classic display of fortitude, tactics and hard work, with the unit covering just more than 3000 kilometres during the course of 33 days, penetrating to within a day's journey (200 kilometres) of Luanda, the Angolan capital. They were back at base two days before Christmas with only two of their men killed in action.

Several months later saw the formal establishment of 31 Battalion. Having proved itself under fire, it was decided that a permanent Bushman base be built, ultimately known as Omega. It was officially opened on 17 September 1977 by General Constand Viljoen, Chief of the Army.

During 1978 Vasekela soldiers were sent to Bushmanland to form the nucleus of 203 Battalion, the second 'Bushman' battalion, with its headquarters at Mangetti Dune. Its first commanding officer was Commandant Pinkie Coetzee. Later that year 31 Battalion Omega had its name changed to 201 Battalion.

Thereafter, the two Bushman battalions, 201 and 203, participated in almost all subsequent major operations as well as numerous smaller strikes against SWAPO. Their operational successes resulted in a ratio of 50 enemy killed or captured for the loss of a single Bushman soldier.

The two battalions launched their final operational strikes during the large-scale SWAPO infiltration of April 1989.

United Nations Resolution 435 followed shortly thereafter with independence for South West Africa and the establishment of the state of Namibia the following March.

What soon became clear was that conditions within Namibia were not suitable for providing a permanent home for the veteran Bushman force. A large group of 372 Bushman soldiers asked Pretoria to relocate the community to South Africa. Under Operation Mattress, approximately half of the community was airlifted to their new rural settlement to the immediate west of Kimberley.

Commandant Scholtz van Wyk took command of the unit in April 1990.

These were not happy times for the Bushman unit. The battalion was finally disbanded in March 1993, with the newly ensconced African National Congress all but washing its hands of the community that had so resolutely opposed SWAPO for almost as long as the Bush War lasted.

The trouble was, the Namibian 'liberators' had always been strong allies of the ANC and they were hardly likely to respond to a call for help from a former enemy, even if both were fellow Africans. South African author Alf Wannenburg phrased it succinctly when he wrote:

> But for the Bushman hunter-gatherers there can be no last-minute deliverance. It is the season of the sun which is the death thing. The forces of change, whether welcome or not, cannot be resisted. The tablets have been cast, the brown hyena has fallen upside down. But after death comes rebirth, although the footprints in the sand of the future will not be the same...

The announcement of the demobilisation of 31 Battalion was a 'death thing' for all its members, but, with the relocation of this society to new locations in South Africa, as some of the old veterans commented, something akin to a rebirth was taking place.

CHAPTER 2

Task Force Zulu – First Battles

The fact that Operation Savannah even took place is remarkable.
   If ever an invasion was under-manned, under-supplied and under-armed, this was it. It was also a military campaign about which nothing was made public at the time. In 'domestic' South Africa, it was the 'non-event' of the decade and only years later did most of the details emerge, and then sporadically.

Task Force Zulu, the main component of Operation Savannah – a South African invasion force – entered Angola's Cuando-Cubango Province from Caprivi on 14 October 1975. It was the first of several South African military columns designated to destroy a succession of MPLA communist-backed elements that had been surreptitiously moving into much of the country from Luanda, the Angolan capital prior to independence.

In his original manuscript Colonel Delville Linford explains that two South African fighting units, Combat Group Alpha (two companies of Bushmen), led by himself, and Combat Group Bravo (three companies of Chipenda [FNLA] faction Angolan soldiers) headed by the mercurial Commandant Jan Breytenbach, were at the forefront of the onslaught northwards out of South West Africa. He goes on:

Hand-over-fist, we took on everything hurled at us by Angola's field commanders. We all came to know the newly created military wing of the Marxist MPLA as FAPLA, an acronym for the People's Armed Forces for the Liberation of Angola, or, more correctly, *Forças Armadas Populares de Libertação de Angola*.

Within my Combat Group Alpha, I had a few hundred men that included a Flecha battalion, a unit composed largely of dissident Angolan FNLA soldiers – who had changed sides in the civil war and offered their services to the South Africans – as well as two Bushman companies. They, in turn, were backed by two Eland armoured cars with mounted 90mm guns. These air-portable, light fighting vehicles based on the French-built Panhard AML (that also came with 90 mm cannon) were supplemented by a single 81 mm mortar platoon and a 140 mm artillery platoon.

Breytenbach didn't do much better, though he did have an additional Eland and some howitzers. Taken together, this was not exactly an exemplary force with which to invade a neighbouring state, never mind try to overrun an entire country militarily, especially one as big as Angola, twice the size of France or Texas. Yet, in the end, we almost succeeded.

Both combat groups moved fast, pushing back Angolan Army forces from their earlier gains in short shrift, largely because we relied on the element of surprise to excellent advantage.

Having first taken the southern town of Ongiva, our two fighting groups then went on to capture the old Portuguese regional capital of Vila Roçadas (Xangongo today). That was achieved by 20 October, which was roughly three weeks short of when the entire operation was due to be terminated: Angola would be declared fully independent on 11 November 1975.

Sá da Bandeira (Lubango) was occupied with minimal losses by 24 October and four days later the southern port of Moçâmedes was ours, again with little opposition. After this, FAPLA, under Cuban Army direction, regrouped and things got tougher.

Less than a week later – having fought our way halfway across one of the biggest countries in Africa and having covered almost a thousand kilometres in the process – we found ourselves in the beautiful coastal city of Benguela, a fine old colonial conurbation that would hardly be out of place along Portugal's Algarve coast.

There were a few interesting events along the way in this early period that are worth recounting. After Ongiva, the first real battle in which Alpha was involved was at Vila Pereira de Eça. It was a full-scale conventional textbook attack with Combat Group Alpha left of the main road and Bravo to its right.

Once the attack got going in earnest, the enemy started to bombard our advancing troops with reasonably accurate mortar fire. When the first 82 mm mortar bomb landed among our troops and sent them scattering, the Bushmen stopped dead in their tracks.

The next bomb fell a short distance behind us and the Bushmen needed no more encouragement. They stormed the objective in a manner that would have done Balaclava's Light Brigade proud. They attacked, probed, exploited and consolidated all in an ongoing, fluid operation and with that, my Bushman troops experienced their baptism of fire.

In the process, we acquired several nice Mercedes trucks that had been abandoned. Our tiffy (motor mechanic) got them going in no time, and from then on we were full in business.

I used the opportunity to reorganise my transport: A Company was mounted on three grey Mercedes trucks with B Company on three blue vehicles. I couldn't help thinking that Alpha was beginning to regain some of its previously-held illustrious image.

At Vila Roçadas we met up with a squadron of armoured cars under the command of Captain Toon Slabbert. An enormous man with flaming red hair and obviously in the process of growing an equally conspicuous red beard, Slabbert and his armoured cars was yet to save us many hardships as well as lives.

From Roçadas we turned north again – destination Sá da Bandeira. This expansive colonial settlement had once been a beautiful town, lying on the single main road running north-south from Pereira de Eça to Nova Lisboa and Luanda. In part, it had a certain significance because it was strategically placed on the Moçamedes–Serpa Pinto Railway Line and also had an adequate airport which was later used to good effect by the Angolan Air Force. From the start Sá da Bandeira was a prime target.

From then on northwards, we encountered little enemy resistance, and with Bravo leading most of the way, we made good progress.

It was about then, accepting that my Bushman troops had sparse knowledge of conventional operations, that I thought it appropriate to try to teach them the basics. The next day I formed up the unit on an open airstrip and we spent the rest of the morning practising the drills on the airstrip until everybody could virtually do it with eyes closed.

With a lot more confidence we took off for the next village – Humpata – striking the place late afternoon where we erected a roadblock on the approach road just outside.

Apparently an enemy patrol had returned from somewhere and was surprised by my troops at the roadblock. I saw some movement in the darkness, and bringing up my rifle, I was about to fire in that direction, when out of the dark appeared a little boy, surely not yet in his teens. What was worrying was that he had a machine carbine aimed directly at me.

I somehow managed to kick the weapon out of his hands, but not before he was able to send a string of bullets flying over my head. My second kick caught the little guy square in the seat of his pants and sent him off into the night.

Just when I thought it couldn't get worse I heard a blood-curdling cry from somewhere within our lines of defence. It was the heartfelt shriek of a woman in terrible distress.

For the second time in several seconds, the icy fingers of fear gripped my innards. I followed the direction of the cry and traced it to a large truck. Whipping the door open, I pointed the muzzle of my rifle inside. The screams increased in intensity.

It turned out to be a woman who was in the process of giving birth. Though caught short for a moment or two, I was relieved that I hadn't found somebody being murdered. I told her to hang on and made it at top speed to where I thought the MO would be located. The doctor delivered a healthy baby, but I never heard whether it was a boy or a girl.

That night I thought was bad, but the next morning was a lot worse. I got up early and scouted around the area and came across a deserted Land Rover that had obviously run off the road the night before. On closer inspection I found the vehicle to be packed with groceries, women's and children's clothing and toys – many of them obviously intended for the forthcoming Christmas festivities. The owner of the vehicle was found dead some distance away.

These are some of the memories one would like to go away, but somehow they just don't.

Not long afterwards we joined up with the rest of the force at Rotunda just short of Sá da Bandeira. Intelligence had told us that there were enemy guns placed on the mountain which dominated the town as well as some of the roads leading to it.

Colonel Koos van Heerden, Zulu's OC, gave orders for the attack on this big town – in fact, is was almost a city – and it was Alpha's job to put the guns on the mountain out of action while Jan

Breytenbach's Bravo took the airport, which was apparently heavily guarded.

After Combat Group Bravo had secured the airport, Alpha was instructed to move down from the mountain and clear up whatever was in the town.

I called the company and platoon commanders and explained what I had in mind. I allowed sufficient time for all of them to get their orders down to every last man.

The Bushmen were past masters at night operations but their experience until then had always been limited to groups of two or three. In fact, I'd already accompanied them on such excursions and could vouch for their cunning in this sort of operation, but a first-light attack with two companies in a completely strange area was something else.

Fortunately, I had foreseen such a problem and I reckoned the bit of training on the airfield a few days before would surely come in handy.

Once all the commanders had reported they were ready, we went out. The plan worked as if it had been rehearsed a dozen times. The enemy must have got wind of a possible attack and had abandoned their positions in good time.

We waited until first light before we would descend from our positions overlooking the town. While we were having our breakfast, I asked Costa Diaz (one of the Bushman leaders): 'Well, young man, what do you think?'

'I think it is a very good idea, we should do it more often.' He offered me a bottle of French Cognac.

'No thanks, my boy,' I replied. 'I never have breakfast this early.'

Throughout all these events, we encountered very few Portuguese nationals who remained behind to greet us: because of earlier domestic hostilities, most of the settler community had fled, the majority heading to Europe and taking with them only what they could carry. As a consequence, the two combat groups took over in an almost empty city.

What was sad was that all these events took place at the end of Lisbon's five-century colonial tradition in Africa. Africa's history was in the process of being rewritten by a small group of fighting men who stood up to be counted ...

CHAPTER 2: TASK FORCE ZULU – WHAT IT WAS ALL ABOUT 31

Benguela, in contrast to the other places we'd taken, was a beautiful coastal city from where the great inland African railway that stretched all the way to Katanga in the Congo started. Both Jan and I were expecting the place to be heavily defended, but we were surprised when our column drove into town with almost no resistance.

I deployed the troops and I tried to make contact with our headquarters way back from where we had originally set out almost two weeks before, but without success. On the outskirts of Benguela was a tall, isolated hill with on its peak some religious structure from long ago, a structure that resembled a chapel.

We drove up the hill as far as we could, with the magnificent bay on which the city stands, to our left. I left my driver, Corporal Hendrik Bodenstein, to try and establish comms with our generals, most of whom were not yet even aware that we had reached the Atlantic Ocean.

I walked up to the chapel, which stood in the centre of a flat, paved circle with a lovely blue-tiled wall around like those you so often see in places like Oporto or Lisbon's suburbs. On the far side I looked over the wall and was greeted by a sheer drop to a road that ran straight into a village. From where I was perched, I could see the entire spectacle that made up much of Benguela, the distinctive Lusitanian red-tiled roofs on many of the buildings, some imposing white-painted administrative structures that would have done any African capital proud, the modest harbour and, finally, the ocean that stretched away towards South America.

A fresh breeze wafted in from the sea and because of the tropical heat, it was a welcome relief.

I was still enjoying the view, when suddenly from around the little hill on which I was standing, a truckload of FAPLA soldiers arrived. They were noisy, raucous and cocky as hell. What struck me immediately was that this was a pretty grim-faced bunch of cut-throats; they looked as if they were expecting trouble. As the saying goes, every one of them was armed to the teeth, even to their distinctive red cravats, a trait they had probably borrowed from the recently departed Portuguese Special Forces.

It took me only a moment to appreciate what was coming. These soldiers were going to drive straight into the rear end of our column and should that happen, some of my men could get hurt because they certainly weren't expecting any hostile new arrivals.

What possessed me, I still don't know, but I leaned over the wall and emptied the magazine of my carbine into the truckload of soldiers.

'Hey, Commandant, stop that bloody noise! I got the HQ on the air, but with that racket I can't hear what they're saying,' came a shout from Hendrik.

For a moment or two I was nonplussed. Here was I trying to save our boys from disaster and my driver tells me I'm making a noise. He turned back towards his radio.

'Hello Alpha. Where the hell have you people been all this time? ... Where exactly are you now and what are you doing? Over ...'

He listened intently for a few more seconds and then went on.

'We've been travelling due west since we last made contact ... have now reached a coast, the Atlantic ... been doing some fighting with some of the chaps we met over here. Over.'

Whatever the reply was, I would never know. Some serious fighting had erupted in the town below, so I left Hendrik to sort out the problems with Zulu HQ and headed down the hill to see what was going on.

After we'd cleared the town of FAPLA troops, the most important facility that still had to be secured was the airport.

We left Benguela shortly afterwards and headed northwards towards Lobito airport, a logical decision because if those Angolans were going to get any kind of support, it would have to be flown in from Luanda to these two large cities along the coast. The roads, we knew, were impassable in places because of ongoing battles between the various factions and bringing anything in by sea would have taken too long.

We reached an area adjacent to the terminal building and were greeted by an awful lot of shooting and noise. Finally we made our way into the airport building itself. I quickly established what I thought was a fairly secure position on the first floor. From there, I had a good view of the town, and indeed, the surrounding countryside.

Within the broader ambit of my view and not far from the airport, I spotted a great jumble of nondescript structures that resembled a shantytown, which it probably was. From what detail I could make out from my vantage point at the airport, there was clearly a lot of firing from there and we were at the receiving end of it all. Apparently the remnants of the FAPLA force we'd encountered earlier had sought refuge across the way and being a fairly expansive, broken-down sort of place, it seemed a good choice.

Several times during the afternoon, the enemy counter-attacked in a series of misdirected efforts to retake the airport, but the Bushman troops fought back hard. They were so enthusiastic in countering these attacks that FAPLA eventually abandoned that option. They then started to use mortars and rocket fire.

Their weapons were all basic Soviet squad weapons and, judging by the volume of fire, they obviously had a lot of it. Their mortars were 82 mm that, in experienced hands, could be deadly while the 122 mm rockets that zoomed in only helped compound the issue.

Having been fighting for almost two weeks, we were already aware that just about every FAPLA unit was armed with this stuff – that and RPG-7s and RPG-2s, with their AKs making up the bulk of it. All were Moscow's contribution to the Angolan war effort, hardware that was then being used in a couple of dozen insurrections around the globe, from El Salvador all the way through Africa and the Middle East to Afghanistan and the Philippines.

The weapons being used against us were good. The 122 mm BM-21 'Grad' rockets that were incoming that afternoon were usually truck-mounted and fired in salvoes of 40 at a time from multiple rocket launchers mounted on Soviet GAZ vehicles. In Angola in those days, they went out singly or in pairs, their most distinctive feature being a piercing roar as the rocket passed over our heads and finally, an almighty blast on detonation.

The trouble was, us South Africans had nothing like it when Operation Savannah was launched. Most of the more sophisticated weapons systems that came afterwards were developed as a consequence of what we experienced at the hands of what Soviet surrogate forces threw at our men in 1975.

Pretoria's answer to the 'Grad' was the 'Valkiri', a multiple rocket launcher with 24 tubes and firing a 127 mm (five-inch) projectile. That was produced after several Soviet rocket launchers had been captured during the course of operations, sent back to the Republic and reversed-engineered. This remarkably versatile weapon made its first appearance on behalf of the SADF in the late 1980s.

Somehow though, my men and I had to make do with what we had, which was standard-issue R1 rifles in 7.62 mm calibre, a reasonable supply of mortars (until the next batch had been airlifted into areas under our control by South African Air Force C-130s), the versatile but outdated Eland armoured car as well as some World War II vintage bazookas.

At that moment, at this strategic Angolan airport, enemy mortar bombs and rockets rained down on us from the shantytown across the way. They were a much deadlier proposition than anything we had encountered earlier: Indeed, these bombs were exploding all over the place.

With each incoming volley, huge sheets of glass in the building that sheltered us would shatter and deadly shards would streak across from points of impact. Quite a lot of it landed in the area we had secured. Because the risk of injuries from glass became so great, I instructed the men to move a bit further up the building, believing that the higher we went, the less might be the risk of mortar fire. But then incoming rockets negated that.

If one of those things hit the building where we were located, the impact would almost certainly cause a lot of casualties.

Watching these rockets through my binoculars, I could see that they were being fired in pairs. On discharge, they would kick up a storm of dust which made their launchers quite simple to detect, even from a distance. Then, as they got closer, we could follow their long red tails of flame and it was easy to see where they would detonate. In fact, after the first dozen or so, it was a simple matter to determine their course and we were able to take appropriate action.

Looking very carefully through the binoculars, I could see a tiny black spot in the middle of the tail-flame of one of them: in fact, they all had them, which is how the name 'Red Eye' originated.

I pointed this out to Staff Sergeant Lubbe and posted him at a strategic spot on the staircase between two floors, from where he could see clearly and where the danger of falling glass was slightly less. He soon became quite good at it and was able to warn the blokes when a clutch of rockets approached.

In-between all these pyrotechnics, I told the guys a joke about a chap from a local village that was a particularly heavy drinker. Late at night he would pass the village churchyard on his way home. His drinking pals decided to play a prank on him, so they dressed themselves in white sheets and lay in wait for him in the graveyard. At the appropriate time, they jumped up and with ghost-like cries, descended on their inebriated friend.

Instead of being terrified as they had expected, the man drew a .44 Magnum and started firing enthusiastically at the white-shrouded images to the accompaniment of loud shouts: '*Gate toe*! *Gate toe*!' (To your holes! To your holes!) he screamed, shooting wildly.

After that, Staff Lubbe would sit at his observation post and each time he spotted a pair of 'Red Eyes' coming our way, he'd bellow: '*Gate toe*! *Gate toe*!'

This became a big lark and quite a bit of fun because the enemy's aim was appalling. But a bit of slapstick in the airport building was not getting us anywhere and it wasn't long before I started to sense a pall of frustration creep into my bones. I had to do something...

Our mortars had been deployed and because the rocket sights were easy to spot, we began making things difficult for our FAPLA adversaries. But then they would just move their launch positions and carry on with their incessant bombing from elsewhere.

The other alternative, of course, was to send out a patrol to try to take care of them, but with the rockets constantly being shoved about to evade our efforts at counter-bombardment, it would have been extremely difficult – and obviously quite dangerous for those involved. I finally decided to give headquarters a shout and see if they could come up with something.

The two of us then went back to our vehicle and started to make our way across the airfield to avoid any FAPLA soldiers that might still be lurking around. There was a fairly thick plantation of trees on the far side of the runway which offered a bit of cover, so we drove in that direction. Then, quite suddenly, about halfway down the runway, the first of the mortar bombs hurtled in, exploding a short distance away. Aim wasn't all that bright, but the blasts were deafening. Hendrik was positively alarmed.

I turned towards him and in a quiet and hopefully optimistic voice said something about no two bombs ever falling in the same place. I suggested that when the next bomb dropped nearby, Hendrik was to drive straight towards it and we'd sit it out in the hole.

Hendrik looked at me sideways, but he did as I said because more bombs arrived shortly afterwards. And then still more. Whoever was doing the firing must have seen us approach, and with the air all but knocked out of my lungs and my ears screaming, I was suddenly knocked partly senseless. A bright scarlet screen appeared in front of my eyes.

My first thoughts just then were that if this was death, then it was certainly a rather colourful experience. I then realised that my mouth was full of dust, which was when I remembered my driver ...

'Hendrik, are you okay?!' I shouted, surprised that I could even get the words out of my mouth.

'Yes,' he answered. Then he asked, 'What the fucking hell was that, Commandant?'

'I don't know,' I replied, but I told him to make for the trees.

We did, but when we got there, we discovered more horrors. We were faced with a ditch, more or less the depth of a house. Hendrik motored up and down the sides several times looking for a gap, finding none and with more bombs and rockets falling all around us.

'Hendrik, those bastards are going to kill us ... get into that ditch!'

He found a spot moments later where the ditch appeared to be slightly lower than the surrounding countryside; almost without thinking, he took the plunge. It was a hairy drop towards the bottom, but we landed on all four wheels and surprisingly, after all that battering, the old truck was still going strong. I turned towards Hendrik again.

'Pull up tight alongside the wall ... I think we'll be safe here.'

Hendrik gave me another sideways glance, but he did as I'd instructed. We scrambled close to the cover that the wall provided on one side and the vehicle on the other. I lay prone next to the rear wheel with Hendrik choosing a position alongside the front wheel.

FAPLA must have registered the position where we had disappeared from view and they were now deliberately ranging in on that spot. Soon we were being bombarded again, only this time with mortars. Because we were in a ditch, we were temporarily out of range of the 122 mm stuff, but the mortars were coming in at a steady rate.

We were now faced with another predicament. With the guns

and rockets which were being fired at us while we were still in the terminal building, we could more or less predict where the rounds were going to fall. But with mortars – considerably less accurate – the damned things could land anywhere. And when they did, there was always a mighty explosion. This worried me the most, because round by round the bombs seemed to crawl closer to where we were lying.

I looked at Hendrik. He had propped himself up on one elbow, leaning against the wall of the ditch. A short while later he fumbled around in his trouser pocket and pulled out a half-eaten dog biscuit and broke it in half.

'Want some?' he asked, his eyes alight. That he had emerged from his earlier stupor was obvious.

'No thanks, Hendrik,' I answered. 'Not right now.'

He started to nibble at the well-worn crust which was already crumbling in places because who knows how long he'd saved it? All the while, more bombs were coming down and I was amazed that some of the shrapnel didn't get through. What went through Hendrik's mind just then, I couldn't tell. He was too busy gnawing at his biscuit.

I continued to watch him out of the corner of my eye and could see, even in that half-light, that there was a pensive sort of expression on his face. I was trying to pretend I wasn't scared, so I assumed he was trying to do the same, but my heart was bleeding for this boy. We had come a very long way together – almost a quarter of the way across Africa – and I had developed an affection for him like I had for my own son. If something were to happen to him, I thought, I didn't believe I'd ever forgive myself.

Several salvos later, Hendrik started to crawl towards the rear of the truck. I presumed that he was looking for some kind of support, moral or otherwise, and frankly, had that been the case, I wouldn't have known how to react. But before I could utter a word, he spoke in that distinctively quiet, long drawn-out manner of his that I'd come to accept as his personal style.

'Commandant,' he said, pulling himself together. 'You know, I really don't mean any disrespect, but I just want to tell you that the theory of yours about no two bombs falling in the same hole is a lot of crap.'

CHAPTER 3

How It All Started

Colonel Delville Linford, then a Commandant (a 'half-colonel in SADF parlance) has vivid memories of how things developed for him personally in the early days of the Border War. As he related, it wasn't at all easy going …

On a miserable wintry day in August in 1974, he recalls, he was sitting in his gloomy Pretoria office which, like most military establishments, was pretty drab. In fact, the place depressed him. There were lots of people moving about, volumes of jaw-jaw and absolutely nothing happening:

I looked through the window and outside was no better. A cold, bleak wind swayed the leafless branches on the trees on the lawns which faced Potgieter Street with its endless charge of traffic heading in both directions. Vehicle sounds were interrupted from time to time by the shrill whistle and puff-puff of a train that was shunting somewhere in the distance.

To add to it all, the air was heavy with the stench of burning flesh. It was a Friday, when the abattoirs – located nearby – burned scraps of flesh, bones, offal and who the hell knows what else. The result was a mind-numbing stench for miles around.

The telephone rang and I answered to the clipped voice of Brigadier Constand Viljoen, then the South African Defence Force Director of Operations.

Always a pleasant, quiet-spoken man, this senior officer who was to eventually become head of the defence establishment in the country, greeted me in his customary friendly manner. Our brief discussion was clipped and to the point:

'Hello Delville, how are you?' he queried.

'Very well, thank you, Brigadier, and you?'

It was clear this wasn't a social call to enquire about my health, so he went straight into what he needed to know.

'How long were you in Angola?'

'A year and a half, roughly, Sir.'

'How long have you been back?'
'A month and a half.'
'Don't you long for the bush?'
'No question about that, Brigadier.'
'Then you wouldn't mind heading back to where it's all happening?'

'Back?' I retorted, finding myself a little off balance at the prospect. Perplexed, I asked him when I should leave.

'As soon as possible ... the next Flossie (the scheduled weekly C-130 flight to Caprivi's Rundu) leaves Wednesday.'

'Can I go ahead and make my booking?'
'Yes of course, that's the idea.'
'By the way, Brigadier ... where am I going?'
'Come and see me.' Click, and the phone went dead.

I slammed my office door and took the stairs two at a time as I headed up to where all the big-wigs – Brigadier Viljoen included – had their offices. Things were looking up.

In a series of vignettes that couldn't have taken more than five minutes, the brigadier briefly explained that one of the new developments following Lisbon's departure from Angola was that our troops were no longer allowed to operate across the border in order to interdict SWAPO guerrillas from crossing into South West Africa.

'You were there, Delville, so you know that,' to which I nodded.

But, he added, the original Portuguese Army Flechas – the Bushman troops on which I had reported while I was stationed in Serpa Pinto – were Angolan nationals and they could legally operate in Angola.

Essentially, his words were to the effect that the Bushmen that were originally fighting for the Portuguese security police were fleeing southward from Angola in fairly large numbers, desperate to seek refuge in South West Africa.

Looking directly at me from where he sat, his instruction was clear: 'I want you to build a camp to accommodate these people, rig them out and train them all. Then we can use them to protect the border areas.'

The brigadier hesitated a moment to ensure that I had understood, which was when I told him that I did. Then he added: 'But I want it kept quiet ... everything you do from now on is classified ... any questions?'

'Where and when is this to happen, Sir?'

'Go and see the Director of *Spes Ops* (the Afrikaans abbreviation for Special Operations) and he will give you everything you need.'

Brigadier Constand Viljoen's final words on that momentous morning that would completely change the course of my life were a simple 'Goodbye and good luck'.

I said nothing to him about not believing in luck.

A hand shook me by the shoulder. I opened my eyes and looked squarely at the two brass buttons on the tunic of the pretty young SAAF girl who manned Movement Control at Pretoria's Waterkloof Air Force Base.

'Sir, your aircraft is about to take off, everybody is waiting just for you.'

I felt terrible. The night before I had paid a final visit to all my favourite pubs and said a series of goodbyes to what I thought at the time must have been every single barman in Pretoria and, in particular, the barmaids.

I was only to discover later that while I slept peacefully in the terminal building and all the passengers heading to Rundu were about to board, that somebody drove his tractor into the side of the Hercules that was scheduled to take us there. The collision resulted in a substantial dent. It also meant that the entire cargo had to be reloaded onto another plane coupled to the usual jargon about being ... 'sorry ladies and gentlemen, but due to a slight accident there will be a short delay' ...

Once on board the replacement Flossie, I was greeted not by the usual smell of hydraulics and octane, but an odour that mingled with the sweet, oily emissions of cologne from a plump lady who was seated opposite me. To my right I was all but overwhelmed by the garlic breath of a rather overweight man who had obviously dined very well the night before.

The effect was nauseating, so I strapped myself in and went straight back to sleep.

The pain in my cramped legs finally got the better of my hangover and slowly, painfully almost, I emerged from my slumber, only to discover that I had my knees securely wedged between the dimples on the knees of the plump lady opposite. I gave her an apologetic

CHAPTER 3: HOW IT ALL STARTED   41

look and with as much dignity as I could muster, withdrew my legs and pulled my feet towards me. Her smile was a sweet rosy pink.

Meanwhile, the little round man on my right was staring with rapt fascination at the gently bouncing boobs of the buxom teenage girl seated opposite him, but again, his breath dominated everything. I turned my head the other way.

Curiously, the man to my left was the exact opposite. He was pale and skinny and dressed in the gaudy peacock blue beret and combat 'browns' that smelled of mothballs. What he read in my face was difficult to tell, but he gave me an encouraging smile and a wink. With a thumbs-up he said loudly over the plane's roaring four engines: 'Don't worry, old chap, they say it's not so bad up there once you get used to it.'

Ja-nee, I did my best to smile appreciatively and turned my attention back towards the pink lady's knees.

By now I was also starting to gather my thoughts about what lay ahead. The briefing by the Director of Operations was cursory and added little to what I already knew about the situation on the border. In fact, having spent a lot of time in that region, I probably knew more about what was going on in South Angola than he did. My eighteen months in Angola certainly helped me understand a few of the parameters under which I'd be functioning – which was clearly why the brigadier had tasked me – but there were also a number of imponderables.

What he did do was present me with my orders and send me along to General Fritz Loots, Senior Staff Officer: Special Operations.

In the overall picture of developments, this was the man – rather ominously to us lesser beings – who was later to become known as 'Godfather'.

To understand the full picture of events that lead up to and followed the withdrawal of the Portuguese Armed Forces from Angola, it is essential to understand what had been going on in the country prior to Lisbon calling a halt to hostilities and pulling all its troops back to Europe in 1974.

For many years the three insurgent forces, MPLA, FNLA and UNITA, had been trying to infiltrate Angola with the object of overthrowing the regime and, of course, taking over the Luanda Government. Just which of the three groups would ultimately be the victor was anybody's guess.

SWAPO – the South West Africa People's Organisation headed by a man who called himself Sam Nujoma and who had been kicking up a storm at the United Nations and elsewhere – was also in the race. But this mainly Ovambo liberation group had its eyes fixed firmly on Windhoek, the South West African capital.

For the majority of 'our' guerrillas – those fighting under the SWAPO banner – the Angolan people, once the Europeans had hurriedly left, offered good support, sanctuary, transport and transit to areas dominated by the South African Army. Essentially, as I had already discovered while working with the Portuguese, Nujoma's very successful tactic was to ride on the backs of the three Angolan guerrilla organisations – MPLA, FNLA as well as UNITA – and making a pretty good job of it.

For my purposes of getting involved in the ongoing counter-insurgency effort in Caprivi, there was no question that time spent in Serpa Pinto offered a thorough grounding in the nature of the guerrilla conflict being waged by Lisbon's soldiers and aviators. I had quickly been made aware of many of the ancillary units that were involved in the colonial war.

For instance, besides regular Portuguese military forces, there was also a paramilitary element known as the GE's (*Grupos Especiais*, small paramilitary groups established by the Portuguese in 1966 and integrated into the Armed Forces) as well as the DGS (*Direcção-Geral de Segurança*), the Portuguese version of the security branch of the police force which succeeded PIDE in 1969.

In their efforts to gain information about the movements of the insurgents, DGS tumbled to the idea of using Bushman troops in both combat and support roles, in which the remarkable tracking ability of these little people was put to use.

This was accomplished with great success. The Portuguese security forces trained and organised a couple of thousand Bushmen in fighting groups which were dubbed Flechas. Committed to combating terrorism – because until then they had been persecuted by the African tribes in the south – these little men went on to become a significant factor in the war in Angola's south and soon became greatly feared by the black insurgents. But with the Lisbon army putsch, everything suddenly changed.

It was consequently not surprising that when the Portuguese forces withdrew from Angola and the black liberation forces started to juggle for dominant political roles in the country, the once great Flechas suddenly found themselves threatened. Overnight, erstwhile terrorists became the putative rulers of the land and, obviously, anybody who had been involved with the colonial administration suddenly found themselves the hunted rather than the hunters.

Sadly, the Bushman communities were rather low on the priority list that followed in the wake of Lisbon's Carnation Revolution. Tens of thousands of Portuguese were fleeing Africa in its aftermath, and from Angola alone, the number was reckoned in terms of hundreds of thousands of refugees.

Those who had the foresight and money to see what was coming left the country for Europe early on. Effectively, those who had a future in Portugal, went there. Many more waited to see whether the status quo would change. In a sense, it was a bit like Europe under the Nazis: As the saying goes, just about everybody believed the crocodile would eat them last.

Then, almost overnight, as the elections crept closer, the flood began. Some Portuguese headed for Rhodesia. Others, in long road convoys took the road south to Windhoek and, ultimately, South Africa.

The South African Army was waiting for those desperate groups at the border and some of the scenes were pathetic: debilitated, undernourished children, older people barely able to stand or walk and very few with either money or assets that could be used to buy goods. Much worse were those who went missing, families robbed and killed on remote roads, others ambushed and quite a few children that disappeared.

It was a repeat of the Congo disaster when tens of thousands of Belgians fled after that country became independent in 1960. Again, many didn't make it.

There had obviously been a lot of talk among the Portuguese in Angola about what was termed 'a black takeover', with many people recalling events that took place in what had previously been known as the Belgian Congo.

Belgium, almost like the Portuguese, suddenly decided in January 1959 that the Congo should become independent, in spite of the fact that almost all senior positions in government were in the hands of white colonials. Worse, there were only six or seven university graduates in the land. Shortly afterwards, the Belgian King Baudouin declared in a radio address that his country would work towards the full independence of the Congo 'without hesitation, but also without irresponsible rashness'.

It didn't work out that way. Having 'tasted blood', self-appointed black Congolese politicians, headed by a firebrand young postal clerk Patrice Lumumba who had close ties with the Soviets, pushed for 'freedom immediately', and after the Leopoldville riots of 1960, full independence was granted in June that year. The country's major security body, the Force Publique, mutinied within days and in the macabre and bloody consequences that followed, there were tens of thousands murdered.

Looking back on these events in both the Congo and Angola, one would have thought that Lisbon would have been hesitant in granting a largely uneducated, totally unprepared African majority an overhasty taste of freedom. The liberation forces were well acquainted with guerrilla conflict. Almost to a man, as well as many of their female fighters, they knew very well how to kill. But, sadly, they knew or understood precious little about running a government, be it socialist or democratic.

I was told that certain influential blacks already had inventories compiled ... whose car, whose house, whose wife was to be whose when the takeover took place. To some of the primitive Angolans who had taken up arms, those were the priorities: a car, a house and then a woman, usually the wife or daughter of the *patrão* who had originally employed him ...

This, basically, was the reason for the great exodus from Angola which was not restricted to white people. Many of those who took to the road were *mestiços*, of mixed blood, and quite a few families refused to leave their faithful black employees behind to face an uncertain future.

As a result, those who could get to the RSA headed in that direction, but in the end, everybody – more or less – found some place to go. Except, of course, the unfortunate Flechas. The Bushman people suddenly had nothing to do and no place to do it. Too soon they became the victims of marauding gangs of black 'liberators' and ran the risk of being exterminated completely.

I came across many stories of these unfortunate people, how the Bushman boys were castrated in order to prevent propagation and the girls and women used as concubines and slaves. But fortunately for the Flechas there were still quite a few DGS operators around who remembered the good these people had done and realised their plight.

José de Oliveira, my friend and former colleague (the last inspector of DGS in Angola) was one of our original sources. It was largely through his doing that the plight of the Bushmen was brought to the attention of Military Headquarters in Pretoria. De Oliveira stressed that if they were not helped, South Africa might lose a valuable future component of its military ability in one of the most unsettled regions on the planet.

That, basically, is why I was called to the office of Brigadier Constand Viljoen that morning...

CHAPTER 4

New Experiences in Kavango

B rigadier Constand Viljoen was dead serious about getting the Bushman show on the road in Caprivi and I was on my way within days.

My thoughts were interrupted by the squeal of tyres as the Hercules C-130 touched down on the tarmac runway at Rundu, a modest town that faced an increasingly hostile Angola across the Kavango River. Rundu was also the Kavango capital and headquarters of 1 Military Area (1MA). This was from where my operation was to be controlled and supported.

I unhitched myself from the blue and red safety belts and trundled out of the Flossie. Outside it was warm, sunny and still. You couldn't miss the military base because it squatted alongside the runway and from where I viewed it just then, there was much activity, not all of it, as they say, militarily organised.

The headquarters consisted of a number of tarpaulins, all joined together and stretched over square cubicles of canvas. It was pretty neatly partitioned and the end result formed several offices. The setup resembled what I imagined to be something of a man-made-rabbit-warren.

I walked into the headquarters, but there was nobody that I knew. So I made my way to the office of the commanding officer, a square four-wheeled caravan that had been positioned under another huge spread of tarpaulins.

1 Military Area's commanding officer, a colonel, was a short, thick-set man in his fifties. His thick muscular neck made his head look small in comparison with his enormous shoulders hidden within the confines of his army browns. He had a ruddy complexion, piercing blue-grey eyes, topped off with snow-white hair, regulation short back and sides, of course.

I was greeted with just the right amount of friendliness, but the man had little more to say except that I was to report to 'Punchy', who would give me 'a complete briefing'.

Major 'Punchy' Botha – his name dated from the days when he

was the heavy-weight boxing champion of the SADF – was the staff officer responsible for logistics and, according to the colonel, he was also in control of the operation. This surprised me. Customarily military operations in any army fall under the control of 'operations', or failing that, 'intelligence'. But logistics?

Anyway, I thought, while it hardly made sense, it didn't matter who was driving as long as we got the show on the road.

Punchy was a really fine specimen of a man. Well over six foot tall and powerfully built with quick eyes and a ready smile, he couldn't help but exude confidence. Had Punchy taken that route with his short, very curly and ginger hair coupled to an abundance of freckles scattered generously over his face and arms, he could easily have made a career for himself as a Hollywood 'tough guy'.

I liked Punchy. He was the exception to all the logistics officers I had known, probably because his most notable trait was that he was helpful and well liked. Always amiable and enthusiastic, the problems that came his way were there to be fixed.

Ask Punchy for the almost impossible, like trucks for a military escort in the middle of the night, and he would reply with something like 'You want it, you got it', his stock-in-trade phrase. More to the point, he always delivered the goods.

Punchy's briefing on what was going on in Caprivi just then was as sketchy as everybody else's. He told me that the project in which I was so hastily plunged was to be known as Operation Alpha. He said we would meet up with a man called Werner Edler at a place called Babwata.

There I would find the first group of so-called Flechas, a fairly large group of Angolan Bushmen that had sought sanctuary from the troubles in Angola. Some would have their wives and kids with them, he confided, adding that the deal was that with the military taking the men, they were also landed with their extended families, though operational demands restricted this only to close family.

Punchy had a drawn map of the area. He'd marked a position with a large black cross which, he declared, was the place where I was to 'build your camp and do your thing'. It was an interesting way to phrase my directive, but I got the gist.

He went on: 'Babwata is a really lovely spot, right out there in the bush and well out of reach of curious eyes … lots of large trees surrounding a water hole and set right in the middle of a patch of green grass.' Utopia indeed, he stressed. It certainly sounded like a Promised Land.

While at the Caprivi Base and after we'd settled formalities, Punchy went on to explain that Edler was, as he put it, 'to be your right-hand man'. Moreover, he was completely in the picture and had been a member of the reconnaissance team that had originally selected the camp site. He was a German-speaking civilian, never having joined the army, and had years of experience with DGS in Angola. He had been recruited by Major General Fritz Loots and knew the bush and the Bushmen 'like the palm of his hand'. Well, I thought, with a right hand like that, who needs a left?

Things started in earnest the next day when we took off from Rundu in an air force Dakota and headed east. I briefly scanned the map that Punchy had given me, little more than a sheet of paper, with thousands of little green circles that denoted trees. The density of the circles varied in accordance with the denseness of the bush. There were also horizontal brown lines that ran from side to side on the map and indicated *shanas*. These were low-level grassy strips – often swamp-like in the rainy season – that could sometimes be as much as several hundred metres wide. These grassy expanses separated the bits of slightly higher ground on which clusters of magnificent Rhodesian teak and mopani trees thrived in abundance.

At that early stage, Punchy's map meant very little to me. So I tried to assess the terrain itself from the aircraft, but the view from a Dakota's side window made it difficult to get a comprehensive picture of the ground below. Fearing that I might miss the Promised Land that he had enthused about, I asked the pilot if I could join him in the cockpit and he was happy to let me come forward.

After the year and a half that I'd been 'commuting' to Serpa Pinto and back with the SAAF when the Portuguese were still in Angola, I'd become fairly well acquainted with many of the pilots. Without exception they were a willing group, always pleased to assist a Brown Job in need.

My new 'home' in the northern reaches of South West Africa was a rather interesting African region, with an intriguing and often complex history that went way back.

CHAPTER 4: NEW EXPERIENCES IN KAVANGO

It included Arab raiding parties operating out of Zanzibar and capturing Africans, who would be sold as slaves. Many of these poor souls – should they have survived – would end up in the New World working white-owned colonial plantations in the Caribbean or what had become the prosperous southern states of America.

In contrast, Caprivi, or the *Caprivi Zipvel* as this narrow protrusion eastwards from Namibia was marked on the charts in German colonial times, had originally belonged to Queen Victoria.

But Kaiser Wilhelm of Imperial Germany had his eyes on trying to link up German South West Africa with the Zambezi, and ultimately, with his imperial possessions in *Deutsche Ostafrika* (Tanganyika). The deal he brokered would offer his regal grandmother the island of Zanzibar (then also in German hands) in exchange for the strip which is many hundreds of kilometres long.

Another clause gave the youthful Kaiser Kilimanjaro, Africa's tallest mountain, which, until then, fell within the British colonial Kenya's boundaries. If you look at today's maps of East Africa, you cannot help but notice Kenya's strangely shaped southern border which includes a loop that places Kilimanjaro on Tanzanian soil.

The Great War of 1914–1918 followed and South African troops invaded and captured South West Africa, which, after the war, it was tasked to administer as a League of Mandate Trust Territory. After World War II, when the United Nations abrogated that trust and demanded that South West Africa be given home role, Pretoria refused to yield.

After much discussion and haranguing at the United Nations, the black South West African political leader Sam Nujoma decided to take matters in hand by launching a guerrilla force which he called SWAPO. It was those insurgents – armed and abetted by the Soviets, the Cubans and many of the more militant African countries – which the South African Defence Force now faced.

My job was to prepare a large force of Bushman fighters to help repel the onslaught.

Kavango, with Rundu as its capital, was (and still is) bordered on the north by Angola, part of the border being a long, almost perfectly straight stretch of open bush that was referred to in local jargon as the 'cutline'.

Further to the East, the great southward-bound Cubango River swings out of Angola, turns towards the east and for a short distance forms Caprivi's northern frontier. From Mucusso the river once more turns south to form the boundary between the Kavango and the Western Caprivi. At that point it changes its name to the Kavango River.

The Kavango – an enormous Central African waterway – is one of few larger rivers of the world whose waters never reach the sea. Instead, it flows through the northern part of Botswana and disappears into Botswana's famous Okavango Swamps. It is said by some Bushman elders that for a long time these swamps were home to a tribe that was never seen by a white man.

From Rundu, as far as Katima Mulilo in the eastern Caprivi, runs the Golden Highway. From the air it looks like a white chalk line drawn between the Angola and Botswana cutlines. At Mucusso the line is interrupted by the Kavango River, but traffic is ferried over on a large pontoon, manned by a contingent of South African engineers.

The Golden Highway crosses the Cuando River by means of a metal-framed Bailey Bridge and for some of its distance is dotted on either side with tiny native villages. But these settlements thin out toward the east and disappear entirely in the Western Caprivi. Only Babwata – 'The Place of the Clear Water' as the Bushmen named it – stands out clearly and in splendid isolation.

Like the highway, the runway at Babwata was a strip of white chalk, very distinctly etched out against a background of verdant green bush. As the aircraft circled towards the downwind side, I had a glimpse of the local military base at Babwata, a square clearing surrounded by a sand wall interspersed with what appeared to be weapons positions.

The base was enclosed by a three-metre tall security fence with a gate on the south side. Our Dakota touched down and as it turned and began to taxi toward the base, the propellers sent a jet stream of white powder into the surrounding bush.

Once on the ground again, I was greeted by a small sinewy army captain. He had high cheekbones, a sandy moustache and bandy legs. Somewhat insignificant-looking at first glance, there was something about his bearing that told me that this was somebody different from the usual run-of-the-mill army officer. For a start, taking charge of

CHAPTER 4: NEW EXPERIENCES IN KAVANGO 51

the new arrivals, he was definitely a no-nonsense little man. He wore a faded green Infantry beret that sported the famous South African Infantry Corps Springbok head.

I didn't miss his quick glance at my navy-blue artillery beret with its gold braid Staff Corps badge.

As an old soldier I had a long time ago become accustomed to the age-old rivalry between the different corps of the Army, but I got the impression that to this young captain, the things they said about gunners were more than idle jest.

A square-shouldered, square-headed man in army browns walked up and clicked his heels in typical German fashion. With his round face, round mouth, round cheeks, round eyes and a sharp pointed nose, set off against a once pink, now red complexion, he was a picture. The Caprivi sun had obviously not been good to him.

The captain introduced him as Werner Elder. He bowed over my hand courteously and said in clipped tones: 'Your troops are formed up and ready for your inspection, Commandant!' He clicked his heels again and indicated with a sharp jerk of the head that I was to follow him.

Also a no-nonsense man I thought, so I excused myself from the infantry officer and formed up beside him as we set off at a brisk pace.

I was still contemplating the sardonic smile on the captain's face when we rounded the far corner of the sand wall. The sight that greeted me stopped me smartly in my tracks. Formed up in three ranks and dressed in brand-new army browns, a gang of black faces stared at me. I sensed a very distinct element of uncertainty from the gathered throng.

Behind the ranks was a crowd of women and children dressed in European clothing, probably recently arrived and much of it not fitting too well. Behind them was a crazy confusion of suitcases, cardboard boxes, blanket rolls and bundles of various sizes and shapes.

On my right, once I turned my head in the other direction, I was greeted at the edge of the bush by another horde of little brown people – men, women and children. The males were all small and seemingly underweight and with sinewy limbs and round heads. All were 'dressed' in skins or lengths of cloth stretched between their legs and tied front and rear all the way round the waist with a rawhide thong. Each of them carried a bow and arrow and what, at first glance, resembled a miniature bush axe.

The women wore skirts of cloth made up in different layers, so that the skirts flared out, almost vaguely like the skimpy outfits worn by ballerinas. Above the waist, all the women were naked, but around their necks they wore strings of beads, some holding a rectangular bib of plaited beads between their breasts. Almost every one of them was either pregnant or had a fat round baby on the hip.

What appeared to be young girls, were dressed in similar ballerina-type skirts with a sort of 'sun top' supported by shoulder straps, much resembling today's boob tubes. The young boys wore nothing.

Obviously, I'd never experienced anything like this before and for several moments I was spellbound. That was when I began to understand the smile on the young company commander's face.

I looked at Werner and asked: 'What are these men?'

'Your troops, Commandant!' he replied confidently.

'Who are all those people?'

'Their families, Commandant.'

'And those ...?' I asked, pointing at the nondescript collection of little brown people on the right.

'Also Bushmen, Commandant – just onlookers ...'

'Alright, tell them who I am, and that we are leaving at first light tomorrow. Also, get a dozen able-bodied Bushmen that are willing to go along and serve as labourers. Come around to the mess later and I'll give you detailed orders.' With this I saluted and walked to the entrance of the base.

Above the gate was an arch of timber with the skull and horns of a buffalo. On a board were the words: 'Babwata, The Land of Milk and Honey.' In small print underneath I read: 'Bring your own cow and bees.' At that stage the humour escaped me.

Babwata Base was much like any other army establishment on the border. In the middle was a parade ground surrounded by tents on four sides. The mess and what passed as my future headquarters was on one side with sleeping quarters on the other. Ablutions and transport made up the rest.

Seeing the flag hanging limply from a pole outside one of the tents, I knew that that was company headquarters, so I set off in that direction. Inside I found the captain and a few other young officers

CHAPTER 4: NEW EXPERIENCES IN KAVANGO

and my old friend José. He was dressed in army browns and sported the rank of major.

This came as a slight surprise. The last time I'd spoken with him was in the Cuando-Cubango Province of Angola and he was the DGS inspector, a formidable man holding an equally formidable national security post. Now he was a South African Army officer with the rank of major.

Obviously I was genuinely pleased to see him, even though the circumstances were very different from before.

Under the circumstances, all I could mutter was: 'José, what the hell is going on? I was told that I was going to work with the Flechas and what do I see: a bunch of black Africans with hordes of camp followers ... there wasn't a single Bushman or woman in sight.'

I stopped to catch my breath and then realised there was no point in going on. The company commander's grin broadened, but he said nothing.

José began to explain. There had been some sort of misunderstanding at Rundu. The officer who had been delegated to organise the show had apparently never seen a Flecha and when a mob of blacks from Angola swarmed across the border, he assumed them to be members of that Bushman unit they were waiting for and promptly absorbed them into the system. Most were members of the Portuguese Citizen Army and not Flechas at all. Nothing I could say was going to change matters, so I let it ride.

We spent the evening chatting in the Officers Mess and I told José that I was going to look up my neighbour-to-be, Commandant Jan Breytenbach, at Fort Doppies the next morning and that I would rejoin the Alpha expedition later.

José elected to accompany me and so after a few final instructions, I found my sleeping bag, quietly crept in and closed my eyes to the 5th day of September 1974.

Before I drifted into oblivion, I looked again into the sardonic smile of Captain Louis Kotzé, Babwata's company commander.

I was up early the following morning and caught the first rays of dawn streaking the sky between some tall trees on the periphery of the camp while trying to start the Land Rover allocated to me by the able Werner.

As the reluctant engine coughed and spluttered, José appeared and we started off in search of the mysterious Fort Doppies, the base having already achieved certain notoriety in local military lore. I didn't have the vaguest idea where my opposite number had established himself, but according to the directions, 'you cannot miss it'.

The words were to the effect that we should 'just follow the Golden Highway for several kilometres. You'll see a track turning south. Follow this track for several more kilos and then you'll find it.' We did exactly this.

The journey was hardly uneventful. As we progressed southwards along the track, I saw more and more notices painted in red on the lids of ammunition boxes and nailed to the trees. These read, alternately: 'This is a restricted area', 'Beware of mines', 'Don't go off the road' or 'Beware – firing exercises'.

Then quite suddenly behind a tree was a gate attached to a formidable-looking barbed wire fence. There was no question, this was Doppies, but the gate was locked with an enormous lock and there was no sign of life. What to do but get out and walk towards the gate where I spotted a field telephone housed in an ammunition box beside the gatepost.

I lifted the phone, turned the handle and waited. Nothing. I turned it again and waited. Still nothing. It went through the motions once more.

Eventually just as I was about to turn away in disgust, a body appeared from behind the bush. Built like Apollo and brown as a berry, it wore a faded brown army T-shirt, faded black army PT shorts and sand shoes. Over its shoulder was slung an R1 army rifle with its muzzle pointing down. The man looked at me, then at José and finally said '*Ja?*'.

'I'm looking for Fort Doppies,' I explained. '*Ja?*' he again replied quizzically.

'I am Commandant Linford and I came to see your commander, Commandant Jan Breytenbach ... can you call him?'

This time the troop emitted a more determined '*Ja*'. He unlocked the gate and we drove into the awesome Fort Doppies.

The camp was a delight, placed in a particularly dense clump of enormous trees. Unlike many other army camps, it was apparent that Jan had determined that no trees be removed when the camp was built. Good use was made of natural woods, with the walls of the mess and quarters constructed of tree trunks planted vertically in the ground and about a metre high. The rest of the walls were open up to the roof, which was made of timber and thatch: buildings were literally built around the trees.

We were met at our vehicle by Jan, by then a man of considerable significance in the SADF. Like the others around him, he was tanned nut-brown and built like an athlete. Like all the others who had come forward to see who these newcomers were, he had an R1 rifle slung over his shoulder, muzzle pointing downwards.

I had known about Jan Breytenbach for a very long time, almost from my days as a young recruit. He was a cadet in the Marine Corps at the SA Army College, way back in 1953 when I was a student instructor. Later he disappeared from the scene and I never saw him again, until 1969 when I was on the directing staff of the Army College.

Captain Breytenbach had been invited as a visiting lecturer to speak on irregular warfare. His address, I remember, was most irregular. So much so that some of my colleagues could hardly find words to describe what they thought of Jan Breytenbach and his crazy ideas. Not everybody was aware that he'd already served in the Royal Navy, much of it with flying crews on board British aircraft carriers.

Little did those who attended his talk know that this crazy young captain was to become the most successful operational commander in the Bush War.

Contrary to the general consensus among the staff, a lot of Captain Breytenbach's crazy ideas made sense to me, and I wasn't afraid to say so. Even now I still have a sneaky suspicion that this could have contributed to my subsequent transfer to the Castle in Western Province Command as an army administrative officer.

Be that as it may, Jan Breytenbach disappeared out of my life again, until this moment when I met him again, face to face at Fort Doppies. He invited us inside and we sat in the cool and spacious mess, talking idly of this and that. Had I only been aware then that this tough and resolute man and I were still to walk many an adventurous mile together …

José and I were introduced to some of his men as they trooped in in pairs to have tea. Every one of them was dressed in what was clearly the requisite faded brown army T-shirts, faded black PT shorts and worn-out sand shoes. There wasn't one that didn't have his R1 slung over his shoulder, muzzle pointing downwards. They were a formidable squad, strong, brown and sharp.

It didn't take long for us both to become aware that Jan's men looked at us rather indifferently. In fact, they hardly spoke to us. I wondered about the fact that the commandant introduced them by their first names only and he addressed them likewise. Much later, even though I had come to know many of them better, I never got to know their surnames. And now, sadly, many of them are no longer with us and I never knew who they were.

We spoke for a while but, as the morning wore on, I learned little, if anything, of their activities. Most of those who were prepared to talk spoke mostly about the bush, wildlife and their pet golden eagle. I also learned that the base was named after a little grey monkey that was an ardent collector of cartridge cases: he'd hoard them like squirrels hoard nuts. So it was not all that surprising that he soon answered to the name of 'Doppies' and, for lack of something else, the base was named after him. Fort Doppies became a legend in South Africa's Bush War.

After tea and 'doggies' (army jargon for dog biscuits) we greeted and left. As I cast a last glance over my shoulder at the tranquil peace of this lovely bush camp, I was not to know that the next time I'd visit the place, Fort Doppies would be a charred, black ruin.

CHAPTER 5

'As the Crow Flies'

With our duty done at Fort Doppies – and still none the wiser about the actual role of Commandant Jan Breytenbach and his curiously unresponsive troops, we returned to our original objective: making a base for our Bushman recruits ...

We found Werner Edler's expedition neatly parked on the Golden Highway, about 40 minutes' drive west of the Babwata Road. It was a really delightful scene with women in brightly coloured dresses and head scarves brewing coffee over open fires.

The men, almost all locals, were standing in clusters, smoking and talking. In-between there were dozens of children running and playing exuberantly. No question, there was a picnic atmosphere all around. Even the Bushmen had picked up the vibes and there was an excited bustle of activity in their little group.

We drove towards the head of the convoy and found Edler pensively sipping a large mug of coffee. He offered to share it with us, which I declined, but José found a mug and one of the troops poured him a good measure of the strong dark brew.

'Is this the point where we leave the Highway, Werner?'

'Yes, Commandant, from here on we travel south for about 15 kilometres to the camp site.'

I looked at his map. He had made an X on the Golden Highway directly opposite the X which marked the camp site. The road we had been travelling on had run straight as an arrow for miles and, judging from the distance indicated on my Land Rover's odometer, I somehow got the impression that we were more towards the east than where the cross indicated.

'How can you tell, Werner?' I asked, adding that according to the Land Rover we should be in a different area. I pointed to a spot on the map, but got no further.

'Commandant, you cannot go by those mileage metres in vehicles. They hardly ever work accurately ... you can't rely on them. I took the time we travelled and estimated our speed, so we are here,' he declared firmly. 'I am sure of that.'

'How would you get to that spot through this dense bush?' I asked.

'As the crow flies, Commandant. But don't worry, I know the bush.' His mien told me that he'd said his piece.

So much for my interest in the matter. I was a greenhorn and it was beginning to show, so I kept my trap shut from then on.

When everybody had taken refreshment and had answered the calls of nature, Edler gave orders to mount. He climbed into the passenger seat of a battered old three-ton army Bedford and stuck his head and shoulders through the observation port on the passenger side, produced a magnetic compass and took a bearing. Moments later he gave orders for his driver to turn left and drive straight into the bush while I sat in my Land Rover and watched the vehicles pass – six battered old army Bedfords – all sporting large letters 'BLR' on the driver's door. In army jargon: Beyond Local Repair.

How Werner had got these old wrecks going, let alone travel for miles and miles, was something that always mystified me. But that he was able to do so was pleasing.

The trucks were driven by six South African servicemen and the picnic spirit continued. Women and children were babbling while the men heroically struggled to keep the thorny overhead branches from scratching the exposed bodies on the trucks. José said not a word.

I drove off behind the last truck, just following in its tracks, as it had done with the vehicle ahead. With the Land Rover in four-wheel drive and in first gear, the old girl plunged on willingly. Soon my thoughts started to wander.

I was with a group of young soldiers and we were standing on a barren hilltop in Voortrekkerhoogte outside Pretoria on a cold, wintry day, 20 years before. In fact, the hill on which we had gathered was the same one on which the magnificent headquarters building of old ISCOR stands today. Our instructor had just given us a lecture on navigation by compass.

'All right men,' he told us authoritatively, 'you are a dispatch rider with your Harley Davidson, and you are to deliver a message to your commanding officer at the Voortrekker Monument. How far would you travel and how long would it take to get there? Work it out and give me your answer on a scrap of paper!'

'Staff,' one of our group called towards the staff sergeant.

CHAPTER 5: 'AS THE CROW FLIES'

'Yes, Combrinck.' (Harry Combrinck was a fellow student on my instructor's course.)

'As the crow flies, Staff?' Combrinck queried.

Our instructor's generous eyebrows bristled and his bushy moustache twitched as his rasping voice cut through flesh and bone.

'To hell with the crow, you idiot. Can you fly through the air with a motorbike?' None of us dared to laugh because we were more terrified of Staff Sergeant 'Twak' van Wyk than we loved him. These days I am able to smile at the memory, but not then, in part because of what the fellows called him. Everybody referred to him as 'Twak' because he was never without his tobacco.

'All right men' old 'Twak' continued, 'now I'm going to teach you how to navigate through the bush when you are alone and you don't have a compass.' He pulled one of those old wind-up watches from his pocket.

'You take the thing like this ... but make sure that it shows the right time. Then you take a grass stem and hold it so that the shadow falls over the 12 and the 6 on your watch ... like this,' he demonstrated. Then you bisect the angle between the hour hand and the shadow and that gives you true north. Simple! Any questions?'

'Yes, Staff.'

'What, Combrinck?'

'Staff, if you are alone in the bush, how would you check if the time on your watch is right?'

I smiled at the memory.

My mind went back to Edler, head and shoulders popping out of the Bedford, compass to his eye and Staff Sergeant Van Wyk's rasping voice shattering the quiet.

'Combrinck, what the hell did I tell you about taking magnetic bearings near metal objects?'

Combrinck replied immediately: 'You must be 20 paces away, Staff. I am exactly 20 paces from the truck, Staff.'

'I can see that, you fool, but you are standing next to a telephone pole, you idiot!'

With Werner taking a compass bearing from the cab of his truck I was obliged to smile again, which was when my thoughts were interrupted by the easy voice of José. He had not spoken all the while and I was shaken out of my reverie.

'You are a very funny man, Commandant,' he said quietly.

'What do you mean, José?'

'Well, I mean that I sit here in the middle of the bush with a bunch of women and children and broken trucks, and that idiot hasn't the vaguest idea where he is. I am terrified and you just sit there and grin. What kind of man are you?'

I said nothing. José looked dejectedly into the bush. A worried expression clouded his faded blue eyes and his brow wrinkled into a frown, which was when I turned my attention to the present and for the first time I took an interest in the goings-on.

From time to time the convoy would stop and when we moved off again, I somehow got the impression we had changed direction, which was when I looked at the gear lever of my Land Rover and noted the direction in which the shadow lay.

I then placed an imaginary clock-face around the vertical lever, checked the time, bisected the angle – between the shadow and the figure 12 and came to the conclusion that we were not heading south at all. In fact, according to my calculations, we were moving roughly in a south-westerly direction. As we progressed still further, I started to get the impression that we were zigzagging our way through the bush instead of 'as the crow flies'.

At our next stop, I drove ahead and found Edler taking his bearings. 'Hey, Werner, can I borrow your compass a moment, please?'

He tossed the instrument down. I walked 20 paces and brought it to my eye, turned until the figure 180 moved under the indicator and I found a prominent tree on that bearing. That done, I brought up the compass again to check the reading and an enormous air bubble virtually obliterated the figures on the dial.

'Now men, always remember,' old Twak had said, 'if you have an air bubble in your compass, the compass will have an error. This error can cause you to go around in circles until you crawl up your own...'

I looked at the lid of the compass and read the letters, laughing, and handed the compass back to Edler.

'Werner,' I said, do you know what BLR means?'

'No, Commandant, why?'

I burst out laughing. 'Never mind.'

As I walked to my Land Rover I overheard one of the black women say to another: 'This Commandant is very nice, he is friendly and laughs much.' Just to please her, I gave her a special grin and walked on.

By now the sun had long since passed its zenith and was rapidly on its downward path towards the west. I was not particularly worried that we had not found our Promised Land yet, because somehow I'd had misgivings on this score from the outset. But what did begin to bother me was what we were going to do that night, and where.

I was still contemplating this when the convoy stopped for the umpteenth time. Now it was more than a compass reading that caused the halt and impatiently I moved ahead and found the lower half of Edler's body hanging from the open bonnet of a Bedford. The upper half of his body was inside the engine compartment. Perturbed, I climbed onto the bumper and peered inside. Edler had the fuel pipe unscrewed and was in the process of removing the carburettor.

He looked up and said: 'Don't worry, Commandant, it's just a fuel problem and I'll have it fixed very soon.' I couldn't help spotting his 'tool box' precariously balanced on the engine block. It was a cardboard rations box and comprised a worn-out pair of pliers with one handle bent at 45 degrees, a claw hammer with a broken handle, a worn-out shifting spanner, a bent and oval-pointed screwdriver with a cracked black wooden handle, and an odd assortment of nuts and bolts together with bits of wire and pipes, old spark plugs and an oily rag.

My heart gave a lurch and I jumped to the ground. 'Don't worry, Werner, take your time.'

I looked up at the human cargo on the truck. The gay chatter and laughter had ceased. The friendly smiles had also disappeared. Bloodshot eyes stared out of sombre black faces, some pleadingly, others disinterested, and a few with open hostility. The party was over.

At that point I turned around to Major De Oliveira. 'José,' I said, 'this is going to take time, so I think we should pitch camp here for the night. Will you please do the necessary?' I believe he was relieved; at least he got an opinion out of me, if not some sort of direct order. José nodded and turned to the soldiers.

Moments later, everybody alighted and stretched arms and legs and vigorously tried to rub the numbness out of the parts mostly affected by the hard benches of the jarring and bouncing army vehicles. The women were muttering in undertones and disinterestedly started fidgeting with their belongings. Some of the men disappeared into the bush and returned with armfuls of fire wood. Fires were built and pots of water put on to boil.

Meantime, Edler had abandoned his repair job and, on José's instructions, had started handing out cans of bully beef, baked beans and mixed vegetables. These were emptied into pots and warmed up, producing what is commonly known in the bush as chow-chow.

While the soldiers and their women and children were gloomily swallowing huge spoonsful of grub and washing it down with coffee, I walked over to where the Bushman community were preparing for the night. The contrast between these people and the blacks was astounding. The place was a hive of activity.

The men were chopping long thin branches and ripping off strings of the bark. Wooden frames were constructed, several metres in diameter and about a metre high. Large grass mats were draped over the frames and as I watched, a Gulliver village of little huts sprung up before my eyes. In-between, the women were cooking their rations and somehow the aroma from their pots smelled different.

I walked closer and discovered the reason. They were adding roots, leaves, pieces of dried-out meat and a messy, greasy, pulpy substance of unknown origin, probably some kind of animal fat, I wasn't sure. The young girls and boys were playing a game of which I couldn't make head or tail of and the toddlers were running, jumping, shouting, falling and being fallen over by everybody else.

I surveyed this amazing spectacle as if in a dream, and then I heard José's voice behind me.

'Hey, Commandant, you have seen this before, yes?' He pointed to a lot of chickens huddled together in a heap. Their legs were bound together with bits of rag. Slap bang in the middle of this feathery mass, sound asleep, lay a tiny runt, a brown and white mongrel puppy. This was too much and once again the craziness of the situation got to me. The Bushmen did not know what I found so funny, neither did they care. They clapped their hands and laughed with me. They were happy people – my kind of souls.

I turned around and we joined the others who, in the meantime, had produced their own version of chow-chow and coffee. So we, too, had our first real meal in the bush, more or less in gloomy silence.

As dusk settled in and more wood was piled onto the fires, everybody was beginning to make their sleeping arrangements. I wondered idly whether José or Edler were going to arrange a sentry system for the night. Nothing indicated that they had or were going to do so, and in fear of showing more ignorance of the bush, I just let it be, dragging my kit a short distance from the fire and unrolled my sleeping bag. Fully dressed, I lay down on it.

I tried to think about what had transpired that day, and more important still, what I was supposed to do the next morning. Try as I might, all that came into my mind was a black crow. For some time I tried to figure out the significance of the crow and eventually my mind drifted to the story of the jackal and the crow.

This didn't make any sense so I pried further, until my mind focused on the Biblical story of Noah and the crow. I tried to conjure up a picture of what took place on that day in the ark, so many millennia ago.

'Look chaps,' I thought Noah might have said, 'that pigeon has dropped us. Let's face it, it's not coming back and we can't just sit here, we must do something, but what?'

His son would have answered: 'You know, Dad, I never did trust a pigeon, so why don't we send out a crow? Maybe we'll have more luck with him.'

'Excellent idea, son, we'll do that, send out a crow first thing tomorrow!'

Meantime, lying there under an African sky, the heavens had turned to black velvet. I located the Southern Cross, multiplied the length from the head to the foot by four-and-a-half and drew a vertical line down to the horizon. That indicated true south, old Staff Twak had said.

I turned the bottom end of my sleeping bag to face south, took off my boots and instantly fell asleep. I slept like an infant: a babe in the woods, you might say …

CHAPTER 6

My Bushman Experience

Having been introduced to the southern African Bushman society in general, I had to narrow my prerogatives to those members of this community with whom I was tasked to deal. As with most things linked to the military, it wasn't easy.

In order to properly understand them, and what it is that motivates them, we need to briefly follow the tracks of the Bushman people since they arrived in the southern tip of the African continent who really knows how long ago.

But for our purposes we have to start in the mountainous regions of Estcourt in what was once known as the Natal Province of South Africa. Historically, their tracks run in clockwise fashion almost in a semi-circle through the arid Karoo, the Kalahari Desert and its adjacent Bushmanland, as well as vast stretches of what we know as Namibia today. From there they moved north into Angola's southern reaches.

Their place in Angolan history has been if not well recorded, then adequately enough to follow their movements, which is how we know they were put to the sword in large numbers by the black tribes of that country, almost like Australia's Aborigines were hunted by the early (and not so early) settlers.

But from then on, the trail grows cold and almost nothing has been put to paper because the Bushmen were illiterate. We have some documents written by explorers and religious people that mention them, but nothing substantial.

Still, as a community they have been noticed and many people have walked the road with numerous Bushman communities in the past century.

My Bushman experience covers the history of the Bushmen from the time they left Angola, through the Caprivi and Schmidtsdrift to Platfontein.

It is not intended to relate the military history of the Bushmen, as this can be found in several works that have been written by well-known authors. They have all done extensive research and have given detailed account of their army exploits, both good and bad.

That said, there is often confusion as to the terminology used in classifying them, for there are many Bushman tribes, subtribes, affiliates, clans and so on. The name Khoi, for instance, which is inseparably linked to them, means quite simply, in their own language 'people' or 'person'. It is perfectly understandable that they would have referred to themselves as 'people', considering that aeons ago they were the only humans in southern Africa. All other living creatures were 'wild'.

My views are largely empirical and based on personal study and hard experience. I have lived, worked and fought with these people and had intimate knowledge of how they did things, or even sometimes thought and expressed themselves, no easy task considering cultural implications. Obviously, there will be those who differ with my interpretations, but in a nutshell, I give you this:

Their tribal organisation is simple. Each band or subtribal entity consists of a few families; they live independently in a large territory within which the tribe alone has rights.

From my own observations, without trying to appear condescending, I have found them very intelligent, musical, fond of dancing and great mimers. They can also be shrewd and crafty when occasion demands, these traits neatly slotting into the basic need to survive. Moreover, when they put their minds to it (as both the Portuguese and South African military discovered) they fight with a frightening determination.

They have no concrete concept of a divine being or a god as we understand religion, though their legends indicate a vague belief in an 'All Father' figure. Indeed, the Bushman religion revolves around idolatry and forefather worship.

Game and plant life have always been their sole means of existence: hence they were (and still are, when in outlying reaches) exclusively dependent on rain. It is therefore understandable that the rain god and the rain dance would play a primary role in their beliefs.

It is said that being exclusively hunters and gatherers, they were unique in that they were the only people who could survive from hunting and gathering alone. In fact, it is this hunting skill that brought the Bushmen into conflict with the other tribes in their vicinity.

The black tribes who later came from the north were largely cattle farmers, and to the Bushmen there was no difference between antelope and cattle: both were an easy prey. As a result they were driven from areas where the black tribes had settled. Because they have never been aggressive by nature, they tended to move out of harm's way when there was conflict and eventually settled in the semi-desert regions further north.

With the arrival of the Dutch and English settlers, the Bushmen were seen as vermin and were ruthlessly hunted and killed. Once again they migrated further north and large groups started arriving in what we today know as Namibia, Botswana and southern Angola.

The Bushmen that originally lived in the original South West Africa were very often badly treated by hostile colonialists. Many were shot out of hand when they 'trespassed' onto 'white' farmland, a situation that was particularly acute when the region was a German colony. There are many stories on record that show how they were hunted and, it is said, a copy of a hunting licence can still be seen in a museum in Windhoek. For this reason the Khwe moved into Botswana.

Nicolas Tenda (the deputy chairman of the Khwe) consulted the 'old people' on the origins of his people. He found that the Hambukushu tribal people that lived along the Okavango River gave the Bushmen the name of Hambarakwengo (also written as Mbarakhwengu). It means 'People of the King' because they lived in close proximity to the king's palace. This is apparently where the name Barakwena originates.

The Bushmen that originally lived in Botswana were known as the Mbarakhwengu but are also sometimes referred to as Waterboesmans (Water Bushmen).

Black tribes killed many of them and took their women and girls as concubines and slaves. Apparently it was the custom that black chieftains take Bushman women as wives. Nicolas Tenda maintains that one of his ancestors was a black chief.

As a result of interbreeding, the Khwe became larger in stature and darker in colour, some are nearly black. They believe strongly in ancestral spirits, the rain dance and witchcraft. Their language differs totally from that of the !Xun in that it has fewer click sounds, which are prominent in the !Xun language.

The group that had settled in Angola is known as the !Xun. When pronounced it sounds like Xung or 'ghung.' These !Xun people were also ill-treated by the black tribes in Angola and, with time, a bitter hatred developed between the two races. In contrast, the !Xun and the Portuguese settlers got along very well. This friendly relationship between the Portuguese and the Bushmen was to play an important role in the history of Angola.

The !Xun and the Khwe lived in central and south-east Angola and although the two tribes were in different areas, their history followed a similar pattern. They lived under primitive circumstances and derived their livelihood from cultivating *mahango*, an African millet species which was their stable diet.

Generally, these folk lived in small family groups seldom more than 50 strong. As with the other tribal groups, their lifestyle was simple and conflict seldom occurred. When conflict did occur, it was resolved within the family group. Only very serious matters were referred to the elders of the community. One of the tribal stipulations was that one person was never more important than another and the oldest individual in the family was the leader and the decision maker.

The Bushman people are a lot more astute in their understanding of the human psyche than most would give them credit for. I picked this up fairly early on and remember an event – or rather, a series of events – that affected those members of the unit involved with tracking, especially in hostile country.

I must preface this by the fact that Bushman combatants in 31 Battalion had not yet been issued with rifles at this stage. There were those in Pretoria (like the French before, who also believed the Vietcong was incapable of fighting an effective war) who believed they might not yet be ready to use them effectively. That, in spite of the fact that there was a mountain of evidence to the contrary.

While these 'Little People' served in the Portuguese Armed Forces, they were issued with the ubiquitous Portuguese Army G3 which used NATO 7.62 mm ammunition and were most effective with this weapon.

Once the Portuguese Army had pulled back to Europe, the war along the South West African border with Angola escalated substantially, with fairly large Bushman communities relocated southwards. Most of their men had been assimilated into SA Army units, but they were still not given weapons with which to defend themselves.

It went on like that for a while, with Bushman trackers involved in a number of follow-ups. While things went well to start with and there were successful contacts in which numbers of enemy combatants were killed, some of the Bushmen asked for guns but were denied them.

Matters then came to a head when several South African groups were close to make contact, but suddenly the trail went dead. There was no explanation asked for or given. Enemy tracks had simply disappeared in the desert sands and long grass.

Thereafter, the word got about that the Bushman trackers were not nearly as good as they were purported to be. Some of the South African units had been following spoors pointed out to them by their Bushman trackers and then, suddenly, there was nothing.

Eventually a Barakwena delegation of Bushman leaders – Keppies, Jack Bambo, my good friend and driver, and Johani Jam – asked to meet with me at Alpha Base in Caprivi. There were many gripes, and the weapons issue – or rather, non-issue – was only one of them.

Earlier, Bushman leaders had demanded to know why black troops out of Angola – the Flechas – had been made fully fledged fighters with the SADF: they had been trained and issued weapons needed to fight a war, but why, asked the Bushmen, hadn't they been treated in the same manner?

What I wasn't able to tell them then was that my hands were tied. Pretoria remained intractable about issuing guns to what some of Pretoria's stuffed-shirt bureaucrats referred to as 'primitive people'.

Johani Jam, regarded as a strong man in the community and somebody that I would often listen to, presented a strong case.

'Commandant,' he said, 'when I say these things I don't mean that we Barakwenas are better than the others. Neither do I want to say that we can do the things that you say we can do better than they can, but I want to tell you that when it comes to walking in the bush, there is not a man in this camp that can walk further and faster than Jack and me. There isn't a man in this camp that does not know that.

'I also want to tell you that we have already had good experience of going on patrol with white soldiers [at Babwata]. Many times we have found tracks and many times we have led them to the terrorists. These things are not strange to us.

'I agree that we cannot shoot with guns, but we can shoot with bows and arrows, and if one can kill a buck at a distance with a thing like that, then will we not be able to shoot with guns? If the Commandant will teach us, I am sure that we will be able to do so as well as anybody else.'

When Johani Jam paused, I saw my opportunity. This outburst was given with such conviction that it needed to be properly answered.

Yes, I said, I had heard of their tracking exploits with the white soldiers of the Babwata and I had also heard reports that they were not as good trackers as some had thought them to be, adding that I had also been told of instances where the tracks had led directly to the enemy and then suddenly been lost.

'How is it,' I asked, 'that if you are as good as you say you are, that you can lose a track when you are so close to the enemy?'

For a moment Johani looked embarrassed. He lowered his head and seemed to study the ground at his feet.

'Do you deny that the story they told me is true?'

Johani looked up and this time I could see determination in his face. He started slowly: 'No, Sir, I do not deny that the story is true. But there is another story I must tell you that others have not. There was a very good young man that I knew well. He was one of the best trackers in the bush. He could see spoor in the most difficult ground and he could follow it no matter where it went. This young man was one of those who went with the soldiers on patrol.

'Then one day he found a track and followed it. The soldiers were so excited that they kept on chasing him. Because the Bushman was eager and because he was young, he did not take enough care. He realised he had run right into a trap that the enemy had made for the soldiers. Of course the young Bushman was right in front and he had no weapon, so that when the enemy started to shoot, the young tracker was the first one to be killed.

'From then on the Bushmen didn't want to do the tracking anymore. That is why they decided to find the tracks and to lead the soldiers, but because it was dangerous, the Bushmen left the tracks when they got too close,' Johani Jam concluded.

I took the man at his word, but he wasn't satisfied. I asked Johani about honour and the fact that they took the soldiers' money and then deliberately led them away from the enemy because it was too dangerous.

'That is not only dishonest, it is cowardly,' I said to him sternly.

'Yes, Sir, that is true. It is dishonest, but not necessarily cowardly. A man that evades death when he sees it coming is not a coward. He just isn't stupid ...'

Johani also admitted that because of the original incident in which the tracker was killed, he never went on patrol, adding that the white soldiers didn't take the Bushmen out again because they said they were bad trackers.

'But that is not the truth. If they had given us guns, we would have killed many terrorists.'

The seriousness in the face of the man, coupled to the simple honesty with which he told his story was moving. I was not able to say anymore on the matter. For the umpteenth time I realised that the Bushman people might be illiterate and uncivilised, but they were not stupid.

Not long afterwards, on my first return to Pretoria, I took the issue up in person with one of the most senior generals in the South African Army. Shortly afterwards the Bushmen got the weapons they so eagerly sought.

With that, everything changed ...

CHAPTER 7

'Masters of the Unpredictable'
Al Venter

Enough then of history, hearsay and legend, except where the Bushman community found itself implicated in a succession of tribal wars in Angola, culminating in the liberation struggle that finally ousted Lisbon from Africa. The trouble was, because they had always been persecuted by the African tribes, the Bushmen in that country looked to the Portuguese as their protectors, having sometimes been subjected to slavery under some traditional black leaders.

Once the modern war started to gather pace, both the MPLA and the FNLA regarded the Bushman people as sworn enemies and thought nothing of hunting them as and where they encountered them in the bush. As mentioned already, they had their men castrated to prevent them propagating (and made concubines of their women), but that is another story, and then only if the male was considered useful as a slave. Old Bushmen and women who were regarded as 'non-productive' were killed.

What did eventually take place was that Bushman fighters found themselves battling the same insurgency then being countered by Lisbon's troops, usually as scouts and trackers and by some accounts – including FNLA and MPLA military intercepts – they were remarkably adept at killing.

One MPLA cadre, in a message to Luanda, made the point that guerrilla units should be especially wary if there were any Bushmen attached to government units in their areas of operation. 'They are ruthless, and extremely efficient as murderers,' he declared.

And so they were, as former Portuguese intelligence officer Oscar Cardoso told me. We met after I had returned with him to Serpa Pinto in a small plane sent to fetch me from N'Requinha, in the extreme south-eastern corner of Angola.

'They first establish where the enemy has his base and after dark they like to get in close, usually moving silently across the ground on their bellies ... and within a very short time they will have slit the throats of enemy sentries encountered,' Cardoso explained.

Colonel Delville Linford has similar stories to relate from the time that he commanded 31 Battalion. 'They had been persecuted by the black tribes for so long, they regarded those tasks as a form of payback,' he said.

But one needs to get close to the Khoisan community to understand many of the mores, customs and traditions that dictate the lives of this society, much of which is integral to their ancient history.

They have a remarkably complex language characterised by the use of click sounds. While they have no collective name for themselves in any of their dialects, they identify as a larger group with such names as Ju/'hoansi and !Xun (punctuation characters representing different clicks).

Their physical and spiritual worlds have always been centred in the bush environment in which they survived. They have their individual gods, linked essentially to this milieu and all Khoisan people reflect strong metaphysical beliefs. This is one of the reasons why traditional Bushmen practise shamanism, conjuring animals with sacred songs. According to one source, there are those among them who perform almost magical healing.

One of the senior members of the group attached to Colonel Linford's group was regarded as a witchdoctor and there was nobody within his ambit who would dare to contradict the man. He wasn't the brightest fellow on the block, but what he said, went!

Bushmen hunt enthusiastically in their ancient fashion. They are good marksmen and use small bows and tiny, unflighted arrows whose barbs are smeared with poison from the larvae of *Chrysomelidae* beetles.

They use a manual communication system while hunting and are often out several days at a time, since big game like the kudu or eland may take four or five days to become exhausted before they can be killed. Most prized is the eland, the largest antelope in southern Africa, which is significant not only because of its size but also because of its fat, very important to the diet of the Bushmen. They also believe it has supernatural potency.

Their women, in contrast, are the gatherers, their methods usually simple and effective. They use a hide sling, blanket, and cloak called a *karos* to carry foodstuffs, firewood, smaller bags, a digging stick or young children and perhaps a smaller version of the *karos* to carry a baby.

Empty ostrich shells are used to collect and store water following good rains, in anticipation of the hot, dry season.

An un-named Bushman warrior from Angola said it best when he declared:

> A long, long time ago, we, the Bushmen, roamed these mountains, masters of the unpredictable ways of nature. We were nomads then, moving with the great herds of game and the changing of seasons. When the animals migrated we followed, leaving no houses or roads to mark our presence here. All we left behind was our story painted in the rock, in the shelters, the story of sacred animals and our journeys to the spirit world. These mountains once gave us shelter and the herds of antelope gave sustenance and meaning to our lives. Especially the eland, for it is the animal of the greatest spiritual power. For us, it is the animal of wellbeing and healing, of beauty and peace and plenty.[1]

These hunters had their own bush navigational systems and the Bushman communities living 'wild' still use them.

If you get lost in the daytime, they will tell you, look in the palm trees for the nest of the red-billed buffalo weaver which always builds on the west side of the tree. You can also watch for termite mounds whose tips mostly lean towards the north-west; that would also help with finding your way if lost.

Possibly the most interesting of the ancient customs still in use today, though to a much lesser degree, involves birth. In his notes, Colonel Linford tells us that having children is not a problem.

'When the time is right, they go into the bush, accompanied by their relatives and friends. No man is allowed in the proximity but what I gathered is that the "midwives" would do the necessary. After the birth, they would rub the baby down with sand, tie a string of beads around its belly, wrists and ankles and hand it over to the jubilant mother. Any excessive haemorrhaging on her part would be arrested by plugging up her vagina with sand.'

As he says, when he first heard this from a nursing sister Steyn who was attached to the sick bay at Rundu, he was appalled and determined to do something about it. The nurse had been called in to deal with an exceptional case of post-natal haemorrhage which sand had clearly done nothing to help.

Linford's Barakwenas, it seemed, were related by a different tribal category – Bushmen – but with a more forceful identity, which slotted in well with his needs as a military man.

The Bushmen are monogamous and adultery is punished by a heavy fine, but some say that in former times a most savage death followed infidelity. Women are rather jealous: they often reprimand their husbands and even beat them.

Colonel Linford recalls further: 'The abhorrence of incest is so great that no son-in-law without children will dare address his mother-in-law and he can only look at her from a distance, as I have had the opportunity of observing.

'The parents' love for their children and vice versa is one of the most impressive manifestations among these folk ... they are so kind to their old people (and to their children) that, in fact, they prefer their father's company to their mother's! Parents pay special attention to their children, which is why they usually look better nourished than the elderly.'

During many visits in the course of the Border War, I visited Linford's Bushman base several times. I found it a welcome respite from the authoritarian rigmarole that characterised some of the bigger bases like Sector 10 Headquarters at Oshakati or even the more modest Rundu. Though literally 'carved out of the bush', the place retained its original simple 'bush' identity, which was surprising for a military establishment.

The base lay almost within walking distance of the Angolan frontier which meant that security was tight. White troops bivouacked in their own area apart from the Bushman settlement which eventually became a thriving little village with a clinic, schoolrooms and a community hall where children as well as adults would spend many evenings entertaining each other and those white troops who might have been interested in their culture.

I spent an evening exchanging war stories with some of the young officers in charge and it was clear that they enjoyed their roles. Certainly they got on well with the Bushman soldiers and entrusted many duties to the ethnic NCOs who were regarded by the Bushman youngsters in the unit with an almost avuncular reverence.

Afterwards we decamped to the office-cum-sleeping quarters of one of the captains, also a young man but obviously somebody who had already experienced a good bit of action both in Angola and in the former mandate. On the corner of his desk was a human skull, clean as a whistle and clearly sun-dried over what must have been many seasons.

The head had originally belonged to one of the local Africans. He'd apparently joined the guerrilla movement some years before and it had been brought to him by one of the trackers after he'd died in a contact with the unit. He said he remembered its original owner, the little man confided.

The dead youngster had been charged with looking after the kraal goats, but as the tracker explained, using language of his own, 'the silly bugger wouldn't listen, so look at the fucking mess you're in now,' he declared, looking severely at the skull on the desk.

For a while, the story became part of the barrack lore and I heard later that the skull had many visitors. That went on until a senior officer visiting the base from Pretoria told those in charge to get rid of it.

One of humorous vignettes that did the rounds about 31 Battalion – for several years in fact – involved the school that Commandant Linford established at the base. All the children were required to attend in order to learn 'the three R's', with young conscripts – mostly university graduates doing their national service – teaching, almost all of it in Afrikaans which, whatever the colour of your skin, was the SADF lingua franca at the time.

There were always several classes on the go during the week and by all accounts, there were even tests arranged for the children at the end of each quarter. The Bushman school was a success story on its own and eventually attracted the attention of the educational authorities in Windhoek.

On a prearranged day a school inspector was escorted to the base to do his own assessment of the school and, by all accounts, he was mightily impressed. He only stayed one night and chose to attend a class being given religious instruction by one of the young white soldiers, in Afrikaans, of course.

On the blackboard in front of the class were two large drawings, one of a devout figure who was clearly Jesus, and the other with a set of grim-looking horns protruding from its forehead. The 'teacher' waited for the inspector to settle himself at one of the desks at the back of the class and then went on, pointing at Christ.

'*En wie is dit?*' (And who is this?) he queried, pointing with a long bamboo stick.

The class answered in unison that it was Jesus, sounding out in a loud chorus: '*Prys Hom … prys Hom*' (Praise Him, praise Him).

Turning to the horned figure, he asked once more who that was. Again the children answered loudly, almost as one voice: '*Dis die duiwel … fok hom! Fok hom!*'

Which needs no translation.

---

1 Quote from http://kwekudee-tripdownmemorylane.blogspot.co.uk/2013/06/san-bushmen-people-world-most-ancient.html.

CHAPTER 8

In Search of the Promised Land

As Delville Linford commented, pursuing the Holy Grail of a mythical Promised Land proved elusive, but when the quest was on, if 'you and others can't find it, you then must try to create it'. And that means effort: lots and lots of it. He recollects his thoughts and takes us back:

It was dark when I woke on my second day in the bush. The camp was totally quiet as I crawled out of my sleeping bag and pulled on my boots. Because I'd pointed my feet southwards the previous night, I was easily able to orientate myself. I turned about and walked quietly into the bush, roughly in the direction we'd come from the previous day. I hadn't gone far before the night sky brought me to a halt.

Before me, to the east, the horizon was beginning to glow with a faint, pinkish light. Etched in sharp black lines in the middle-distance was the stark silhouette of a tree.

Unmistakably, it was an old, dry camelthorn, its boughs long since stripped clean of leaves and twigs, probably by elephants. The trunk formed smooth black lines against the backdrop of a soft greyish tinge and presented a picture of extraordinary beauty.

Almost like a revelation, it came to mind that this tree surely had to be the only thing on earth that, even long dead, could be so beautiful. Standing there, in the quiet dawn and totally isolated, I felt the serenity of the bush creeping into my soul. How close one felt to nature at a time like this.

Gradually other things around me caught my attention. There were nightjars and a single owl that called, and somewhere in the distance a lonely jackal made a final effort to attract a mate, only to be ridiculed by a hyena from somewhere beyond.

Then I heard a strange humming noise, accompanied by a faint crackling sound. Straining, I eventually traced it to the branch of a small tree near to where I was standing. I couldn't immediately see what it was, but clearly, something there was working very hard.

There I stood, perplexed and totally awed by the magnificence of this primeval world as the first illuminations of dawn started to spread across the sky.

At that point, the uneasy mutterings of a human presence reached me. There were voices and rasping coughs and in the still morning air these sounds jarred, almost like harsh hammer blows. No question, a new day had started.

And with a degree of irritation, I rallied, feeling that my privacy had been abused. But then, I thought, that's life …

I made my way back to the camp where I found people emerging from their sleeping bags and disappearing into the bush. Others were already building fires while still more sat around watching water boil.

José looked up from where he lay on top of his sleeping bag and said in his quaint Iberian-tinged drawl: 'Hey, Commandant, don't you sleep like other people?' I chuckled and greeted Edler who had marched up with a mug of coffee in each hand.

'You must be careful, Commandant,' he said, stressing that the bush around us was treacherous. 'Especially at night, and it could be dangerous if you walk about in the dark.' With that, he smiled condescendingly.

I thanked him for the coffee and wondered how long I was going to be able to remain slotted into the role of greenhorn. What Edler saw in my face, I don't know, but he made the observation that it was going to be hot again today.

'We must get an early start. Major, will you please get the people to strike the camp while I fix that truck. Then we can move on.'

I might as well have been sitting in an office in Army Headquarters for all he cared, which was when I thought, to hell with the greenhorn! 'No, Werner,' I replied, pulling myself erect, 'You go and fix the truck and leave these people alone. I believe the place we're looking for is to the immediate west of here and right now I'm going to drive that way and see if I can find anything.'

'Do you want me to come with you?' asked José.

'No thanks,' I replied. 'These Bushmen are supposed to know the bush. Find me one that I can take along. You take care of the camp – just see that Edler gets that bloody wreck going and we'll decide what to do when I get back.' I turned to Edler: 'Werner, bring me your map and get me a rifle with a full magazine, but try and find one without the letters BLR on it.'

It suddenly dawned on me that this little outburst must have been the most words I'd spoken consecutively in the past 36 hours and I didn't miss the look of surprise on José's face.

I studied the map closely and was still trying to figure it out when Edler marched up with a Bushman at his heels.

'Commandant, this Bushman's name is Jack Bambo. He is able to speak some Afrikaans and he seems to be the brightest of the lot.'

I looked at Jack with mixed feelings. He was tall for a Bushman, with a lean body and a strong face with a rather square jaw. He stood upright with shoulders straight and he looked me squarely in the eye.

In answer to my questions, the man told me that he'd slipped into the country from Angola with a group of East Caprivian contract workers, and consequently found his way to a gold mine in South Africa. And that was where he'd learned to speak Afrikaans, which was good enough for me.

I took the rifle Edler had offered and got into the Land Rover. With the aid of the sun and the shadow of the gear lever, I determined in which direction I'd need to head if we were going west.

'Hey Jack, where is Rundu?' He pointed straight ahead.

'Right, that's where I want to go.'

Jack looked at me in surprise but said nothing. He made as if to climb into the passenger seat, but I told him no, he should walk. 'Now go!'

He looked at me in great surprise, but then turned around and headed into the bush at a brisk walk. I drove after him. Dodging left and right to by-pass thick undergrowth, I soon lost sight of him. After several hundred metres I stopped and called out to him. His answer came from directly abreast of me, but some distance further to the south. This was exactly what I wanted to determine.

Through the bush, dense and in places almost impenetrable, I was making, on average, about the same progress as Jack. Judging his walking speed at about five kilometres an hour I was now able to determine our progress with a reasonable degree of accuracy. I called Jack and told him to climb aboard.

I noted beads of sweat on his forehead, but sensed the look of relief, rather than seeing any signs on his stark features.

It was a good start and while I didn't have the slightest illusion about locating the Promised Land, I did have a burning need to establish just where in Africa I was. So, with gear lever and watch in hand, I navigated as accurately as I could manage.

From time to time, Jack would jump off and run ahead, all the while indicating the best route through a dense forest cluster. The rest of the time I just filled by talking to Jack.

It didn't take me long to discover that my newfound travelling companion was blessed with a wealth of knowledge of this vast and primitive country that we traversed. I learned as much about the bush and the native Bushmen as what the time available and what Jack's limited vocabulary would allow.

After we'd travelled what I estimated to be about 20 kilometres, much to Jack's surprise, I turned hard north. I reassured him, but I didn't have the courage to try to explain my theory which centred on the fact that approximately 20 kilometres west of the cross that Edler had made on his map, the highway turned sharp left for several kilometres and then swung right again.

I sensed that Edler might have turned off the road too soon. My instincts told me that if I travelled west for about 20 kilometres and then cut north to the highway, I should locate the bends in the road.

This might sound presumptuous to anybody not familiar with the Caprivi's many quirks, but to my mind it made sense. So I wasn't too surprised when we hit the highway. Then, heading east a few more kilometres, we came to the two bends that were indicated on the map.

By calculating both time and distance, I was able to locate the point where the convoy had turned off the highway with reasonable accuracy. In as few words as possible, I explained to Jack that Edler had been travelling zigzag and he agreed. I asked him to walk ahead and attempt to cut a route 'as the crow flies'.

It was about mid-afternoon when we returned to the temporary camp we had pitched the previous night. José and the others greeted me enthusiastically. Did I find the Promised Land they asked, almost in chorus.

'No,' I replied with a smile, but I did manage to work out exactly where we are and it is not where we think we are.' José merely raised his eyebrows, but said nothing. Edler was a lot more difficult to convince. Frankly, at that stage I really didn't care whether I'd won him over or not.

I turned to my Portuguese friend. 'José, do you remember yesterday we drove past a big camelthorn tree and I told you that I wouldn't really mind pitching my tent under it?' He nodded assent.

'Well, I can tell you now that that magnificent tree is less than a kilometre along the track we came.' I hesitated a moment before I added: 'And I would still like to pitch my tent under it. So, will you please move the convoy back there and pitch a temporary camp. We'll stay there until we find our elusive Promised Land. In the meantime, while you move camp, Jack and I will take a look towards the east.' The rest of the group seemed to be getting used to my long speeches because no-one said a word.

Jack and I motored due east and then turned north. A few kilometres later I stopped before turning the nose of the Land Rover towards what I thought was slightly south of west and asked Jack where our camp was. He pointed directly ahead.

Obviously, I was delighted. My gear lever trick was working. However, estimating direction by means of all sorts of gimmicks was one thing, but finding a particular point the size of a rugby field in that bush, was another, so I said to Jack, 'Okay, let's go home – you show the way.'

Jack took me straight back to our original camp. I found that my tent had been neatly pitched under the camelthorn tree, and inside, a rusty old army bed complete with a tatty sponge rubber mattress and a lumpy pillow with narrow, barely visible black stripes awaited me.

What more could a man ask for – except perhaps a tall glass of gin and tonic with two cubes of ice. But I was not complaining.

I will always think fondly of this day as 'The Day of the Crow'.

Creating a permanent camp with the kind of equipment that Edler had scrounged at Rundu was something else again. Confusion reigned!

Tents, cooking utensils, bedding, rations, furniture, medicines of sorts, tools, building equipment, weapons, ammunition, fuel and every other conceivable bit of what-not he could lay his hands on had been piled in total disorder onto the trucks.

What with 39 black troops together with their families (15 wives and 11 children) and belongings under Corporal Anthony Lloyd, as well as 15 Bushmen with their wives, 27 kids and belongings piled on top of everything, made for total disorder. After this lot was offloaded and dumped in piles on the ground, the tents were extricated and pitched. Then came rain and as much as possible was carried into the tents. There was no order to it all, no system ... just taken in and out of the rain.

Complaints followed. Almost immediately I was inundated with issues ranging from coughs, temperatures, fever, headaches, unwanted pregnancies and threatening miscarriages, to diarrhoea and constipation. Overnight, I'd been transmogrified into the village physician, but with my limited knowledge of medicine, I felt a lot more like the village idiot.

I started by searching frantically for the unit's medical supplies, but it was not easy. Much of the stuff had been trampled, crushed, melted, dissolved or crusted with mud. Quite a bit, it later transpired, had been lost or misplaced. But I did eventually locate some supplies that had been crammed into a few plastic lilies (the army term for field urinals). These were more or less intact and hopefully uncontaminated.

In the end, I seemed to manage with most of the ailments. I'd raised my two boys well into their teens and was consequently vaguely acquainted with quite a few of the symptoms and that helped. Fortunately, some of the medicaments had labels indicating their use and dosage.

Finally, we seemed to muddle through and with a few days of warm weather and sunshine, things started looking up again.

One of the biggest problems we faced was literally 'feeding the masses'.

Because there were no shops in the vicinity where the people could purchase food, the entire population of Alpha had to be fed on army rations.

This was easier said than done. In a normal community, I suppose this would have been a simple matter. All you had to do was compile a list of the soldiers with their wives and children. Then calculate the number of adults and children and break up the rations accordingly. In this community, however, it was not so straightforward.

CHAPTER 8: IN SEARCH OF THE PROMISED LAND

With some of them preferring to take more than one wife, though it was against traditional custom, the matter was more complicated, and to try to keep record of who was whose wife and which children belonged to which mother (and whose wife she was) ... never mind the rest of the conundrums that waited to unfold, was an impossible task. I just had to accept the fact that under the circumstances it wasn't easy. So I set about devising a plan that worked well once we had got it properly sorted out.

I'd already made specific lists of the people involved, classified them into families and photographed them in their groups. I had also issued each soldier with a dog tag which he wore around his neck. The next step was to dog-tag each of the soldiers' wives. On those tags were the names of their husbands and the number of children.

When the rations gong was sounded, the women gathered in their respective companies and were issued their food according to their dog tags. Other dependants were individually dog-tagged. On their tags were their own names plus the names of the soldier to whom they were attached.

In order to justify army rations for these people, we took them into service on a temporary basis. They became known as what I termed 'the Chelsea Pensioners'. Their job was to keep the camp free from litter and do other useful jobs in and around the base.

Some were employed as hygiene personnel or scullions and to make fire in the 'donkeys' which supplied the kitchen and bathrooms with hot water. For their services they were paid a salary from the Unit Fund, and they were also issued with rations. In this manner we were able to keep tabs on who was who and made sure that everybody got equal rations.

As soon as the situation was reasonably under control and I might risk leaving Edler and the camp, I mustered six young servicemen and we sallied forth into the wild unknown. Our search was still on for the Promised Land.

After blundering through the bush all morning, noon found us once again with a faltering engine. The driver of the Bedford, promptly got stuck into the engine and the troops on the back of the truck got stuck into their rations. I sat in the front seat trying to catch up with my diary I had started at Babwata, but due to circumstances, had fallen in arrears.

My thoughts were interrupted, not by a particular sound, but rather a lack thereof.

I threw a quick glance at the troops on the back of the truck. As if mesmerised, they just stared ahead, eyes fixed and unblinking. One soldier had just taken a spoonful of food and he sat there with his mouth full and expression almost uncomprehending. I followed the direction of their stares and froze.

Ahead of the truck, some 30 paces away, were the first enormous grey-brown hulks of a herd of elephant. Then more and more of these magnificent creatures arrived, and still more. There were hundreds and they moved silently, straight towards us!

There we were, everybody sitting on an open Bedford truck with a crook engine. While we remained motionless, a sea of grey-brown, round-humped jumbos completely surrounded us, almost as if we weren't even there. Fortunately, they barely spared us a glance, moving quietly and gracefully to get past. There wasn't a tad of aggression from any of them.

The elephants must have taken only a few minutes to get passed us, but it seemed much longer. Then they were gone.

For some time afterwards we could hear them chomping branches and foliage as they moved along. Only after the stragglers had passed did I start to breathe normally again, as did everybody else on the truck.

Then, quite unexpectedly, an enormous elephant bull emerged from the bush immediately ahead. Unlike the rest of the herd, he looked at the truck and stopped. Stalemate followed as he gazed at us with much interest, because we all sat transfixed. Again!

Of elephants, their habits and predilections, I knew absolutely nothing. Werner beside me, who supposedly had a wealth of knowledge of the bush, wasn't talking. Consequently, we had no way of interpreting the intentions of this great monster when it raised its trunk and slowly started to flap its ears slowly. Ideally, we should have simply driven away, but our vehicle stood there, immobile and with its hood open.

I did not know at the time, but found out subsequently, that an elephant only behaves like that immediately before it is about to charge.

Of elephant psychology I knew nothing and cared even less. But

I did experience indescribable relief when the great beast lowered its trunk and seemed to lose interest. He strolled past with no more than a sideways glance at us.

As if by pre-arranged signal, everybody came to life at once. Each one of us carried on with what he'd been doing or pretending to do. It was almost as if nothing had happened.

As if fate played a hand, the engine almost magically coughed and spluttered and we moved on. Outwardly we gave the impression of being casual and unworried, but inside, it was something totally different.

I looked again at the almost boyish faces of the youngsters around me and my thoughts turned to my own two sons. Their turn for National Service lay ahead in the not too distant future. Surely there must be another way of doing this, I thought. To run the risk of kids being trampled by an elephant was not the way …

From here on in, I thought to myself, I would find the Promised Land on my own.

From that day on, the two of us set out every morning with our Land Rover, a rifle and a box of rations, with Jack often preferring to walk ahead in thick bush country.

We found many big trees, numerous water holes and enough patches of green grass to feed vast herds of cattle, but never the combination of all three together.

It was on one of these excursions, while travelling along a *shana* and quite close to the verge of the bush, that we had an unusual experience. It had been raining the previous day as well as during the night and now and again I had to detour slightly to miss large pools of water. Near one of these puddles my eye picked up something moving, so I slowed down and approached carefully.

Once close, I saw a baby warthog playing in the mud and obviously so engrossed in what it was doing that it didn't notice the approach of my Land Rover. What possessed me to do what I did then, I have never yet been able to explain, even to myself. I guess everybody does foolish things from time to time, and I was no exception.

Telling Jack to step back a little, I stopped the vehicle and got out. Carefully, step by step, I stalked the little creature. It was completely oblivious of what was going on around him, so I had a marvellous chance to get a very close-up view of the little fellow.

Having been raised on a farm, I have a great love for animals, all animals. Piglets, lambs, chickens, ducklings and pups were always the most important things in my life. This little one was the exception. It was without doubt the ugliest little creature that I have ever laid eyes on. Its head was far too large for the scrawny tapering little body and its spindly little legs hardly looked capable of carrying its modest weight.

But it was the face that really got me, and the expression 'a face that only a mother can love' suddenly made a lot of sense.

Just then, caught up in a moment of delight, I wasn't aware of Mother Pig coming out of the nearby bush, obviously checking on how her baby had gotten on with his bath. It was only when I heard an enraged snort and looked around that I saw the danger. Mama, hair bristling, tail erect, was already at full charge.

I don't know how far from the vehicle I was at that stage, but I very quickly discovered that I could outrun a warthog over that distance.

Going out of the camp into the Caprivi wilderness every day, I would quite often take Jack along with me. His knowledge of the bush always proved to be of help, sometimes immeasurably. Blessed with an uncanny knack known and understood only by Bushmen, he seemed almost instinctively able to smell out water holes.

We criss-crossed that corner of the Caprivi and I learned a lot. Jack was not only my tutor, he also became my friend, and I never ceased to marvel at his incredible senses and instincts.

One day we were having our lunch in the shade of a cluster of enormous trees, talking of this and that when suddenly he stopped in the middle of what he was saying. He listened intently, head cocked and hand raised. I looked at him enquiringly. But he did not speak, not yet, anyway. Then his raised hand took on the shape of a giraffe's head and he indicated with his fingers that there were three of them.

With that he bunched the tips of his fingers and pointed to his mouth: the giraffe were eating. He glanced up at the trees and pointed at the branches overhead.

I looked at where he was pointing and sure enough, his fingers indicated where the leaves had been cropped quite high up in the trees. Then he pointed at their dung on the ground and at the other trees. His sign language was specific: this is where the giraffe come to feed.

Suddenly he pointed at his ears and again simulated the head and neck of a giraffe, but this time the animals were on the run. Jack dropped his gesticulating hand and smiled. The spell was broken.

'They sensed us and they ran away,' he explained a little later.

All through Jack's silent commentary of the animals and precisely what they were doing, I neither saw nor heard a thing. I didn't even catch a whiff of their presence, even though giraffes have a distinctive odour of their own in the wild.

On another trip in this remote bush I picked up a puncture. To my horror I discovered that somebody had removed the wheel spanner from under the seat of my Land Rover. Try as we might, there was just no way to remove the flat tyre.

I cursed my own negligence for not having checked my tools personally, but partly consoled myself with the fact that we were on the Golden Highway and passing traffic would soon enough offer help.

By evening not a single car or truck had come by and there was nothing to do but to sleep off the night and hope for better luck in the morning. I stretched myself out on the seat of the Land Rover and tried to make myself comfortable.

This was impossible. Soon my legs became cramped and it wasn't long before a cool night breeze sent a chill right through my bones. I could hear Jack fidgeting around, but in the dark I couldn't figure out what he was doing. Then I heard him quietly calling me in the dark.

When I got out, I found him under the Land Rover and he beckoned me to crawl in too.

Taking me by the shoulder, he pushed me gently down beside him, where he was lying. 'Lie here, it is warmer,' he said.

Somehow he had managed to dig a shallow trench in the loose sand and had piled it up between the rear wheels of the Land Rover, which was when he motioned that I should crawl into the shallow hollow. Then he lay down alongside the trench, opposite the sand bank.

To my surprise, the rear wheels, sand bank and Jack's body formed a perfect shelter from the wind and the temperature was consequently several degrees higher.

I woke up several times during the night, more by sense than because of any specific sound. Once it was the click of the safety catch of a rifle. Jack was staring intently into the darkness, weapon ready, every fibre in his body alert. I didn't dare to speak, so I quietly drew my 9 mm pistol and waited.

After an immeasurable period of time I felt Jack relax and heard him slip the safety catch back on. He reached out in the darkness and the slight pressure of his hand on my shoulder said it all.

When I recall incidents like these, only then do I realise how much I grew to love Jack and how much I came to miss him after he'd so tragically been killed in a landmine explosion. But that, like so much that went on in this terrible war is a story for another day ...

Anyway, we never did find Punchy's Promised Land.

CHAPTER 9

Locating Our Promised Land

The days sped by and pleasant as it was roaming around the bush, I was getting nowhere. The rainy season was coming and my patience depleted. What, I asked myself, was so important about this particular spot in the remote Caprivi bush that Punchy Botha had selected?

I decided to take a trip to Rundu to find out, so I instructed Edler to come along, just in case, and it was good that I did. We hadn't travelled two kilometres when we finished up with a flat tyre. I left Werner to handle the problem and walked off into the bush.

I hadn't gone far when I came upon another beautiful camelthorn tree, with a bunch of sparrow-weaver nests hanging precariously from some of the lower branches. This one was even statelier than the camelthorn tree I'd discovered in my earlier meanderings through the area.

About 15 metres high, it was a splendid specimen, with its bark rubbed off in places, probably by an elephant. The wood's dark reddish-brown texture was clearly evident.

What did catch my attention was a circle of about ten metres in diameter around the base of the stem, which was covered with elephant droppings. Aha! I thought, this was the home of the lone tusker we had come across from time to time. He must surely sleep under this tree. There was a strong scent of elephant which means that he couldn't have been gone long. I could even make out signs of a spoor – fairly fresh.

I strolled on a bit and found a small clearing in the dense bush. It could have been twenty or thirty paces in diameter. Right in the centre was the thick stem of a tree, long dead, standing at a slight angle. I stood motionless in the clearing and marvelled at how still it seemed with birds breaking the silence.

I looked up into a cloudless sky and I let the ambience seep into my soul. What a fortunate man I was.

To spend my days, stripped to the waist, with all this beauty around me when I could still have been sitting in that dreary office at Army Headquarters…

How long I stayed there I don't know, but eventually I became aware of an intense drone of noise not far away. I followed the sound and spotted clusters of bees disappearing into a hole in a tree not far away.

'The Land of Milk and Honey' the nameplate at Babwata had read. 'Just bring your own cow and bees'.

The idea of Babwata eventually stripped bare of trees, encircled with sand walls and barbed-wire fences made my mind drift back to Fort Doppies and all those trees and shrubs.

My thoughts were suddenly interrupted by a bang some distance away as Edler threw the flat tyre into the back of the Land Rover. So I ambled back to where I'd left him. He looked at me enquiringly as I pulled my pistol and fired several shots into the trunk of a tall tree next to the Land Rover.

'Is anything wrong, Commandant?' he asked, eyes wide.

'No, everything is fine, Werner, because we have found *our* Promised Land and I'm going to call it Canaan. Come, let's go home. We will find it again by the bullet holes in the tree.'

'What about Rundu?'

'Bugger Rundu, let's go!'

Once back at the camp, I called the six corporals together, and gave orders. I was going to lay out the camp and they were to go out in search of mopani bush and thatch-grass. I told them we were going to build a camp at the place where the elephant sleeps under the tree and we were going to call it 'Canaan'.

They could sense my enthusiasm when I said that we would start to build camp almost immediately. But the name Canaan never really caught on and our new home became known as 'The Place Where The Elephant Sleeps Under The Tree'. Later it was the 'New Camp', and then, Omega.

What the hell – what's in a name! To me it will always be the Promised Land.

After an early lunch I dispatched the corporals in search of suitable trees, each with a truck and a number of troops. I took one too, together with some Bushman labourers to start clearing the bush so that I could plan the camp's layout. That was easier said than done.

I went back to the tree where the elephant sleeps and thought that were I to walk in a large circle, beginning and ending at this point, we could cut away the dense undergrowth. I would then have a suitable clearing in which to set the outlines of the buildings we intended to build.

My first problem arrived with the bush itself: the undergrowth was so dense it was just impossible to walk in a straight line, let alone walk in a circle and finish up at the original starting point. After several attempts I gave up. At that point I heard what sounded like somebody chopping down a tree. If somebody cuts down a tree in this place, I thought, I'll kill him!

I walked quickly in the direction of the sound, and it brought me back to the clearing I'd found earlier that morning.

The Bushmen were standing round a tree in animated discussion. I looked up and then I realised that it was the same tree into which I had seen the bees disappear. Halfway up the trunk a young Bushman had chopped off the branch that contained the bees nest and was handing down large handfuls of honeycomb to his mates on the ground. He was smeared with honey from head to toe. I was furious, but the damage was done and I'd achieve nothing by kicking butt.

Then an idea struck me. I told Jack to climb into the slanting tree in the middle of the clearing and whistle continuously. I walked into the bush listening for his whistle until I could barely hear him. Then I stopped, made a 90 degree turn to the left and started walking. By listening to Jack's whistling, I was able to judge very roughly where the centre of my imaginary circle was. I'd brought a roll of toilet paper from my Land Rover and I used this to mark my progress through the bush.

Then, after hacking my way through the undergrowth with a panga for an hour or more, I eventually caught sight of my original 'Elephant's Tree' and I knew that my circle was complete. Torn and blistered by the thorny scrub, I made my way back to where Jack was whistling away merrily among the branches. And that was how that particular tree was to become known as 'Jack's Tree'.

By this time the day was far gone, but I was satisfied with my progress. And then I caught sight of the wretched little Bushman that had destroyed the bees nest. I should have killed the little bastard when the idea first struck me. He was busy rubbing sand all over his honey-smeared body. My stomach lurched.

'Jack, tell the men to mount,' I ordered. I got into my Land Rover and drove off, horror-stricken.

The next morning, soon after daybreak, I issued pangas to every able-bodied man and we set about hacking away the undergrowth in the area I had marked the previous day. This was a tough task in extremely difficult bush, and the troops soon proved not to be too good at it. But a good part of the area had been cleared and there was debris that had to be carted away, so I put the black troops onto this. Meantime, I left the wayward Bushmen to go on with the clearing.

The work was hard and progress slow. I could see that this was going to take ages and I was becoming increasingly despondent. What had I let myself in for?

The second morning I was surprised to see just about all the Bushman women had climbed onto the trucks along with the men.

When I asked Edler what it was all about, he explained. 'Commandant,' he said, 'Bushmen are not accustomed to doing this kind of work. That is work for the women. They are very good at it, and we will achieve much more with them than with the men.'

I was surprised, but said nothing. And he was right, because the women got stuck into the bush with their little pick-axes and before long, an area the size of a rugby field had been cleared. All the trees, according to my instructions, had been left untouched.

After the clearing operation, I divided the corporals into two teams. One team with the troops was to cut trees for huts, and the other, with the women, cut grass for thatching. And so it happened that the first huts were built in the 'New Camp.'

From the outset, I had private reservations about constructing a training camp using poles and thatch, but I had become acquainted with this sort of accommodation in Angola. Although it was basic and formed a reasonably comfortable shelter against the elements, it had very little else to offer.

Each hut was circular in shape, the walls formed by planting poles three or four inches in diameter against one another and leaving a gap for the entrance. The walls were about two metres high, with a single, longer pole in the centre that served as a support for the trusses. That, in turn, supported the thatch.

In spite of my misgivings, I let the building operation continue. It was now full summer and in the heat, almost always stifling, even when it rained, it made for a gruelling task. Add to that millions of insects that clung to your torso, while others crawled into your eyes, nose and ears and almost all could either bite or sting or both. It was all grime, sweat and *goggas* ...

We started early in the day to make good use of the cool hours, had a kind of siesta towards noon and then went on with it until fairly late in the afternoon.

Manual labour in this environment and climate might be acceptable if one lives under reasonable conditions. But even back at Alpha, our conditions were rough.

We slept in tents, on beds, mattresses and sleeping bags, ate our warmed-up canned rations out of mess tins and sat at 'tables, folding, six foot,' and on 'benches, folding, six foot'. And that was about it. This was what Werner thought an expedition of this nature would boast in the way of 'home comforts'.

When the troops returned to base each evening, sunburnt, weary and caked with sweat and dust, they weren't able to have a bath, because we had none. Water, too, was a problem, because it was transported all the way from Babwata.

I showed the youngsters how to improvise. You dig a hole in the ground and spread your groundsheet over it, fill the hollow with water, get in and do your thing. Lacking all else, this was at least a way of staying reasonably clean and hygienic. Trouble was, we didn't even have a few cans of beer to complete the picture.

I gave the driver of the water truck to Babwata some money and told him not to come back unless he brought some beers with him. He could buy a stack of cans from their mess. The message came back that they were virtually dry themselves, but they could spare us a case.

We decided to ration our precious supply to one beer per man per day, but when we opened the first can, it spewed out a shower of froth.

The following day I applied myself to solving one major problem: cooling our beer down to a temperature where it would not 'blast off' when one cracked the can. I searched the supplies tent and came across four canvas water bags.

After a lengthy contemplation of all options – coupled to a stroke of genius – I cut a horizontal slit across the top end of each bag. Edler wasn't happy, but I had my way. I filled them with water, put two cans in each bag and hung them in the shade of the trees. I said nothing to the troops and that evening after the unit's 'bath time', I invited the boys for a cold beer under my tree.

They thought I'd had stroke, but the expressions on their faces when I produced cans of relatively cool beer, stays with me.

For all that, the tasks in which we were involved were still clouded in secrecy, a vital aspect where Operation Alpha was concerned. Very few people knew of the existence of the camp, let alone what was going on in there.

The very idea of using Bushmen in wartime was repugnant. It went off extremely well in the Portuguese military, but this was the South African Army. As a result, radio comms were kept to a minimum and, anyway, there was never any mention of our activities.

At the point where our track met the Golden Highway, I'd erected a tent and had a telephone installed. Anyone who had any business at Alpha would phone from the tent, and then whatever could be arranged over the phone was appropriately handled. Otherwise I, or whoever was involved, would meet the person in the tent and transact business from there.

I didn't need to worry much though, because nobody ever visited us, and very decidedly, no outsiders were allowed.

As summer progressed and the heat became more intense, life became almost unbearable without some kind of cooling facility. After endless requests and motivations about health hazards with food, medicines and that sort of thing, we were eventually provided with a fridge and a deep freeze. We had no electricity – that was somewhere in the future, so the apparatus operated with paraffin.

Like most other things the army sent to Alpha, the appliances didn't work. After much haranguing, Rundu agreed to send out a fridge mechanic, their proviso that we evacuate the camp so that the mechanic wouldn't see the true purpose of our activity.

I couldn't argue – not that I saw any purpose in doing so – so I swore solemnly to do this, and diligently set about executing my plan on the specified date. The only thing that bothered me was lunch: I would have to feed my troops as well as the bugger who was coming a fair distance to repair the fridges.

I considered issuing everybody with dry rations, but that presented its own set of problems. Besides, the mechanic was only to be there for an hour or two, at most. I couldn't see any harm in keeping

Padua (who had become our chef) in camp to prepare lunch, so I briefed him.

'Padua, now you must please do your thing right,' I instructed him. Only come into the kitchen when necessary and no matter what, don't talk to the man who is coming here. I will explain to him that you are deaf and dumb. Okay?'

'Okay, Commandant, don't worry.'

Everything went well, and I was watching the guy doing his thing, when in trooped Padua. The mechanic looked up and politely greeted him. Padua was deaf as a doornail and dumb as an ox. I explained to the technician that he was deaf and dumb, but because he was such an excellent chef, we were glad to have him. I was such a convincing liar that the chap gave Padua no more than a sympathetic little half-smile and carried on working.

At this point Padua broke into a merry song while cleaning his pots and pans. Fortunately, it was something in Portuguese and nothing that made sense to the surprised mechanic. 'Don't worry about him, the old chap ... unfortunately, he is also half mad and when he gets excited he makes those weird noises,' I told the man from Rundu, adding that it usually preceded an attack of epilepsy. 'Excuse me,' I said, which was when I grabbed Padua by the shoulder and half-dragged him out of the tent and marched him some distance away.

'Padua, you stupid bastard! I told you not to say a bloody word!'

'But ... Commandant, I was singing.'

'Well don't sing, damn you! As a matter of fact, get the hell away from here.'

I returned to the kitchen and explained to the mechanic that I had put the poor fellow to bed until his fit was over. But whether the mechanic was convinced or possibly saw through the whole charade and just played along, I'll never know.

That night one of Padua's buddies called to him and said, 'Hey Padua, I hear that secrecy can make a man mad.'

For a long time he was unable to live this down.

CHAPTER 10

Alpha's Irrepressibles

Jack Bambo was not the only character of note. Some of the other characters that arrived at Camp Alpha would have been worthy of a book on their own. Most arrived from Angola with only their clothes on their backs.

The temporary base in which we had settled became known as Camp Alpha. In the beginning, the young servicemen were in high spirits and there was a lot of conversation.

They spent a lot of time talking about school, which was to be expected because the majority had emerged from school desks straight into army uniforms. There was even more about their basic training.

One particular story never failed to amuse me, so typical of military life in general. The youngster's name was 'Vaatjie' van Heerden, I recall thinking about the name, which, in fundamental English means chubby.

I looked at him closely as he spoke and thought that during his basic army training he might well have earned the name Chubby, but while at Camp Alpha he was a willing soul, he threw himself into everything he did with a furious macho gusto and as a result, this young man had trimmed down considerably. I fact, he'd emerged as a pocket-size Tarzan. His parents would have been proud of him.

Nut-brown muscular shoulders tapered into a narrow waist and were set off against a powerful pair of legs. He had light-brown hair, it stood out because it had been bleached by the sun. There was always a hint of a smile lurking somewhere around his mouth and it was quick to break into a wide pleasant grin.

I listened to one of his stories from a distance and it was interesting. He'd been standing in the queue at the Quartermaster Store, waiting for his kit, he explained to his buddies. 'As luck would have it, the guy in front of me was issued with the last bush hat, and the NCO doing the issuing called for a fresh supply from the store. When the bundle was broken open and the hats shaken out onto the counter, I could see that the hats were different in size and shape to the ones that were given to the guys ahead of me.

'The NCO threw one of them at me. "Hats, bush, brown – one!" he sang out to the clerk checking my kit list. I looked at the hat with its broad rim and square top, and said, "But, Sergeant, this hat is different".

"Yes, lovey," he replied, "that's because you're different."

'And from that day on my life became hell on earth. Fate had it that I was the only man in my company with a hat like that. I became known as "the man with the hat".

'"Hey, you with the hat! Pick up that matchstick"; "Hey, you with the hat, come here at the double!"; "Hey, you with the hat, go tell Van der Merwe there's a telephone call!"; "Hey, you with the hat, fetch me this or that!"

'I tried everything, but there was little I could do because I was the one with the hat that was different. And there was no way I could rid myself of this terrible curse.

'At last, in sheer desperation, I decided to lose my hat. I would rather face the corporal's wrath than go on like this, but even that didn't work. A guy I didn't know from a bar of soap, came up to me and said: "Hey, isn't this your hat?"'

Another of the youngsters at Alpha had been in the United States the previous year on a student exchange programme. His name was Lloyd and he had an endless stock of tales from across the sea which the guys would listen to with great interest because he was the only one among them who had been to America. One of these involved an embarrassing experience he had because of different cultural connotations sometimes attached to words.

He said something about being in a mixed class of boys and girls and they were apparently doing a writing exercise. 'Everybody was concentrating like mad and the class was quiet. You could hear a pin drop,' he told his mates as they sat under a mopani tree munching doggies.

'I'd made a mistake with my writing and wanted to erase it, and where I come from, we call an eraser a rubber. But in America a rubber means a condom, or a contraceptive. I turned to the desk nearest to me and addressed the girl seated there; you can imagine what went through her mind when I said, "Say babe, can I borrow a rubber from you?"

'In spite of my whispering the request, just about everybody heard it …'

And so, that evening, as the men whiled away the time until supper was ready, they all swopped stories and some made quite good sense. These youngsters, new to the army, were a willing, uncomplaining bunch and took most things in their stride.

Werner had become a sort of camp commandant, unofficial that is, and with it he inherited the job of cooking our meals, and I use the expression lightly. He would empty a lot of canned rations into a pot and bring it to the boil. There were also dog biscuits and he'd mix them up with a cereal, canned fruit and coffee. That was supper. But it was also breakfast and lunch depending on what time of day you ate it.

There were other times when Werner's duties would keep him out of our improvised kitchen, and he would prepare dinner sometimes so late that we would eat food in the dark because we had no lights. The youngsters were just too tired to kindle a fire, so they gobbled up whatever came their way and crawled into their sleeping bags.

On my part, because I had to do some writing at night, I needed a light, so I made a lamp for myself. I filched a peanut butter jar from the rations tent and emptied it, and from Werner's toolbox I obtained a length of copper petrol piping as thick as a pencil. I cut about two inches off and fixed it through a hole in the lid of the glass jar. I cut a strip of two-by-four flannelette that we used for cleaning our rifles into thin ribbons and fed the length through the copper pipe.

I poured half a cup of dieseline into the jar, screwed the top on with only a short length of flannelette protruding and the rest saturated by dieseline in the glass, and behold, there was light!

It was during one of those dark suppers that I made a promise to my troops. We were all huddled around my lamp eating our rations out of billy cans on barren tables and they were making smart-arse comments about our 'Five Star Hotel'. But somewhere, deep down, I could sense the first signs of tension.

'You guys here might not experience it,' I said, 'but I can tell you with confidence tonight that the day will come when those who follow after you, will dine in this camp in splendour.' The boys didn't laugh because they could see I was serious. I continued:

'We'll have five-course meals, served in grand style, by waiters wearing white gloves and bow ties and drink chilled wine from hand-cut crystal, on green lawns.' At that point they laughed.

CHAPTER 10: ALPHA'S IRREPRESSIBLES

But those who visited Omega in the good old days that came later, will know that I kept my promise.

I never did find out exactly how many people there were in Camp Alpha at any one time. Officially there was Edler, myself, six South African Army corporals (Wouter du Plooy, Phil Erasmus, Chris Kies, Anthony Lloyd, Vaatjie van Heerden and Lance [surname unknown]), about 39 black soldiers and 13 Bushman labourers. That meant 60 males in all. Women and children could have numbered a hundred or more. All the black troops had been documented at Rundu, but in order to keep track of the Bushmen, I tried to draw up something that resembled a population register, but this proved impractical because it was not possible – for me, at any rate – to physically write their names. There was no way that I could interpret their clicks and clacks and all the other sounds they used.

Jack was alright and so were Johnny, Keppies and Skyfie. But the rest and their women and children were not. So, from nowhere, we got hold of a Polaroid camera. I then arranged the Bushmen – men, women and children – into family groups and photographed them. After everybody had had their requisite sittings, there was a little boy left standing to one side.

Exactly what his story was, I never did quite figure out. However, I got the impression that he'd been orphaned, and although he hadn't exactly been adopted by any particular family, he had more or less become community property. The kid lived in the family group of one particular family, but they had not formally claimed him.

I had been very explicit in my instructions to Edler about camp followers – *only* blood relatives were allowed! There were to be no hangers-on, no friends, no distant cousins or uncles.

I looked at the little boy. He was slender but not frail; in fact, he was quite well formed. His face was clean-cut, with well-shaped features and a set of very white and healthy teeth. It was his eyes that first caught my attention because they implored whenever he looked at me. I sensed at the time that he must have been aware that his future at Alpha was in jeopardy.

I called together the Bushman families and they all sat in groups in an open clearing towards the middle of the camp. I handed each man the photograph of his group and the reaction was indescribable. Having come straight from an extremely remote corner of Africa only weeks before, what they saw before them on a tiny strip of photographic paper could have been nothing short of a miracle to these primitive folk.

But not even that hubbub and enthusiasm could draw my attention away from the forlorn little figure of the Bushman boy standing forgotten in the middle of the excited crowd. Being a child, he must have been desperate to be a member of one of those families – to be displayed, like everybody else, on a photograph with a mother, a father, and possibly brothers and sisters. Each time that there was a burst of exuberance from the children when they were handed a picture, his little face would light up in a smile and he would make as if to join in the jubilation. But he had been told to stand apart and he did as he was told. Then, after a few moments, his explicit smile would disappear and his eyes would return to where his little black toes were burrowing in the sand.

There was mistiness in his eyes when he next lifted them. Then I spotted a tear rolling over his cheek.

I could stand it no longer. 'Jack!' I called loudly, 'this little boy will stay in the camp, even though he has no father nor a family. I will be his father and I will give him food and clothing.'

I turned towards the photographer and told him to take a picture of the two of us together. For the record, because I couldn't spell his extremely complex Bushman name, I wrote 'Bokvoet' on the photo.

The delight on that little boy's face when I handed over this picture was indescribable. The other children crowded around him and the lonely stray instantly became the heart of attraction in Camp Alpha. I vaguely remember the story from childhood about the *Ugly Duckling*, and strangely, the parallels fit.

How simple life could be, I thought. How simple it was to turn misery into happiness and desperation into hope. All it needed was a little compassion and a few seconds' thought...

From that day on, Bokvoet became my alter ego, my shadow. I sent money with the rations driver and asked him to buy the boy some clothes in Rundu and so, days later, dressed in a red T-shirt with black shorts and washed squeaky clean under the supervision of one of the women, his little black-brown face shone like polished mahogany. Then his white teeth could be seen everywhere, and invariably in a grin.

CHAPTER 10: ALPHA'S IRREPRESSIBLES

Since then Bokvoet followed me everywhere, and I taught him many things. From his previous contact with the troops at Babwata, the boy had learned to speak reasonably good Afrikaans, so communication wasn't a problem and I soon became impressed with the little boy's initiative.

Using a salmon tin, the wooden plank from a tomato case and some nylon gut, he somehow contrived himself a little guitar, something he'd seen in some other camp. Quite ingenious, it worked. In the evenings he would bring out his little instrument and sitting on the bench in front of my tent he would sing and play.

Jack had another kind of instrument. It was a flat piece of wood with nails, the ends flattened and slightly curved. One end was fixed onto the plank so that the metal pieces lay side by side. The flat ends were loose and standing slightly apart from the plank, with the nails cut to different lengths so they would resonate at several different pitches whenever the ends were strummed with a finger. By twitching the flat ends of the nails, Jack was able to conjure up an amazing repertoire of tunes from his little bush-harp.

Many evenings, when the sunset glowed gold and red through the trees, he and Bokvoet would take up impromptu positions in front of my tent and play and sing. I made several tape recordings of their music and with great intent they would listen to the recordings.

It also surprised me when Bokvoet would make adjustments to his instrument, and then different sounds would emerge, with smiles of great satisfaction on his happy face.

Something that did cross my mind early on, was that the other children might become envious of Bokvoet's newfound status. I overcame this by giving him employment. Then he was no longer a camp follower or hanger-on, but a fully fledged employee.

I made him my batman, showed him how to polish and shine my boots and also how to prepare my shaving water. He also brought me morning coffee at sparrows each day. Bokvoet was happy because he was handsomely paid for his services and he soon became the only child that possessed his own money. Unlike other people I know, the money didn't go to his head. Indeed, Bokvoet was a very happy little guy.

He also had quite a sharp sense of humour, which I hadn't really expected and, I must admit, I didn't always understand. What he enjoyed a lot was to sneak up on me in the mornings without waking me and that caused a problem or two because I'd become a very light sleeper. In fact, my senses had become so keen that I was able to wake up at the sound of Bokvoet's naked feet on the canvas doormat outside my tent. When Bokvoet would sneak into my tent in the darkness and approach my bed, I was already awake and, with time, this became an unspoken contest: how close could he get to my bed before I would open my eyes. How was the poor little fellow to know that this innocent game nearly cost him his life.

He must have tumbled to the idea that it was the canvas doormat that gave his game away, so one morning he somehow removed it without my being aware of it. Anyhow it happened. Bokvoet was able to enter my tent, sneak up to my bed and put my coffee mug down quietly without me waking up. How proud the poor kid must have been with his achievement. It was only when he reached out his cold little hand and touched my shoulder, that things nearly went seriously wrong.

In a single, fluid movement I grabbed the pistol beside my pillow and pointed it at the shadowy figure before me. The youngster took terrible fright and ran like hell, screaming. We never played that game again.

During the census there emerged another unforgettable personality – a Bushman girl this time, probably twelve or thirteen. She was tall and on the skinny side of slender.

Like Bokvoet, her position in the camp was also complicated, as were most of their domestic affairs. Technically, she was a camp follower and, consequently, would have to be sent back to the bush.

But things were a little different with her, because I didn't stand up for her, but the community did. A deputation approached me on her behalf. Her name was unpronounceable, so I said, 'Okay, from now on we'll call her Twiggy. Now tell me about Twiggy …'

Slowly, bit by bit, the puzzle began to unravel. It seemed that Twiggy was not a blood relation of any particular member in the camp and what had become of her parents was not quite clear. What we all knew was that she'd been living with one of the families. I was told too that a member of this particular community group was away in South West Africa, where he was employed as a shepherd.

This chap, whose name I never did find out, the deputation leader told me, was betrothed to Twiggy. And never mind that she was barely into her teens, a marriage of sorts did exist. More to the point, it had been decided (though nobody could say by whom) that he would return and claim his bride when he had made enough money to close the 'bride price' deal with what could have been described as her foster parents.

Anyway, now that the family with whom she had been living had moved to Alpha, it meant that Twiggy would either have to move or become destitute.

There were two other issues that muddied the waters. First, because the host family had made a solemn promise to take care of Twiggy while her betrothed was tending flocks in distant South West Africa, they couldn't just abandon her: it was a matter of tribal honour and come what may, that made the issue sacrosanct. Secondly, because Twiggy was betrothed, and because her fiancée had been supporting her for some time until then, it was not really proper for her to take up with another man. This, I was told quite forcibly would be tantamount to a breach of promise … it couldn't happen in tribal terms.

I could see what was coming because these people were a lot more astute than one realised.

'Jack,' I said to my aide, 'I want you to find out if there are any other people like Bokvoet or Twiggy in the camp.'

He didn't hesitate, 'Yes, Commandant, there is still one more and his name is Rooikat.'

'Okay,' I said, 'tell me about Rooikat.'

'He is not related to any of us. His relatives live at Congola (another distant Bushman settlement).'

'Okay,' I replied, and I told him to listen to me very carefully. 'Twiggy will be employed as my laundry girl and keep my tent tidy. I will pay her out of my own pocket. Under these circumstances she can remain, but she will be the responsibility of the family that has taken her in. But Rooikat is another matter. Because he has relatives at Congola, I'm sorry, but he will have to return to the bush. That is my decision, now are you satisfied?'

'Yes, Commandant, you have made a very wise decision,' he declared visibly relieved, and his reaction quite made my day.

And so it happened that I became the master of two young people: Bokvoet, my personal batman, and Twiggy, my housekeeper. I ordered more T-shirts and skirts from Rundu and Twiggy discarded her ballerina-type skirt and boob tube. In the end she looked quite resplendent in her new red outfit.

Twiggy was a rather pleasant little individual. Although neither of us knew what the two of them were saying to each other, she always smiled and nodded and carried on doing whatever she was busy with at the time. Nothing I said appeared to have any influence on her activities.

Bokvoet, however, intervened on my behalf from time to time. Although he was younger than Twiggy, his linguistic advantage gave him the edge.

In the beginning I always told Bokvoet to inform Twiggy what I wanted her to do, but this turned out to be a mistake, because essentially, Twiggy didn't take kindly to him issuing instructions. Like all girls of that age, Twiggy had a sharp tongue and she didn't hesitate to use it on poor Bokvoet.

I then decided to talk directly to her. Obviously she didn't understand, so in a bit of a panic, she appealed to Bokvoet. He interpreted and this time it worked. Somehow, she didn't seem to mind Bokvoet interpreting my orders, just as long as he was not *giving* them.

Eventually there was order and harmony of sorts in my somewhat bizarre household.

As far as the housekeeping was concerned, well this was another matter. Twiggy didn't have a clue how to make a bed. Neither did Bokvoet. I tried to show her, but it didn't work. She was eager to learn, but try as she might, she just couldn't master the problem because she just wasn't able to put a sheet over the bed so that it hung down at equal lengths on either side.

First she would have one side dragging on the floor, with the other side barely covering the mattress. She would look up expectantly and when I shook my head, she'd rip it off and try again. This time the sheet would end up more or less diagonally on the bed. In desperation, I'd call for Jack to help.

'Jack,' I said, 'go and fetch your wife. I'll show *her* how to make my bed and then I want her to show Twiggy.'

Would you believe, Mama Jack couldn't get it right either and I subsequently discovered the Bushmen as an ancient culture do not understand the concept of symmetry: crooked, skew, parallel, diagonal, it was all the same to them. They simply couldn't see what in the world I was driving at.

Then, to my horror, I discovered that Jack did not have a clue either. I gave it all up and settled for my sheet hanging one side up and one side down. What the heck, as long as the thing was on the bed.

Whether my wash basin was in the middle of the table, on the side or even under it – as long as it was somewhere in my tent – ended up not mattering at all.

Twiggy, like Bokvoet, earned her own money and, like him, she soon enough assumed a certain air of importance within the community. That pleased me enormously.

Early one morning I was called to the sick bay. It was urgent, the messenger said. From a long way off, I could hear women and children shouting and screaming.

When I arrived at the medical tent there was mayhem. Apparently a pot of boiling porridge had been spilled over a nine-month-old baby. The scalding porridge had clung to the infant's skin and had caused horrific burns on its tiny body. The scalding stretched more or less from under the armpit, down the side of the body, to the leg and foot. I was distraught because this was something completely new and frightening to me.

As was their custom, they had rolled the baby in the sand and regardless of what the medical profession might have to say, the sand did cool the porridge which dropped away from the child's skin.

As coincidence would have it, a short while before, I'd been severely burned when a smoke grenade exploded in my hand. It was a bit of a mess, but the doctor at Babwata applied gauze soaked in paraffin wax to the wound and this had proved so successful that the burns very quickly healed. With this experience to guide me, and an adequate supply of paraffin gauze available, I set to work on the Bushman baby.

Having adequately cleaned the wounds, I covered them with paraffin gauze and then covered everything with great swathes of bandages. Then I broke a strong pain tablet in two and mixed half with sugar and a bit of water and got the baby to swallow the mix, or most of it. Just to make certain, I cut open a black and red capsule, mixed half of the contents with sugar and also fed this to the infant. I set a routine and had them bring her to me three times a day.

And to the surprise of all the others, it worked. Soon the wounds turned bright pink and before I thought it possible, the skin started to heal. It was tough, but we somehow muddled through, and the baby got well and was spoiled rotten in the process. With three visits a day to the sick bay, she soon became accustomed to the condensed milk, raisins, dried fruit and whatever else could be scrounged from the ration tent.

For easy reference I called her Snowy. Anyone that had dealings with Snowy soon became attached to her because she was an adorable little creature. She was eventually to become a well-known little character in the history of Alpha.

Having been cursed from my childhood with some kind of claustrophobic problem, I find life quite unbearable when my T-shirt clings to my sweaty torso. Life became impossible for me when the movement of my arms and shoulders were constricted by clammy, sticky material. So, in a moment of exasperation, I'd usually cut away the sleeves of my brown army T-shirts and throw them out.

How Snowy's mother had got her hands on those sleeves, I don't know, but one day she presented the little girl at the sick bay dressed in her customary bangles and beads, and instead of the usual string of beads around the waist, she sported a natty army-brown cotton skirt. On closer inspection, I discovered that her mother had threaded a piece of string through the ribbing of the sleeves of the T-shirt. Along the ragged verges where the sleeves were cut away, she'd sewn coloured beads. The drawstring was pulled tightly around Snowy's waist and the 'skirt'– with the beaded hem – flared out like that of a ballerina.

Anyone who hadn't seen Snowy in her army browns cannot vaguely imagine the picture. She had enormous black eyes, and like all Bushman babies, she was blessed with a fat, round belly. Even at that early age, the characteristic, bulging buttocks of Bushman women were evident.

On my routine daily inspections of Alpha's Bushman quarters, I made a special point of looking in on Snowy. Because she was still suckling, her mother was exempted from grass-cutting and she invariably spent her time with the other mothers, laughing and talking and playing with the babies.

CHAPTER 10: ALPHA'S IRREPRESSIBLES   107

Because of regular visits to the clinic, Snowy had somehow been kept a little cleaner than the other children. But one day I found her in a particularly filthy state.

Using Jack as an interpreter, I strongly reprimanded the mother. Brushing aside her excuses, I took a 50 cent coin from my pocket and offered it to her. I instructed Jack to tell her that she was a bad mother because she does not take care of her child. First she was negligent when she burned her child with porridge and now she doesn't keep her clean like I showed her.

Without ado Jack passed on the message. The mother dropped her eyes and hung her head in shame.

'Tell her also,' I said sternly, 'that because she does not look after the baby, I will pay her 50 cents for the child and I will take it upon myself to look after her properly.'

Jack interpreted and the woman's face brightened momentarily. But then it clouded over again and began speaking in undertones to Jack, pointing at her enormous breasts with her hand.

'She says the baby is too young to sell now, she is still feeding the baby,' Jack told me. I kind of got the feeling that my little joke had backfired, so I gave the coin to the baby and walked away. I was intrigued by the woman's remark, so I brought it up again with Jack and then learned that Bushmen sold their daughters in marriage, even at an early age. It was only after his explanation that I realised what a complete ass I'd made of myself.

Before I left Serpa Pinto in 1974, I'd appointed a young black boy as a servant in our house, nicknamed Makatees (sounding like the Afrikaans for 'make tea!') – an offensive term as I only realised much later.

He was still only a teenager, but very nice, always smiling, pleasant in his demeanour and very keen to learn. Because of the army mutiny in Lisbon, we all pulled out in a hurry and I left him there.

Much later, in Rundu, Commandant Punchy Botha mentioned that there was a young black fellow at his house looking for me. That surprised me. He said the little chap had shown his face in Rundu and started asking around for a certain commandant that had been in Angola. He told those who were prepared to listen that the man he was looking for had a beard and long hair. Eventually somebody referred him to Punchy's house.

When again asked to describe the person he was looking for, Punchy immediately knew it was me. He kept him there until I pitched up at Headquarters on one of my rare visits. Obviously, I was delighted to see the newly appointed youngster and he me.

On being questioned as to how he had crossed the border, it appears that when the MPLA took over Serpa Pinto where the Portuguese military and security elements had their headquarters, the first thing they did was kill my house cat and then they went after anybody who had anything to do with that house.

Makatees was fortunate to get away with his life. After an enormous struggle travelling weeks through the bush he eventually made it to Calai on the other side of the Kavango River and then got himself across the river to Rundu.

His real name was Manuel, and later Sergeant Major Jock Irving, a Scotsman who couldn't pronounce the youngster's difficult name, rechristened him 'MacTavish'.

When Bokvoet went on to become a schoolboy, MacTavish took over his duties as batman, and he also eventually became the barman in the Officers Mess.

Later he 'graduated' to medical orderly, a job for which he showed much promise, and eventually he became a very dependable and much relied upon member of the medical staff.

CHAPTER 11

Expanding the Operational Profile

As soon as I could arrange my affairs, I went to Rundu and discussed several new developments with the OC of the Military Headquarters. I was referred to the Staff Officer of Communication Operations, Commandant Jimmy MacAdam.

MacAdam was an impressive man. He was big and broad and square-shouldered with a large forehead that ran well into where his hairline would have started, if he had one, that is.

He was a delightful person with a quick brain and a very good sense of humour. I was glad that he was on board. Jimmy was going to initiate the ongoing project with me. We'd already worked together many years before and I'd always found him competent and cooperative.

We managed to discuss some of the outstanding details before I returned to the camp. The intention was that he would join me as soon as possible so that we could get our recruiting drive under way.

Meantime, in order to determine where and how we should start, Jack and I set out on an initial reconnaissance mission. We started at the one side of the Caprivi and worked our way systematically across the region.

I made a rough estimate of the number of able-bodied males in the different kraals and explained to the tribal leaders what we were looking for. It was obvious to me that this matter had already been discussed in great detail and that the subject was more or less known to most of those involved, but I went over the more salient points again: after all, this was war. Surprisingly, we were greeted with great joy everywhere we went.

Only once it didn't go too well. As we entered the kraal, we were greeted by a very old Bushman woman. We all went through the usual procedures, only this time it was as if there was something missing: there was no sparkle to the occasion.

The old woman greeted Jack in the usual manner, but before he had the opportunity of launching his well-rehearsed harangue, the old woman cut him short. And she was merciless. I was astounded at the ferocity of this little creature.

Small as she was, one was inclined to overlook her at first. But only until after she'd launched into her tirade did one take any real notice, because she had a lot to say. And that, for a very old and somewhat withered Bushman lady.

Like all the females, this enormously forceful character was dressed in a front-and-back skin skirt that was tied around the waist with a rawhide thong. Because of her age – and obviously her status in the community – she was richly adorned with beads around her neck, waist, arms, knees and ankles. Her hair was turned into dozens of little black wormlike strands a few centimetres long, threaded through with numerous white beads. According to tribal tradition she was bare-breasted like the rest of the women.

It was her face that immediately caught my attention: like the rest of her body emaciated but contrasted by two piercingly black, snake-like eyes.

As she lashed out at poor old Jack with her rasping, almost cackling voice, her little black eyes would flash with a vehemence that was matched by a vicious tongue. Jack was overwhelmed.

Bravely and quite exasperated, he tried several times to make some sort of a stand, but she cut him down with a torrent of words. Finally, he gave up and quite helplessly just stood there.

When it looked as if the old woman had run out of breath, I said to him: 'What the hell is all this about, Jack, why don't you tell her to shut up and listen to your story?' That was a mistake. The woman turned her wrath in my direction and for the first time I was made aware of the terrific surge of power that emanated from that tiny body.

Almost as if rehearsed, she planted herself squarely in front of me. The fact that she barely reached up to my waist didn't daunt her in the least. Prodding me in the midriff with the first two fingers of her left hand – like you do with prize bulls at an agricultural show – she said something in her own language to Jack.

He translated: 'She asks why you don't give her some cigarettes?'

'Tell her I don't smoke and neither should she if she wants to live much longer.' And that was the second mistake.

Her reaction was indescribable. Fortunately, I was unaware of her vituperative utterances which were delivered with great dollops of spittle, but Jack wasn't.

Eventually he held up his hands in what looked like a sign of surrender and surprisingly the old woman stopped. Jack turned round to the Land Rover and from the stowage box under the seat he recovered cans of beef, coffee, milk, sugar and everything else he could get hold of. He handed everything over to the old crony, talking all the while.

When he, too, had run out of breath, he turned to me and almost breathlessly said: 'Now, Commandant, we must go.'

'But, Jack, we haven't yet done what we came here for.'

'I know, Sir, but I will come here again later when she is not around. But right now we must go quickly.'

I didn't need much persuasion and we started off in great haste. When we got to the Golden Highway I turned in the direction of our camp, which was when Jack looked at me questioningly and asked where we were going. 'There are still more people in that direction,' he said.

'Yes, I know, but now that you have given away all our rations, what do you suggest we eat? Or are we going to live off the veld?'

He paused a moment or two before going on in a quiet voice: 'Commandant, you must not blame me for what I have done ... believe me, I did what was best and for you it was a great favour. One day you will be very glad about the rations ...'

Of course, while I didn't care a hoot about the food and rations, I was still curious about what exactly had gone on at that kraal. 'Okay, Jack,' I said, 'but now you tell me what that was all about?' Then the truth emerged.

'Commandant, that little old woman is a very influential person in the Bushman community. She is really a very nice person, but she can be vicious – as you have just seen – and everybody is cautious of her when she is angry.'

'Okay,' I retorted, 'but what was it that made her so bloody angry?'

'She says that we have taken her son from the kraal and have left her alone. Now she must sit in the bush and suffer while he is earning money and squandering it on the strange women from Angola. That is why I gave her the rations. I said it was from the men in Alpha, as a present for the women in the kraal and they would soon be sending more food and money.

'Also, I thought that was the only way that we could get the consent of the old woman to recruit more men, because I can tell you now that if she doesn't agree, we can forget about getting anybody else from there ... she is very powerful.'

My response was that he had obviously done a good job and that I was pleased. 'You are a good diplomat.'

'What's that?' he asked, confused.

'Never mind, Jack, but you are going to make sure that whoever it is that belongs to that kraal, sends money and rations. And quickly too!'

'You need not worry, Commandant, I will see to it, for sure ...'

Commandant MacAdam arrived at Camp Alpha in April 1975 and we got started. We made several journeys similar to that on which Jack and I had embarked and took down the details of quite a few likely candidates in each kraal. We told those who we thought might be suitable to report at our camp on a certain day to be tested and, if found suitable, they would be enlisted.

Jimmy and I spent many hours trying to figure out just how we were going to go through these motions. South African Defence Force standards were almost certainly not going to work in the bush with these little folk. But it was clear that we had to lay down some kind of specific standards by which to test them all, or we could end up with a complete shambles. Eventually we established a few guidelines.

First, each prospective recruit had to have two of everything: two hands, two feet, two eyes and two ears. Second, his limbs had to function properly and third, equally important, he must be fit. That meant that he had to be able to run a reasonable distance, without being winded. Also, we had to watch for basic coordination.

The next problem was how to actually determine all the basics we had laid down.

So on the day that the first batch of recruits arrived, we formed them all up in the open space in the middle of the camp, and this was something to observe!

Somehow we'd thought that only the young, willing and able would turn up, but we were sadly wrong. Everybody and his uncle

CHAPTER 11: EXPANDING THE OPERATIONAL PROFILE

and grandfather arrived at Camp Alpha eager to join the army: the young, the old, the healthy, the sick, the lame and the lazy. We even had some who had no interest in the venture but came along anyway. After all, what else was going on in the Caprivi that could not wait until this great and historic occasion was over?

By a process of visual inspection – or a series of them – we separated the probable from the impossible. Then we took what we thought were likely candidates and disqualified those that had any part of their visible anatomy missing. The not-so-obvious would come later.

That bunch was then subjected to the fitness test, which involved forming the men up in single file and have them run around in a circle all the way around the clearing.

After several rounds of this, we ordered them to walk past, one at a time, and with the help of the camp doctor, their breathing would be checked. The problem here was that almost every one of them smoked from a very early age and pulmonary problems were if not commonplace, then an issue that needed to be watched.

Add to that the fact that when they ran out of tobacco (which was often) they would mix up their own concoctions and this could consist of a mixture of leaves, animal dung and certain kinds of roots and herbs. One can only imagine what effect this had on the lungs.

In any event, by listening to their wheezes after having run a short distance, one could form a reasonable idea of what percentage of them were properly functional. Those that were seriously rasping and coughing and obviously winded were out of it. The remainder were put through several 'limb functions' tests.

This largely entailed swinging arms, touching toes and deep knee bends. Those unfortunates who were unsuccessful were then also eliminated and the remainder was subjected to the final and most stringent test of all: coordination.

We'd given this one a lot of thought and what was expected of them was to place one hand palm-down on his head, and the other hand flat on his stomach. Then he was told to simultaneously move the hand on his stomach round in little circles, while his other hand was patting his head. It was the sort of game we all played as children.

Although this is a suitable test to determine whether a person is capable of moving his two hands independently of each other, we soon enough had to dispense with it for fear of failing them all.

In fact, whether they really were unable to do it or whether they thought we were off our trollies was something that was also raised, but we finally settled for those that had got that far.

That was followed by the biggest hurdle of all: registering their details. As previously mentioned, the names were not only hopeless to pronounce, they were also impossible to spell.

We recorded details as best we could and then gave each of them a slip of paper that stated his name and told him that he was a successful candidate. They were suitable for enlistment in the South African Army, though we kept it simple by saying they were hired and would get paid at the end of every month they remained with us.

But now, we said through Jack, they should return to their kraals and only those who had been issued with papers were to return a week later. Of course this led to something that fringed on mayhem and some rather emotional scenes as the unsuccessful ones realised for the first time that they had not been recruited.

In the eyes of the rejected ones, this was tantamount to being robbed of the opportunity of becoming a soldier. It was tragic, of course, but what had to be done, was done.

We explained as best we could, but there was simply no nice way to tell a man that because of something totally beyond his control, he had been deprived of an opportunity to feed his family.

A week later, when the next phase arrived and the chosen ones turned up, we counted them and checked that their papers were in order.

Once we had made quite sure that they were determined to continue, we explained in very simple language that there was yet another step that needed to be completed. Jack told them that they would start with the training process and only after they had been able to prove that they were suitable would their families be brought to the camp to join them. There were quite a few who were not happy with what they heard, and only after I'd explained that if they did not like the things we were doing and the way we were going to do them, they were welcome to give back their papers and leave, did they calm down.

A lot of jabbering followed and I let it go on for a while. Then I drew a line on the ground, more or less as I imagined Lieutenant

Traverse had done on that fateful day at the Alamo, and said that those men who were satisfied with my terms were to walk over the line. My words were to the effect that those who didn't like the prospects could stay where they were and would be sent home.

I also made it quite clear that once a man had crossed the line there was no turning back.

This was the moment of truth and one could see the tremendous strain under which some of them had been placed. They were having to conform to Western standards, and that from a society that was still basically aboriginal in outlook.

It became much easier once I'd asked Jack if he and his gang of labourers would set the example. When they walked over the line, the newcomers followed, one by one, until they were all safely on the other side. There were 23 of them and with Jack and his crowd, it made 36 in total.

It also meant that we could form the recruits into a single platoon, a pure Barakwena platoon and ultimately, the first real Bushman fighting unit in the country.

Although there was very little room for sentiment in this game, I did get a certain feeling of satisfaction that we'd created a new way of life for these people, but the truth was that for them, their world would never be the same again.

This, I thought with a modicum of melodrama, was the way an army is born and it was no different with our Bushman friends.

In the meantime, I'd been advised that a new contingent of Portuguese instructors from Fort Doppies were now fully trained and waiting to be collected from the training camp. These people, all former members of the Portuguese Security Services in Mozambique – like José Pereira, Costa Diaz and Padua – had fled that East African territory when things went wrong.

General Fritz Loots, whom we called 'Godfather' because he was the ultimate *eminence grise* where southern African intrigue was concerned, had originally recruited them. On his instructions they had been sent to Jan Breytenbach's Fort Doppies where they had all been instructed in our way of soldiering.

This was the group of men that had been earmarked to take care of the Barakwena training and later lead them into battle in a series of subsequent operations. I sent word that we were ready and the instructors arrived.

In order to comply with Godfather's security arrangements, every one of the newcomers who were going to show members of the unit how things were done in the army had pseudonyms, which was how José de Oliveira became Joseph Olivier, and João Pedroso Miranda took on the rather inappropriate appellation of Johnny van der Merwe.

Getting our Bushman recruits up to speed, now that I reflect on it after many years, was a much more difficult task than we'd originally anticipated. We were faced not only with a language barrier, but also an enormous cultural gap in the attitude of these people to life generally.

The anomalies were substantial. In the South African Army we were always accustomed to doing everything on the double, particularly as a recruit. Doubling soon becomes a way of life to a rookie, but not so with Bushman rookies.

Though it might seem strange, dealing with a community that was almost solely dependent on their legs for basic survival in the African wilds, Bushmen are really not accustomed to running unless the situation demands. This madness of running all over the show like we from the so-called civilised world tend to do, was just so much nonsense to them. This worried me and several times I discussed it with Jack.

'Commandant, you must try to understand the way we Bushmen think. We are accustomed to walking many miles in the bush. We take our time, because there is so much time and besides, what must you do when you get to the end of your journey?

'When you hunt, it is wrong to run after a buck. In the first place, the buck can run faster than we can, and in any case, if you run, you cannot follow the track properly. So what is the use of running when you only scare the thing? Then you lose the track and finally you will have to give up because you are too tired from running.

'It is a much better plan to walk very slowly and quietly so as not to let the animal know that you are following him. So you track your buck very carefully and you do not have to walk unnecessarily to look for it ... you follow until the animal thinks you are no longer following. Then he will lie under a bush to rest from the sun and that is when you sneak up and kill it.

CHAPTER 11: EXPANDING THE OPERATIONAL PROFILE

'Surely you cannot just run up to a deer and cut its throat? Surely you ...'

'Okay, Jack, I understand all that, I am not stupid. But whatever you say, I still want you and your men to do all the things we say and we want you to do them *our* way. After all, that was the understanding we had when we started this whole business.'

'No, Commandant, we do not think you are stupid, in fact we think you are a very clever man and that is why we all find it so difficult to understand that a clever man like you can tell us to do such stupid things.'

Anyway, with all that, we eventually got the men trained and to our astonishment they turned out to be rather sharp. That is, of course, providing you don't judge by SADF standards.

Let me hasten to add that no matter by whose standards one judged those people, they were not to be underestimated. What comes to the fore most vividly in my mind, even today, is the pride with which these men assumed their new role – the *new* way with which they went about their business; the slight arrogance with which they pulled the tag on their beer can after a long, hard day of training.

They were no longer labourers, no longer inferior, and certainly not to be looked down upon. By the time we had all done our thing, they were fully fledged soldiers, worthy men, able to stand up with the rest, even the celebrated Flechas.

The Barakwenas were now combatants, though their proverbial 'baptism of fire' was still ahead. Right then we were all justly proud.

I remember a day when we took these men on their first fully fledged military exercise. When I say it was hot, I mean it was piping, in the tropical African sense of the word. We had run out of food some time before and were very short of water. I was beginning to doubt the sanity of the exercise. At that stage I believe it was only my pride and determination that prevented me from calling it a day and heading back to camp. Still, I was stupid enough to insist on going along to 'set the example' and to be there to 'encourage the men in case their morale started to flag'.

The platoon commander called a halt and in a state of exhaustion I dumped my pack in the shade of a nearby shrub and all but collapsed, lying with my head on the pack and closing my eyes in absolute misery. How long I'd been prostrate, I don't know, but I was aroused by footsteps and sensed, rather than heard, somebody close to me. I opened my eyes and wearily got them to focus on what was in front of me.

It was old Keppies, of all the people in the world. He stretched out a hand and to my utter amazement it was full of bright little red tomatoes.

'Commandant, we went through a patch that was once a vegetable garden and these tomatoes are now growing wild. Eat them, they will give you strength for the rest of the journey.'

This was just too much, I told myself, looking at him gratefully and in disbelief. But it was not. Along came Skyfie, and when he stretched out his hand, it was full of little brown berries.

'Commandant, these berries are not very nice to the taste, but because they are so sour, they are very good for the thirst.'

I took the berries from the little fellow, hardly more than a boy really and I looked at him through new eyes. I thanked them both and as nonchalantly as I could manage, I tossed the tomatoes down my throat, followed by the little brown berries.

With that, I got up, threw my pack over my shoulder and shouted: 'Come on, you lazy buggers, get off your asses and let's go!'

I stomped off into the bush before the men had even got to their feet to avoid being overcome with emotion. At the end of it, the Barakwenas passed their tests – if not with distinction, then commendably.

The second time I had to fight back the tears was when we strode into base, tattered and torn, starved and dehydrated. Not only had the families of the men turned out to welcome us home, even the Flechas had turned up to cheer them.

Worn-out as the troops were, it was something to see how the men lifted their weary shoulders and pushed out their chests. The pride in their filthy ragged faces was indescribable.

The Barakwenas had arrived!

CHAPTER 12

Some of the Ways of Bushman Society

As already mentioned, I spent a lot of time travelling about the bush, much of it in Jack's company. Although his command of Afrikaans was pretty basic, it was sufficient and we got on just fine. Also, I learned a lot from him. One day I followed up on an incident with Snowy's mother and it was his explanation of how things went in their society that intrigued me.

In bygone days, it appears, when the Bushmen were solely dependent on the bush for their sustenance, it was not always possible for the father to provide food for his children, particularly if he was getting on in years or perhaps not a good hunter. In such instances – if the minor was a girl – the father would strike a bargain with a young man in the tribe to provide food for the baby. This would happen until the girl reached puberty, when the hunter would be allowed to claim the girl for his bride: a kind of lay-by system, so to speak, but in those primitive groups it made a lot of sense.

However, the rest of Jack's story left me wondering. Whether this is true or not I cannot vouch, but this is how he explained it:

Before the girl was presented to her husband, the entire male population of the tribe had the opportunity to initiate the bride in the ways of marriage. Only when this was done would the bride be handed over to her husband.

'Jack, this is unbelievable, is it still like that today?' I asked him.

'No, today when a man wants to take a wife, he talks to the girl's father. They decide on a settlement. If the man doesn't have money he will pay in some other way. The father then selects a man from the tribe, usually his best friend, and this man and the girl are then put together in a hut for a time so that he can teach her the ways of marriage. When she has learned what she is to know, she is given to her husband.'

I actually witnessed this myself later. One of the Flechas asked me to buy a dress for his bride-to-be. I asked him about the size and he was very proud of the fact that he was marrying one of the young girls in Keppie's family. I knew the girl, and bought the dress.

Later, one afternoon, I was surprised to see this girl and another man sitting in the door of a small home-made tent. When I enquired whether she had changed her mind and married another man, I was told that this was the best man and he was teaching her the ropes.

Soon I was to learn how easy it is for us so-called civilised people to take things for granted. We have become so civilised that our children don't know that milk comes from a cow. As far as they are concerned it comes from a bottle. We have become so accustomed to our way of life that we do not know that there are people out there who haven't the vaguest notion of the things we regard as everyday commodities.

My bush education soon taught me not to take anything for granted. Canned rations to a soldier in the bush is like frozen foods to a housewife in the 'States' – as we commonly referred to 'back home' – both of which are completely foreign to a Bushman.

Being nomads by nature, they were accustomed to living off the land. Meat and fat from trapped or hunted animals, berries and roots were their staple diet. Preservation of food was unknown. Meat left over from a kill would be cut into shreds and left hanging over branches to dry. In winter this process worked slightly better than in summer, when it didn't work at all.

Obviously the meat was completely rotten in a day or two and had to be eaten or it went bad. Roots and berries had a longer shelf-life, but they were difficult to come by and it took virtually the whole day for a woman to collect enough of these to feed a family. These people lived from day-to-day and hand-to-mouth, so to speak. They took nothing for granted.

We in Western society grow up with things like motorcars, cellphones, planes, telephones and elevators. Even our children know how to use them. It is difficult to imagine how we would get along without them, and yet there are still people that do not even know of the existence of these things that form part of our everyday lives.

The Bushman people keep dogs to help in their searching and hunting for food. It is said that when times get rough and animals become scarce, food becomes limited exclusively to berries and roots, and the dogs are slaughtered to provide fresh meat.

I was so revolted at the thought that I never did ascertain whether it was the truth or not, but judging by the Bushmen's attitude towards a dog I am quite prepared to believe that this was in fact common practice.

Talking about dogs, these animals were often used in hunting and fed only what scraps were unfit for human consumption. As a consequence the creatures were literally skin and bone. Naturally dogs were always on the scrounge, only to be beaten off or kicked and sent scampering.

I was so disgusted by this maltreatment that I gave very strict orders that unless the dogs in the base were properly treated, fed and cared for, they would be taken away and the owner declared unfit to own a dog. I was determined to see that my orders were obeyed and I was absolutely ruthless in this matter. In fact, I raised absolute hell when I heard a dog yelp.

The message had eventually seemed to get through and although the Bushmen had no idea what it was all about, they eventually obeyed, if only to avoid my wrath.

One morning I was on my inspection rounds and as I approached a group of women and children around the breakfast fire, I saw there was an unusual activity and somehow a little brown puppy was involved in the commotion. When I came close enough to see what was going on, I stopped. A woman had hurriedly poured a can full of Ideal milk into a pot. She had the poor mongrel by the neck and with his snout jammed into the pot.

'Hey Bokvoet, what is that woman doing to that dog?'

'She is trying to make the dog drink because she is afraid you will shout at her because the dog is so skinny.'

I looked at the little creature, its belly was like a football. I was convinced that the puppy's weight problem was definitely not due to malnutrition. I made a mental note to order deworming tablets.

So it came about that a dog's life in Alpha took on a new meaning.

Imagine now, if you can, a bunch of people directly out of the bush. They are given canned meat, Vienna sausages, meatballs in gravy, mixed vegetables, baked beans in tomato sauce, peas and sweetcorn. No bread, but high-protein biscuits and Pro-vita, condensed milk in tubes, Ideal milk in tins, and powdered coffee in little paper sachets. These are common items we take for granted, but we forget that a Bushman has never seen these things in his life.

Imagine what goes through a Bushman's head when you hand him a lot of cans and packets and a can opener and tell him to go and eat. He doesn't know what a can is, let alone what to do with the can opener.

You thought you were confused when you plugged in your newly purchased microwave oven, and book in hand you and your spouse were trying to figure out how the thing worked and what button to press and what to do when a red light flashed and the damned thing started screaming 'BLEEP-BLEEP-BLEEP!', but think for a moment how confused a Bushman is when he is battling to get a cooking fire started with the Pro-vita and army biscuits. How is he to know that they are for eating, and not for making fire with?

We know that peanut butter is a delicacy when eaten with bread, but how were they to know that peanut butter was not a cure for veld sores and most definitely not recommended for cosmetic purposes?

Most children would like to have a puppy for their amusement and take for granted that the supermarket will supply the necessary Pets Delight or Dogmor to feed the pets. We have become so civilised that we do not know that there are people who keep dogs for other purposes than the amusement of their children or as watchdogs.

During the visits to the sick bay I noticed that the black women and children were generally well dressed and clean. They seemed to maintain a reasonably high standard of personal hygiene. This, tragically, could not be said of the Bushmen.

The women wore only skirts or just pieces of cloth wound around the lower half of the body and tied into a knot at the waist, and beads. The children wore only beads.

Nobody ever seemed to wash. The whole setup appalled me to say the least, so I discussed it with Edler who responded, 'Commandant, you'll also get used to it.'

'Not very likely, Werner, I don't think I ever will.'

That Sunday I told Twiggy to bring me the baby that had been born earlier during the week. I prepared a bath of lukewarm water and topped it up with a bit of liquid soap that we used for washing the dishes. I whipped up a nice lather.

When Twiggy brought the woman with the baby, she handed it over with some reluctance. I tucked the baby under my left armpit as I had seen the nurses do and I dipped its head scalp-deep in the water. After I'd finished washing the head, I also washed the rest of him. I dried the infant carefully and dusted it with some athletes' foot powder. To add a professional touch, I sprinkled the little body with aftershave lotion.

I'd found a roll of cotton cloth, cut a piece the length of the baby's body and slipped him inside. Then I pinned the cloth on either side above the shoulders, leaving just enough room for the neck to protrude. The end result was marvellous and the mother was beaming.

From that day on I was presented with dozens of babies every Sunday for their weekly bath. I refused, but offered to bath only those babies that had been born in Alpha! The others were to bath their own.

It did seem to have some effect and for as long as I was available on Sundays to kick-start the operation, it worked, but unfortunately, whenever I was away, no baths for the babies.

As the rainy season set in and with it the wet and heat and heaven knows what else, there developed what seemed like athletes' foot among the children. It was getting so bad that some of them could hardly walk.

On Sundays, I would round up all the children and got Twiggy and some of her pals to bathe the children's feet and apply Gentian Violet. This took about the whole Sunday and just when it seemed to be improving, I discovered that the girls were only treating the children of their friends and skipped the others. I gave it up and got Bokvoet to treat the really bad cases at the clinic.

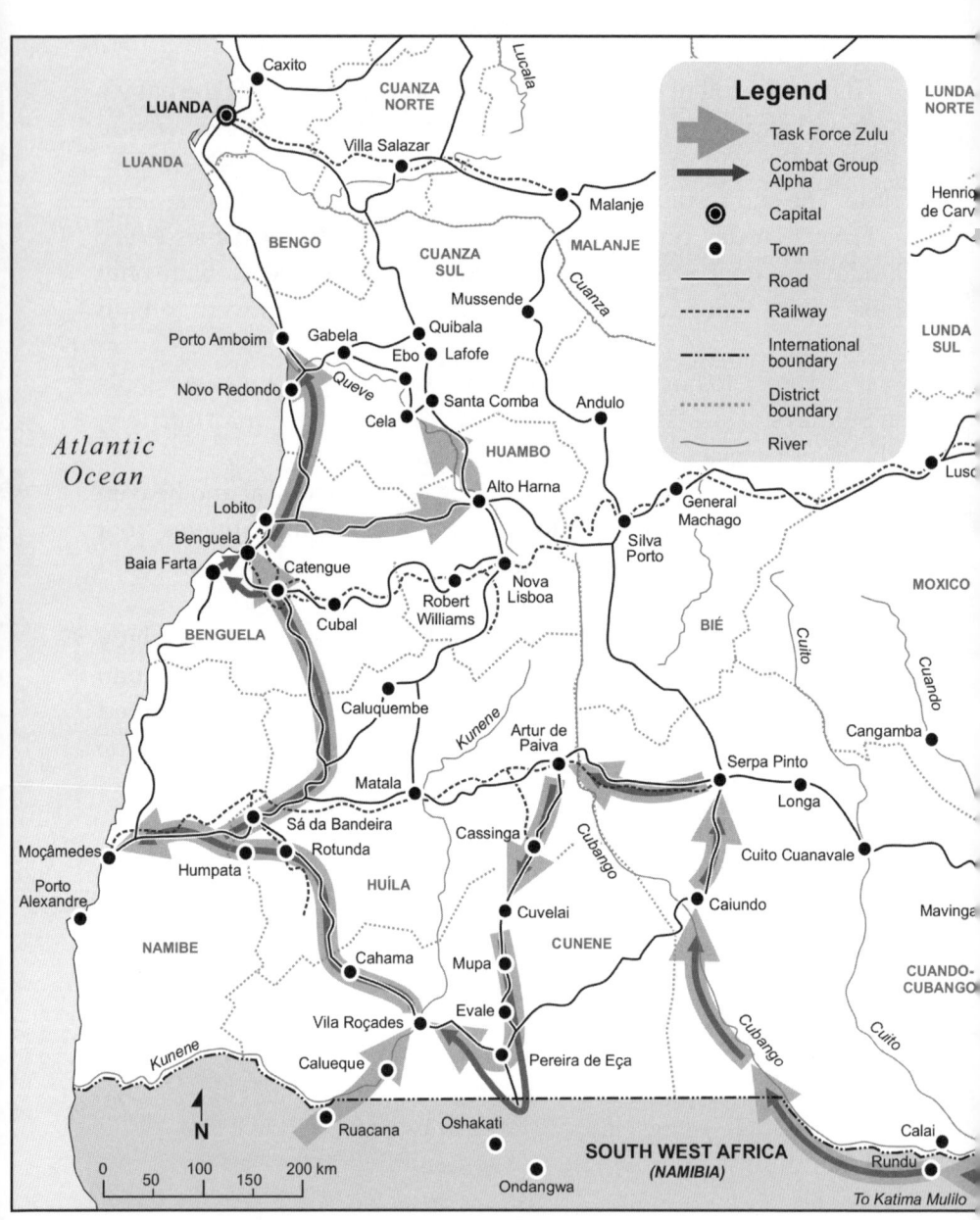

Combat group Alpha advances into southern Angola as part of Task Force Zulu during Operation Savannah.

CHAPTER 13

Operation Savannah

At Alpha there was never a dull moment and before I'd had time to realise it, winter had come and gone. One day, late in August, I was summoned to Rundu. The message came from the brigadier himself, so it was clearly a matter of considerable importance. I was delighted to discover that Jan Breytenbach had also been summoned, but surprised in the sense that we had not been involved operationally before. I also got a rather distinct feeling that my friend Jan knew a lot more than he was letting on. I was burning with curiosity as we walked into the brigadier's office.

Brigadier 'Mac' Kotzé had meantime retired and had been replaced by Dawie Schoeman, also a brigadier. I did not know the newcomer, except that I'd run into him once or twice while he was attached to Headquarters as an agricultural expert, with the task of upgrading the Kavango people's agricultural expertise.

Having been a successful farmer in the Western Transvaal all his life, this was of course his forte, but of his military expertise, I had no knowledge.

The brigadier got straight to the point. It appeared that Jonas Savimbi of UNITA was running into a spot of bother with his erstwhile compatriots MPLA, and that he was looking for help elsewhere. 'Our people' had been dealing with 'his people' and we had come to some sort of agreement.

If we were to help him grab as much of Angola as possible, said Schoeman, this would strengthen his hand when it came to staking claims for government after declaration of independence on 11 November 1975.

In return for that little favour we would be given the opportunity to sort out the SWAPO bases in Angola. I have no desire to delve into the political antics of the leaders of the time, but in order to understand the situation, I wish to mention briefly what led up to this decision.

After the military takeover of the Portuguese regime in Lisbon in April 1975, the Portuguese troops were withdrawn and things happened in rapid succession. To say it was chaos may be an understatement, but as I had left Angola in July of that year, I had no knowledge of what was going on. I could only guess.

The single most important matter was who was going to run the country now that Portugal had withdrawn. There was talk of an election, but then we know about elections in Africa, and it slowly became apparent that the inevitable was to happen. The three so-called liberation movements were rapidly steering down on a 'winner-take-all' situation.

The MPLA was sponsored by the Kremlin, FNLA by the Chinese and UNITA more or less by the USA. Russian support for the MPLA was, however, so enthusiastic that it soon became clear the MPLA was gaining more than just a head start on the other two. This was the part that captured my imagination. If the MPLA ended up running the show, it meant that we were going to have communist neighbours. This boded ill for our fight against SWAPO and therefore had a direct bearing on us.

There was something else, too. Initially SWAPO was riding on UNITA's back to get a foothold in SWA. As UNITA was losing pace, SWAPO started looking to MPLA for support. For me, this made MPLA enemy number two.

The third factor that affected not me personally, but our whole set-up, was the fact that FNLA more or less disappeared from the scene and the 'Chipenda faction' was booted out by the MPLA. These poor souls now found themselves in much the same situation as the Bushmen after the Portuguese withdrawal. They had meandered towards south-eastern Angola and settled in a little place called Mpupa, not far from the South West African border.

Apparently the leader of the ex-FNLA troops, a chap by the name of Pelissa, had approached our headquarters in Rundu for help. This help, I discovered, was in the form of one Commandant Jan Breytenbach. He was to rig these people with kit, train them as I had done with the Bushmen, and then he and I would set forth in aid of our newfound allies: UNITA/FNLA Incorporated. The FNLA's army had by this time assumed the name ELNA.

What the brigadier was proposing here sounded like a fair deal to me, particularly as Dr Jonas Savimbi was anti-communist and from what I could gather, a bright politician and a brilliant soldier. It left me with a nice feeling to have the good guys on my side.

But, the brigadier added seriously: 'I must impress on you that this is obviously a very sensitive issue. Nobody but the essential people are to know about the operation. You are not to be associated with the SADF in any way whatsoever.'

Only now did it begin to dawn on me that I was not chosen for my brains or my military skills, but only because I happened to command a gang of Bushmen that were in fact Angolan citizens and hence the RSA could not be caught with their hands in the cookie jar if anything went wrong. This realisation didn't do much to bolster my flagging spirits.

Also, my command of the Portuguese language was such that I just might pass for being Portuguese.

I recall that one night at a party in Angola, when driven into a tight spot about my background, I told them I was of German parentage from my father's side (hence the name Dieter Lindorf) but he had married an Israeli woman (hence my rather Jewish-looking nose).

I was a kind of vagabond mercenary of no fixed abode and willing to serve any 'noble cause' (providing the money was right). This went down okay then and I decided that it would have to do here also. Fortunately, it never became necessary to resort to this.

Early in October, Breytenbach and I were again summoned to Rundu. This time, there were a few more familiar faces. We were told to book into the mess as there would be a complete order group the following day.

We spent that evening pleasantly chatting to old pals, some of whom I hadn't seen in years, and speculating on the very interesting possibilities of the adventure ahead. Next morning there were all sorts of discussions behind closed doors, to which I wasn't invited, and I spent most of the morning like most other mornings at Rundu trying to scrounge whatever I could from the kitchen, sick bay and QM stores.

When the time arrived, we were all gathered in the OPS room. The plan was briefly outlined. The task force was to be called Task Force Zulu. There was to be a mini-headquarters, comprising the commanding officer Colonel Koos van Heerden, an operations staff officer, Commandant Willie Kotzé, a logistics staff officer, Commandant Shylock Mulder, an intelligence officer, Major Dries van Coller and a signals officer whose name I had forgotten.

The operation, code-named 'Savannah', would be conducted from 1 Military Area HQ. The operational staff officer, Major Coen Upton, and Major Punchy Botha, logistical staff officer, would be responsible for operational and logistical support.

The task force would cross the cutline at 1900 hours on 13 October at Katwitwi and move north as far as Caiundo, where it would laager for the night.

North of Caiundo is a good sand road running from east to west. By moving in a westward direction along this road, the task force could move around the right flank of the enemy positions at Vila Roçadas. This meant that the enemy would be caught from behind.

From there the main road was easy-going all the way through to Sá da Bandeira and Luanda (or anywhere else for that matter).

It was an absolute 'copy book' plan, but there were a few things that bothered me. For a start, I didn't know of the so-called 'good sand road' running from east to west to the north of Caiundo. When I'd left Angola the previous year, the road was in progress, but very far from negotiable. It was unlikely that it could have progressed any further at all.

The second thing I remember vividly was that all the major rivers run more or less east to west, and thus would have to be crossed if we were going to use the main north road to Sá da Bandeira.

We also know that the MPLA were strongly supported by the Cubans and it wasn't difficult to guess what would happen if they decided to blow the bridges.

In an effort to put two years of experience in Angola to use, I suggested that it might be a better idea to move north through southeast Angola as far as Cuito and Serpa Pinto and then west, straight to Luanda.

Rivers are not obstacles in south-east Angola and where they do become a factor, we move in the same direction and don't have to cross them. With Luanda in our hands the rest would be easy... Whether the brigadier had heard me or not, I couldn't tell, but he certainly didn't show any sign. He simply wasn't interested. My thoughts started to wander again.

When I was a small boy, my father, who was involved in World War I somewhere in German East Africa, told me how their advance was halted by a German force deployed on high ground, dominating

Delville Linford with Al Venter in the sitting room of his house on the outskirts of Wolseley, taken early in 2015.

Al Venter in Nova Lisboa late in 1975 with a Portuguese mercenary after he had joined Daniel Chipenda's Chipa Esquadrão. (Photo: Al Venter collection)

Early days at Camp Alpha. (Photo: Wouter du Plooy)

The 'no-nonsense' and 'able' Werner Edler at Camp Alpha. (Photo: Wouter du Plooy)

Cmdt Linford at Camp Alpha – still fresh from Army Headquarters in Pretoria.
(Photo: Wouter du Plooy)

One of the first dwellings erected as instructed by Maj. Gen. Fritz Loots.
(Photo: Wouter du Plooy)

The first two tents pitched at Alpha. (Photo: Wouter du Plooy)

Wouter du Plooy shooting a buffalo for the pot. (Photo: Wouter du Plooy)

Road to Alpha from the Golden Highway. (Photo: Wouter du Plooy)

First permament structures at Camp Alpha. (Photo: SANDF)

Maj. Dries van Coller, Col Koos 'Proppies' van Heerden and Col Linford. (Photo: SANDF)

Maj. Toon Slabbert and his men during Task Force Zulu's advance. (Photo: SANDF)

Task Force Zulu with some prisoners of war. (Photo: SANDF)

Zulu's rapid advance was made easier with a Land Cruiser-mounted Browning machine gun. (Photo: SANDF)

From left to right: Brig. Dawie Schoeman, Cmdt Delville Linford, Defence Minister P.W. Botha and Cmdt Eddie Webb at the hospital at Cela after capturing Novo Redondo. (Photo: SANDF)

High-ranking visitors P.W. Botha and Magnus Malan at Omega. (Photo: SANDF)

Cmdt Linford socialising with two of the Alpha troops. (Photo: SANDF)

Cmdt Linford and Brig. Georg Meiring, who later retired as Chief of the SANDF. (Photo: Coen Upton collection)

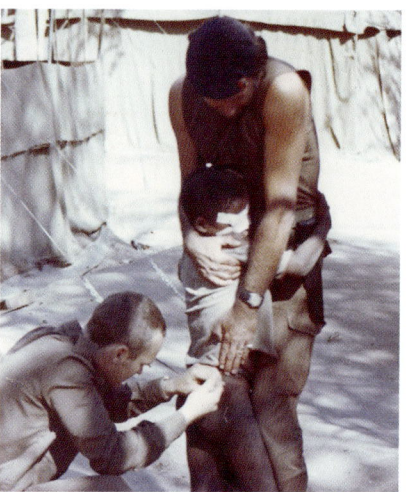

Linford at his happiest in Camp Alpha, where a special bond was formed with the Bushmen people. (Photos: Petrus Roux)

Wuri 'Bokvoet' Tsapau, who later became a teacher at Omega.
(Photo: Scholtz van Wyk collection)

Linford with the adorable Snowy in her natty army-brown cotton skirt made from his shirt sleeves. (Photo: Petrus Roux)

Bushman schoolboys – future soldiers – being trained by the national servicemen.
(Photo: Petrus Roux)

Bushman children singing to Cmdt Linford on his return from an operation.
(Photo: Petrus Roux)

CHAPTER 13: OPERATION SAVANNAH

their axis of advance. Try as they might, they just couldn't dislodge the Germans, and the whole advance came to a grinding halt.

When General Smuts moved forward to investigate the cause for the delay, he said to the commander, 'So what do you want to throw them off the mountain for? Move around them and carry on with the war.'

I was no strategist, but this made a lot of sense to me. It also seemed to apply to this situation. It didn't make sense to me to walk up to a lion and pluck it by the beard – besides, I didn't command that sort of courage. No, I would walk around the lion, sneak up from behind and grab him by the ...

'Gentlemen, I must impress on you once again ...,' the brigadier's voice brought me back to the present.

We were informed that no South African citizens, vehicles, equipment, documents or anything that could connect the task force with the RSA, was to be taken into Angola. Jan and I were to surrender our personal ID cards and even had to assume a false identity.

It is worth mentioning that by then Jan Breytenbach had already assumed the pseudonym of Colonel Carpenter from the then Rhodesia. It went down pretty well, but my problem was more difficult. I could hardly also be an ex-Rhodesian.

The briefing went on for a while longer and ended as abruptly as it had started. As we trampled out of the OPS room, Shylock remarked: 'Ag shame, ou Lin, what a pity that you are now to be shot in Angola.'

'Don't worry, old pal, Confucius he says ... he who shoots first, laughs last.' Having said it, it somehow didn't sound quite as flippant as it was intended.

Finally, it was time to leave Alpha. We had prepared as best we could and what we lacked in 'war-mongering', we made up good with enthusiasm.

Headquarters transferred two officers from somewhere in South West Africa to take charge of the base while we were gone. Captain Pinkie Coetzee would assume command and Lieutenant Tas van Solms would act as second-in-charge. I briefed them thoroughly, bade them farewell and left. I was allocated the rifle range outside Rundu to billet until the next day when we were to leave.

The enthusiasm we had all felt up until then soon abated when my troops were ordered to hand in their R1 rifles, zeroed to perfection, in exchange for Angola's G3's in 7.62 mm calibre, the rifle universally used in Portugal's overseas territories during the colonial wars.

As if to add insult to injury, our German-built Unimogs – in showroom condition and fitted with long-range fuel and water tanks – were ordered back to Alpha. We were issued, of all things, with civilian three-ton trucks. We referred to them as *groentelorries* (vegetable trucks) because they had been acquired from Portuguese refugees who had fled southwards over the cutline to Rundu.

We tried as best we could to test and zero the rifles and started loading the trucks. With weapons, ammunition, rations and kit all bundled onto the three-ton trucks, there was hardly room for the troops, but they managed to perch, however precariously, on top of the kit. The end result was a sorry sight. It looked much more like a convoy of refugees than the proud and well-turned-out unit that had arrived at Rundu the day before.

Not the least of my problems was the briefing of my troops. I ordered the unit to form up and I set about my briefing. This in itself was rather a complicated business.

In order to obviate any misunderstanding due to discrepancy in language, I would issue my orders in English to José. He would then repeat the orders to the leader group in Portuguese. The platoon sergeants, who were Bushmen but fluent in Portuguese, would repeat the order to the platoons in whatever language was appropriate to a particular platoon. (There were three lingos spoken: Vasekela, Barakwena and Cazamba.)

At this point only was it assumed that everybody had received the message.

'Men, it is important that you understand exactly what we are about to do. You know that UNITA is fighting against MPLA. You also know that Commandant Breytenbach from South Africa has organised the FNLA into a battle group which we know as Battle Group Bravo and we and they are going to fight alongside each other with UNITA against MPLA. Is that clear?'

There was a sharp and vigorous exchange of words among the Bushmen and then Kamamma stood up and addressed José.

'Hey Major, there is a very serious misunderstanding here. Please, will you tell our commandant that we are fighting *against* these people, not *with* them. He must surely have misunderstood the situation!' I knew that was coming.

I recollected the story of the Battle of the Alamo, where Lieutenant Traverse drew a line with his sword and invited those who volunteered to fortify the Alamo to step across the line. It worked then, why not now?

'José, tell the Flechas that I'm going to turn my back and those Flechas who want to go with me must remain seated. But they will only go on my terms and they will fight alongside the soldiers that I say and against those whom I say.

'Those who do not wish to do so must get up and congregate by that tree over there. They can go back to Alpha to stay with the women and children. That is all – two minutes!'

I turned around as dramatically as my limited theatrical abilities would allow and timed two minutes on my watch. There was hushed conversation, but I heard no movement. Then I turned and my heart swelled with pride. I searched the ranks seated in front of me till I found a particular platoon and then I saw old Jimmy's face. I recalled the day the Flechas arrived in Alpha. I remembered the broad smile on Jimmy's face.

'I know this man from Angola,' he had said to his compatriots, 'and I will follow him wherever he goes and will fight with him, and die for him.' It was as if he was reading my mind. His face lit up and there is only one man in this world that can smile like dear old Jimmy.

'Okay, Flechas, now we understand each other once again. No, I do not misunderstand the situation, but there are things that you do not understand yet, but let's not bother about that now.

'Let's go and fight these people who want to take our country and who abuse our women and children – no matter who they are. I know them, trust me. But know this: the troops of Bravo do not want your land. They, like you, have found a new home in our country. They are no longer our enemies, they are now our brothers-in-arms.'

I wasn't exactly given a standing ovation, but at least I wasn't booed.

'We will sleep here tonight, and you must be ready to move tomorrow after lunch. When I say go, we go!'

I dismissed the men and started looking into my personal transport arrangements. The only thing that I could safely say for certain at that stage was that I wasn't setting foot anywhere without my garry. We had been together too long for us to be apart now.

Meantime, I bought two cans of brown Duco from the co-op store in town and industriously set about camouflaging my Land Rover. While busy with this task, a lanky chap in a drab green shirt, trousers and a ridiculous-looking green bush hat, walked up.

'Are you the OC of the Bushmen?' he asked.

'Yes, who are you?'

'I'm Staff Sergeant Lubbe from the South African Corps of Engineers.'

'So?' I questioned.

He replied that he was my engineer for the operation.

'If you're an engineer,' I said to him, 'then you must be able to camouflage. Right?'

'Yes, I can.'

'Okay, here.' I gave him the paint. 'Camouflage there!' I indicated towards my Land Rover. When he'd finished, I hardly recognised my vehicle.

'That's very nice, Staff. You certainly know how to handle a spray gun ... I hope you can do as well with the real thing.'

He gave me a sour look and I must confess that I felt a bit foolish.

'Okay, now where's your kit, let's get organised.'

'It's okay, Sir, I am organised.' He glanced in the direction of a sky-blue Land Cruiser standing some distance off. The cab of the vehicle had been removed, but the cargo space was covered with green plastic sheeting and securely tied down all round with rope. He must have read my mind because at that point he grinned rather sheepishly and shrugged his shoulders.

'Oh boy ... this is going to be fun,' I smiled.

The Task Force HQ comprised only a handful of officers. Our commander, Colonel Koos van Heerden, and I were buddies in our Academy days. Although he was an infantryman and I have always been a gunner, we'd kept close contact over the years and remained good friends.

I was delighted to learn that he was going to 'run the show' or, more formally, 'command the expedition'.

Much has been written about this officer and his ability as a military commander has been well recorded. Due to the rapid progress made by Task Force Zulu, Colonel Van Heerden ended up being dubbed Rommel – a rather suitable nickname, I thought.

But we all knew him as 'Koos Proppies'. 'I think I am still one of the few people that know the origin of the name and my tribute to this remarkable individual is to place on record how he actually acquired it. In fact, it had nothing to do with his being short and stocky, as some people believe.

We were both students of military history at the Military Academy, and during the course of our studies it was necessary for the students to research certain historically important battles. That would lead to us having to do a detailed presentation of the battle in accordance with accepted military norms.

On one such occasion Cadet Van Heerden was assigned the task of presenting a certain significant battle from World War I.

Actual details have long since escaped me, but what has remained in my mind all these years was the name of the German commander, Colonel Von Propolow. His level of military expertise still eludes me, but the name 'Von Propolow' was flung about with such reckless abandon, and Cadet Van Heerden expounded the military expertise of the man with such zeal, that it was inevitable that he promptly became known as Cadet Koos van Propolow.

The abbreviation 'Proppies' was a logical result. Koos van Heerden was consequently remembered dearly by all his friends as 'Koos Proppies'.

Commandant Willie Kotzé was a gunner. During my days as an instructor at the South African School of Artillery, I became well acquainted with his keen intelligence as well as a personality that positively sparkled. He was also blessed with a delightful sense of humour.

Willie went on to become a boffin in artillery intelligence and counter-bombardment, though how he got the job of operations staff officer of an infantry task force is anybody's guess.

Commandant Shylock Mulder – the other officer in this rather diverse mix – was an engineer by profession. We hadn't had all that much contact, but I knew him as well-liked and efficient. Strangely, he finished up as the logistics staff officer.

Our intelligence officer was Major Dries van Coller, whom I didn't know at all. But what did strike me as significant was that he was from the Corps of Military Intelligence.

Then there was the unit's signals officer – would you believe, from the Corps of Signals.

The entire complement of personnel was to be accommodated in two Land Rovers. What was notable was the absence of a B Echelon (the component which was to provide logistical support like fuel, rations and ammunition and the rest). But, what the heck, the brigadier had said that we would be logistically supported from Rundu.

How this was to be accomplished was another question, but fortunately not my worry. The always competent Punchy Botha surely had the answer. Besides, the Good Book says that the Lord will provide.

The fighting element comprised our two combat groups, Alpha and Bravo. Bravo was numerically superior and comprised three strong infantry companies, a three-inch mortar platoon and a machine-gun platoon. It worried me that the weapons we were issued with were outdated, but because of the clandestine nature of the operation, anything modern that could be traced back to South Africa was not allowed. In spite of this – and because of the remarkable skills and other qualities of the instructors – everything we had was put to remarkably effective use.

One of the many outstanding qualities of the officer commanding Combat Group Bravo – Commandant Jan Breytenbach – was his initiative. From somewhere, he'd acquired a quite beautiful royal blue 30-ton horse and trailer. On this he mounted four .303 Vickers machine guns broadside onto the trailer, secured them with sandbags and voila! – a pretty effective fighting machine, or as someone dubbed it, 'a mean machine'.

With the aid of some instructors that the commandant had smuggled in from his previous unit, the erstwhile band of marauding FNLA freedom fighters were soon knocked into a fairly efficient fighting unit. Most of the junior commanders were Portuguese – ex-DGS Portuguese secret service people from Mozambique, recruited by Godfather General Fritz Loots. Many of these people really were very tough and able to handle themselves in some extremely tricky conditions.

Then came my unit, Battle Group Alpha. I had been able to muster two strong rifle companies. The first – A Company – was drawn mainly from our Vasekela (!Xun) Flechas. That unit was commanded by a Portuguese fellow by the name of Covacha, originally from Angola. A pleasant, soft-spoken man who, when you first met him, gave the impression of possibly looking more comfortable in a pulpit than on a battlefield.

Being an ex-member of the security police in Angola, he had no experience of this type of warfare, but his leadership qualities were outstanding. Also, he had no qualms about listening to advice.

In contrast, B Company comprised the Barakwena Bushmen from the Caprivi. They were commanded by another fellow from Mozambique whose name eludes me and who was the exact opposite of Covacha: loud, plump brash and a know-it-all.

The platoon commanders were also ex-DGS people and between them all, they knew virtually nothing about infantry tactics. It irked me that the broadchested commandos and paratroopers had all fallen by the wayside and we were now left with a bunch of 'ordinary people'.

The platoon sergeants and section commanders were all Bushmen. Those in A Company had a reasonable amount of experience of combat, acquired in the Bush War in Angola. Though they understood little about tactics and battle drills, at least they had reasonable control over their men. And of course they knew the bush.

My B Company was less fortunate. Although some of the sergeants and corporals had some bush war experience in Angola, the rest were the guys that had started off under my guidance as labourers. Operation Savannah was to be their baptism of fire in the true sense of the word.

Contrary to instructions, I squirreled away three national servicemen in my organisation. Hendrik Bodenstein was my driver, a serious, slow-speaking farm boy from the Free State. He also operated my radio set.

A young fellow by the name of De Witt drove one of the troop carriers. He, too, was a rather reticent youngster with a pleasant smile and always ready to do anything.

The third individual was a motor mechanic by the name of Kapp. He was lanky and hardly ever spoke a word, but then again, it was just as well because the amount of repair work that had to be done to the vehicles with which we were issued was awesome. There wasn't much time for talking anyway. If the truth be known, without Kapp, Combat Group Alpha would not have got out of the assembly area, let alone across the start line.

Staff Sergeant Piet Lubbe was the only man in my outfit who had been properly trained in the job he was expected to do. He had a wealth of knowledge and experience and, as I was soon to discover, was a very nice guy. Tall and athletically built, he spoke in a soft, lazy manner and positively exuded confidence.

So it came to pass that on the afternoon of 13 October 1975, we sallied out into the wild unknown. Our intentions were clear: we were to do battle with those who were called FAPLA.

No question, we were a peculiar bunch you might say. But in the three months that followed, many were the times I was proud to be counted among that number.

We left Rundu sometime after lunch and travelled west along the southern bank of the Kavango River. Bravo led the advance, followed by the Headquarters Group, while Alpha brought up the rear.

We crossed the cutline – as explained earlier, the official border between Angola and South West Africa – which, officially-speaking, was the beginning of our adventure and headed for a little place called Katwitwi, nothing more than a name, where the cutline meets the Kavango River, which is also called Cubango. The only significance Katwitwi had at that stage was that a large refugee camp had been established there.

We had travelled part of the way on the Angolan side of the border and joined up with the rest of the combat group at Katwitwi.

We arrived just before last light and were more than happy to accept an invitation meal at the commandant's HQ. The officer-in-command of the camp was Commandant Vossie Nel, an old gunner pal and somebody I was looking forward to seeing again after so many years. Well, I thought, what a way to start a war!

I was delighted to see my old friend again but somewhat surprised by the rather attractive blond lady who acted as hostess. It didn't take me too long to discover that she was a captain nursing sister from the South African Medical Corps who had been posted to Commandant Nel's outfit to attend to the welfare of large groups of refugees who had fled the fighting in the north.

CHAPTER 13: OPERATION SAVANNAH

It is worth mentioning that when the refugee camp was later moved to Calai (opposite the river from Rundu) she became known as 'The Angel of Calai' because of the magnificent task she did there.

Meantime, our one evening at Katwitwi turned out to be a remarkable and memorable event. What better way to start a war than with a scrumptious meal served by candlelight, good wine and a pretty blond in a long white gown.

We took leave of our host and hostess and settled in for the night. I spread my bed-roll beside my vehicle and lay myself down. As was my habit before falling asleep, I reflected on the happenings of the day, and applied my mind to what lay ahead.

Obviously an undertaking of this nature called for more than 'bush tactics'. In order to do this sort of thing, one would have to endeavour some form of 'advance to contact'. Ideally, having made contact with the enemy, I felt that a more conventional type of attack was called for and possibly a more formal defence system.

Roaming across the African bush, seeking out groups of terrorists and killing them, was one thing ... what our command structure had in mind here was a completely different ball game.

I couldn't think of a more suitable person for this type of job than Jan Breytenbach. He had loads of expertise, good experience and guts – the lot.

But here was I – and I could only smile inwardly. I might have been one of the most qualified gunners in the SA Corps of Artillery at the time, but now I found myself in command of a bunch of Bushmen who had until very recently known only a bow and arrow and had certainly never heard anything louder than a rifle shot. As for the Portuguese commanders, they had not even heard the word 'conventional warfare'.

What worried me most was how these guys were going to react to heavy gun and mortar fire. Facing the enemy, eyeball-to-eyeball, with good rifles and plenty of ammunition was one thing, but charging an objective where your adversary is out of sight and backed by some heavy defensive fire, was something totally different.

Another issue that started gnawing at my mind was intelligence: the military kind. We had no maps, no aerial photos, no reconnaissance aircraft, in fact, none of the things the textbooks said one should have when you go to war.

To me this felt somewhat like blundering into a dark cinema when the show has already started. Everybody can see what is going on, except you.

The last thing that concerned me was the obvious lack of logistical support. I had all the confidence in the logistical ability of 1 Military Area, but – and I'd raised this issue a few times – how the hell were they going to bring supplies forward through terrain that was not properly secured?

What if FAPLA blew all the bridges and ambushed our supply convoys? Air supply, yes, but what if we were not able to secure suitable airfields in time? Also, what if FAPLA destroyed the airfields?

What if … what if …? I recalled an incident at the Army College years ago. We were discussing medical problems in the field. I hadn't been contributing much and the senior instructor asked me for an opinion.

'Gentlemen,' I started, 'our operational expertise is in my view beyond question and I don't think we are likely to ever have much of a medical problem …' Six heads popped up simultaneously – eyebrows raised.

'In all the exercises in which I have been involved, the troops were always fed from an existing kitchen and distances that needed to be covered were such that a vehicle could do the entire exercise with one full fuel tank and ammunition delivered from a magazine, also within striking distance.

'Hence,' I added, 'the expression "administration and logistics, normal".'

'Okay, so what's that got to do with the medical problem?' the instructor wanted to know.

'Sir, we have no experience in logistics in the field and we don't seem to be doing anything about it. I think we are going to starve our troops on the start line and, hence, we won't have any medical problem …'

'Thank you, Major, you may sit down.'

What I thought was a valid point, got me transferred to the Castle as an administrative staff officer, the furthest possible military posting from the College.

On that rather nostalgic note, I fell asleep.

CHAPTER 14

Group Bravo in Benguela

As discussed in the first chapter, Commandant Delville Linford's Combat Group Alpha's attempt to sort out the mess at Benguela Airport caused a few problems. Meanwhile, Commandant Jan Breytenbach's Combat Group Bravo was bringing up the rear. As he explains, after several earlier clashes against FAPLA troops, he and his unit also mucked in at the airport. Breytenbach takes up the story in his book *Forged in Battle*[1]:

By the time we'd returned to Catengue early the morning after our unforeseen scrap with FAPLA the previous day, Delville and his men, Zulu HQ, as well as our entire logistical system had moved on to Benguela. Our orders were to follow on behind.

Meantime, I was told that Nic, second-in-command of the previous unit I'd commanded, had been killed in an aircraft accident the day before. I also knew two of the others who had died in the crash: Piet, the pilot, and Des, an old colleague from Oudtshoorn.

Nic's death touched me deeply. In a way I was glad that Delville would be handling that day's hostilities. I'd decided early that I would rather grieve than rush headlong into another punch-up. Soon our spirits perked and I was able to take an interest in what had recently taken place in some of the areas we traversed. We passed the scene of Delville's very successful ambush, with burnt-out wrecks – trucks and cars – scattered all over the place. There was no sign of Zulu Force, but we were not concerned.

It was good to relax for a while without wondering and worrying about what lay ahead. As it was, the hills ahead looked ominous and who knew what was secreted in the bush, with possibly FAPLA flanks lying in ambush.

We passed through the final line of hills, and after making our way across a narrow defile, we discovered an extensive but unoccupied enemy trench system. Shortly afterwards we emerged onto the coastal plain just south of Benguela. Ahead we couldn't miss the crump of artillery and rocket fire: Delville had obviously run into a humdinger of a scrap.

We were beginning to feel apprehensive about our prospects when, rounding a bend at the end of a long straight stretch of tar road, we could make out the short round figure of a little man standing in the middle of the road next to his grey short-wheel-base Land Rover. Good, I thought, we'd caught up with Zulu and Corky [Colonel 'Proppies' van Heerden] was waiting for us.

As we drew up, he stopped my column by simply making like a traffic cop: the man was concerned about something and he quickly explained.

Delville had picked up trouble on the airport, just south of Benguela. In fact, just then you could hardly miss the almost continuous banging away of heavy guns and the odd column of smoke on the far side of the plain just ahead. Meanwhile, a report had come in that FAPLA troops were abducting Portuguese families onto deep sea trawlers from Baia Farta, a small fishing harbour just down the coast from Benguela.

Corky said he wanted me to make for Baia Farta to try to rescue the hostages. The rest of my battle group would concentrate at the old FAPLA military base – or *quartel*, as it was called in Portuguese – a few kilometres further on because Delville and his Bushmen had kicked the Angolan Army out of the place that morning.

I detailed a troop of armoured cars and an infantry platoon to accompany Toon and myself to Baia Farta while Frank Bestbier would take the rest of our group to the concentration area. So we turned left, off the main Benguela road and sped along a plain, dotted with barren flat-topped hills towards the distant sea to the south-west.

Not far from Baia Farta, which started to appear in the distance, we encountered a Mercedes Benz sedan heading for Benguela. The driver turned out to be a local white Portuguese from the town. He told us that there was no truth in the abduction rumours but FAPLA did however command a small garrison in a single building in the centre of town. The good news was that he was prepared to act as guide to show us the place.

Our advance continued, this time with the Mercedes Benz just behind my Land Cruiser and we entered the outskirts of Baia Farta, a surprisingly big town none of my group had ever heard of before. The main street was flanked by two-storey buildings and shops, but everything was deserted, with not a soul in the streets. Off to the

CHAPTER 14: GROUP BRAVO IN BENGUELA

right was the dockyard area where we could see the tops of masts and rigging of numerous vessels in port.

We immediately set about clearing an unknown number of Angolan soldiers out of their entrenched positions before we could take a closer look at the place. So, under the expert guidance of our Portuguese friend, we arrived at the quartel.

The so-called FAPLA base was perhaps the most unprepossessing quartel I had so far seen in the war. At first glance it looked like an ordinary four- or five-bedroomed house: here wasn't a strand of barbed wire, no machine gun nests, no imposing-looking fortifications built of sandbags or concrete. Nothing!

We rolled into the concentration area as the sun was going down. Frank had deployed Bravo Group in a defensive circle, more or less manning the embankments of the old quartel. Zulu HQ was pulled up under the northern embankment.

Off to the north, Red Eye rockets were mushrooming between us and Delville on the airport. A lot of machine gun and rifle fire came from that direction. Delville was obviously having a rough time and night was coming on fast.

I found a spot inside the quartel, less dirty than most other spots, where I parked the Land Cruiser and proceeded to Zulu HQ.

The quartel had earlier been occupied by Cubans. Some equipment, rifles, ammunition and a lot of mines had been captured by Delville inside the quartel. The place was, however, one big filthy mess. Corky could not use any of the buildings as headquarters because of the filth and the fleas. He therefore pitched his headquarters away from the buildings in an open spot.

There was no doubt that Benguela would be a very tough nut to crack, mainly because it is a largish city with numerous multi-storey buildings and large shantytowns tacked onto the side of it.

Delville had not been able to clear the airport because he was brought under rocket fire from high ground north of Benguela and small arms and mortar fire from the city itself. His troops were all pinned down on the airport and behind the air terminal buildings.

Corky visited the airfield during the day to be able to plan our actions. He refused to be pinned down at the airfield forever and we discussed various possible attacks. An outflanking attack round the east would be in full view of the observation post officers of the mortars and the rockets that have harassed us all day. A direct attack on the city was not feasible as the city was too big, there were too many civilians and it would most certainly develop into the most horrible and costly form of warfare, namely street fighting. Corky eventually suggested a limited attack on the outskirts of the town bordering the airfield to quell the direct fire being brought down on us. That would make us retain the initiative and allow us time to plan subsequent actions.

Eventually we decided that it would be better to try and outflank Benguela to the east and attack the high ground north of the city. That would cut off FAPLA's retreat and put us on dominating terrain. It would also neutralise the FAPLA rocket batteries.

It was agreed that I would send a patrol to find a route around the east and a ford through the river that ran into the sea just south of the high ground. The river was in flood as the rainy season had started inland.

After evening conference, Corky opened a bottle of Smirnoff, one of the few we received from Rundu, and which he evidently saved for a suitable occasion. Delville complained about his Portuguese platoon leaders but nobody took any notice. The Smirnoff gradually made our surroundings, and the smell, more acceptable and I soon turned in in spite of the odd Red Eye going off from time to time.

My patrol went off early the next morning, to find a passage around the east flank, to no avail, however, as there was no suitable river crossing.

The firing had picked up again towards daybreak and Delville had left just as rocket fire was beginning to mushroom between us and the airport.

The Smirnoff had worn off and I was looking at the general situation in the enemy training camp where I had slept the previous night, in the cold light of morning. I was disgusted. Bits of human excrement could be found everywhere and I felt as if I was covered in fleas.

I therefore decided to take my chance with Delville and departed for the airport, waving gravely at Corky as I passed his headquarters.

Keeping the air terminal building between me and FAPLA in the city made it possible to drive right up to Delville's headquarters. He was on the top floor, in fact an open balcony, from where he had a bird's eye view of the city and could also see the rocket positions on the high ground to the north.

CHAPTER 14: GROUP BRAVO IN BENGUELA

The trouble was that he had nothing with which he could reach the Stalin Organs, not even with the 81 mm mortars.

All around us his Bushmen were lying behind cover, hammering away across a stretch of open ground at the nearest buildings of the city.

Groups of armoured cars were clustered up and down the airfield from where they added to the din with their 90 mm guns.

Suddenly an unmarked Dakota appeared over the city, heading for the airport. For a while everybody stopped shooting and then all opened up on the Dakota, FAPLA and the Bushmen.

We were a bit puzzled by its identity, but Delville got his troops to stop shooting as the aircraft was obviously going to land. If it was a FAPLA aircraft, we could capture it on the ground.

The Dakota landed and unconcernedly taxied to the dispersal area behind the terminal building. It was one of our own Dakotas.

Firing had picked up again between the Bushmen and FAPLA so that bullets, interspersed with rockets and mortars, were flying around all over the airfield.

The pilot sat for a while, waiting for somebody to offload his machine but, as nothing happened (fighting kept everybody busy), he decided that he and his crew had better do it, and quickly too. Soon ammunition boxes tumbled out of the rear. By this time the pilot must have realised that we were still fighting for the airport and that he had landed right in the middle of a firefight. Never had an aircraft been cleared so quickly. Within minutes the engines started up again, the Dakota turned around and commenced its take-off run from dispersal across the rough veld ignoring all runways or taxiways. It soon disappeared over the horizon towards the south.

Meanwhile Delville and I were having a second look at the air photographs of Benguela. It was obvious that the high ground north of the town had to be taken. Outflanking to the east of Benguela was out of the question as we could not cross the flooded river. The only way across was by means of the bridge just north of the main city centre.

In order to take the high ground, we would have to clear at least part of Benguela, that part just north of the airfield, so that the 81 mm mortars could be deployed within range of our final objective, the rocket batteries.

We had arrived, at least partially, at Corky's solution. Corky was, understandably disgusted that we, Delville and I, had decided to adopt his plan after our strenuous objections the previous night.

While all this planning was going on, FAPLA was trying very hard indeed to wipe Delville's headquarters off the face of the earth with some rocket fire. Delville therefore placed one of his men as a lookout for incoming rockets while he and I studied the air photographs.

Every now and again a warning would sound 'Here it comes!' Followed by Delville's comment: 'Here comes a pot of crap'.

We would take cover, wait for the explosions and carry on with our planning. Finally FAPLA decided to let go a whole broadside of rockets from the other side. 'Here it comes, a whole lot of them!' Followed by Delville's comment: 'Here comes a big pot of crap!'

We took cover. Rockets exploded all around the headquarters, the building shook, dust and smoke covered us and when it finally blew away, we were still in one piece. The spent rocket motors could be seen sticking out of the ground just in front and behind the terminal building looking for all the world like the army's well-known urinal 'lilies'.

We decided that I would clear the shantytown to the immediate north with two of my companies while Delville would give fire support. Afterwards Delville's Bushmen would leap-frog through, clear the rest of the town while the mortars would re-deploy. The final assault would be done by Delville – to take the high ground to the north.

Frank brought up two of my companies and the remainder of Toon's [Major Toon Slabbert] armoured cars. I joined the companies and we assaulted from east to west across Delville's front, Jack's [Captain Jack Dippenaar] company on the left and Connie's [Lieutenant Connie van Wyk] company on the right.

Corky had joined Delville at his command post from where they had a beautiful view of my companies moving through the outskirts of Benguela.

It looked good, my troops moved well with the armoured cars a short step behind to give immediate and close support where necessary. Unfortunately, there was no resistance. FAPLA had gapped it as soon as we started deploying.

So we decided to clear all Benguela.

Jack's company was detailed to clear the southern approaches and the centre of town, afterwards to cross the river and make for the high ground in the north. Connie's company was to clear the eastern side of Benguela as far as the river.

Gradually the streets began to fill with people and by the time Jack got to the centre of the city, the streets were thronged with wildly cheering inhabitants. He could not carry on with his clearing actions as he was virtually bogged down in the crowds.

Jack therefore requested permission to open fire over the heads of the crowds to disperse them so that he could get his company moving again.

I was flabbergasted, and quickly stopped Jack. Instead I instructed him to ignore the city centre, to drive through in a victorious procession, to accept the flowers, the beer and the cheers and to make for the high ground to the north.

Meanwhile, I made my way to the centre of the city. Everything was in uproar. People stretched out their hands to touch the liberators. Others ran next to the vehicles and spouted away in Portuguese. The troops beamed from ear to ear, especially at the girls.

Connie had cleared his area with far more decorum than Jack, and I instructed him to pull into a very beautifully situated cemetery on high ground, surrounded by thick stone walls, for the night. It was a very strong position, but the troops were somewhat apprehensive about spending a night among the dead of Benguela.

Jack got to the high ground north of the city. The bird had flown and left some entrenchments, rockets, empty boxes and so on behind. They were obviously heading for Lobito.

I slept behind Delville's command post that night. There was no way in which anybody was going to get me back into the Cuban quartel for my last night in Benguela; even if odd bodies of FAPLA could still be running around the airport or in the city, intent on having a go at the widely separated bodies of Zulu troops, cut off from each other by dark and intervening blocks of buildings over which we had no control for the moment.

---

1 From *Forged in Battle* by kind permission of the author Jan Breytenbach, published by Protea Book House, Pretoria, 2014.

CHAPTER 15

Alpha's Battle for Benguela Airport

We take up the story of Commandant Linford's travails on the Angolan east coast where he encountered still more problems...

Combat Group Bravo ran into some serious FAPLA resistance as they approached the city of Benguela. I moved forward on foot until I came across Jan Breytenbach, who'd taken up a position to watch proceedings from a distance.

From a spectator's point of view, it all looked very exciting and he seemed to be enjoying what he was doing. I was quite happy to keep a low profile and leave him to get on with it and was still enjoying the goings-on, when I was summoned back to our forward headquarters.

Once there, the commanding officer indicated a secondary road on his map. Using his index finger as a pointer, he showed that it branched off towards the west and eventually joined up with what was clearly the main 'highway' from Catenque to Benguela.

This was obviously important because Catenque was where Bravo's advance was being held up by FAPLA.

'Take this road and get in behind the enemy ... cut off their retreat once Bravo has pushed them out of their present positions.'

'Ah,' I replied. 'Another one of those ...' The previous day's operation, which also involved a 'cut-off', was still too fresh in my mind. With that I returned to our temporary base.

It was quite late and I'd fallen asleep, dreaming on merrily, when Hendrik woke me up. 'Hey Commandant, wake up! There's a lot of vehicles and things ahead' were his words, little disguised by his enthusiasm.

'Where are we?' I asked, looking at the map.

'Just about where this road meets the main road to Benguela ... lots of trucks and other equipment coming towards us from Catenque.'

This was good news, I thought, and I told Hendrik that he was a champ. Our timing couldn't have been better.

I gave orders to deploy on the side of the main road, just as the first of the enemy vehicles moved into our line of fire. I can only imagine the shock these people must have experienced when they heard our first volley of rifle and machine-gun fire from our hurriedly occupied positions. Being suddenly attacked from the side of the road must have been an enormous surprise.

The initial reaction of those taking fire was impulsive, with many of the drivers trying to turn their vehicles around in what was little more than a fairly narrow road. For the majority of the newcomers, this tactic didn't work too well for them because most of their vehicles were exposed and our guys were not only well trained, but excellent shots.

Some of the FAPLA soldiers hurriedly dismounted and tried to take cover beside the road, but a lot of that was open ground and their actions were pointless, though some of them did discover a ditch along one of the stretches where we'd taken up position.

At the end of it, FAPLA suffered serious losses, with most of their vehicles damaged. Going over the scene of the action afterwards, we did manage to find a few vehicles intact, together with quite a lot of usable weapons and ammunition. I was able to exchange my Czech-made AK-47 which tended to rust whenever it got wet – which was often – for a Russian one. 'Ah, look,' I said, 'the real thing: from Russia with love!'

Generally speaking, the operation came off very well for my group when compared to the dismal failure of the previous day.

While our troops were still rounding up some of the stray FAPLA soldiers who hadn't been accounted for, Hendrik and I drove a short way down the road along which the FAPLA column had arrived, in part to ensure that there weren't more of the buggers heading in our direction.

On our return to our position, I was suddenly surprised to see two of these chaps walking alongside the road. We spotted each other at exactly the same time and they were obviously as surprised at the encounter as we were and, obviously, something had to happen.

By the time they'd lifted their AKs to fire, we were alongside them and there was simply no way that I could retaliate from a sitting position because Hendrik was in the way. It took me only a moment to accept that if they fired, my radio operator would take the brunt of it, so I hastily shouted for him to duck, jumped up and raised my rifle to fire. But it was not to be...

The small mat inside the vehicle cab at my feet slipped out from under me and the next moment I was flat on my butt back on the seat. At that precise moment the two FAPLA soldiers fired simultaneously. One of their bullets whistled harmlessly over my head while the other lodged itself in the metal frame that supported the windscreen of my garry.

I tried once more to retaliate. This time Hendrik was crouched low and not in the way.

I fired a long burst of automatic fire at where the two men had been and was delighted to see them disappearing in the middle distance. I didn't know a man could move that fast, but then, there's no accounting for what can happen when the adrenaline really starts pumping.

'Shoot, Commandant, shoot!' I looked at Hendrik, who was bent forward in his seat and peering warily over the dashboard. He reminded me of a very small Italian taxi driver in Naples. If I hadn't been so scared I would have laughed.

'Okay, Hendrik, you can come out now, they've gone.' It was already late afternoon and I'd had enough excitement for that day. I gave orders for the men to form a laager for the night.

With time, on this operation, it had become normal practice to position our logistics echelon – together with my HQ such as it was – square in the middle of the defensive circle that was created by the troops. I'd mentioned before that we had acquired a brand-new five-ton Fiat tip truck earlier on, which we used to transport our rations, usually proudly driven by Padua.

Unfortunately, Padua had a tendency to become somewhat unpredictable, often at the most unexpected times. That evening, in order to get his rations truck at the heart of our defensive position, he tried to engage his four-wheel drive, but with all the excitement, Padua pulled the wrong lever. Five tons of bully beef and mixed vegetables were suddenly and unceremoniously dumped in the middle of the main road to Benguela.

Obviously, with the prospect of them having to load it all onto the truck again, everybody in the camp was furious. Padua was shouted at from all directions and in several languages, including several

CHAPTER 15: ALPHA'S BATTLE FOR BENGUELA AIRPORT

Bushman dialects and Portuguese. But I'd got over my fright and I thought it was hilarious.

Laughingly, I walked up to Padua, who by now was expecting the worst and looking rather foolish and apologetic at the same time.

'Don't worry, Padua my friend,' I said as I addressed him directly. 'Worse things can happen to a man – so we'll get the troops to load the stuff and get on with the show.'

His reaction was a scream ...

Our attack on Benguela Airport followed and, as mentioned earlier, how we actually got out of that mess almost unscathed, is proof enough that when God decides to give you his support, you're in pretty safe hands.

It was late when we arrived at Zulu HQ. I spent a little time explaining my problem but I somehow got the impression that they didn't really feel much for it. The entire headquarters staff had managed to get their hands on a large can of Russian pork and somebody had rustled up a meal with that, together with whatever else they could scrounge. At least they invited us to share the meal, which resulted in a relatively quiet evening, particularly as I had a constant ringing in my ears from all the near misses over the previous few days.

The next morning as we were about to leave, I was standing beside my garry when I saw what looked like a Dakota circling over the airport at Benguela.

'Hey Willie,' I called to the OPS officer, 'have we got any of our planes flying around in this area?'

'No,' he replied and asked why I'd asked.

'Because there's one circling Benguela right now, and if it's not ours, then what is it doing there? The guy must be mad.'

'Search me,' he retorted and reiterated that it was definitely not one of ours.

I immediately got on the radio and told the company commander I'd left in charge at the air base to shoot the bloody thing down. Fortunately, we had no anti-aircraft weapons, but the troops let fly with everything they had.

In spite of a fairly awesome display of firepower, the pilot didn't appear to be too worried and continued to manifest his determination to land. I told my troops to stop firing and then ordered them to capture the plane intact. I could do with an aircraft just nicely.

The aircraft landed and we were advised that it was indeed one of our own Dakotas. It was on its way back to Sá da Bandeira, but when they saw nobody there, they assumed the entire task force had moved on to Benguela. Unknowingly the aircraft had landed slap bang in the middle of a firefight.

The crew dropped their cargo and the plane quickly took off again. Apparently this was the first time in the history of Angolan aviation that a Dakota had taken off across a field.

Later that day I was pleased that Jan joined me at what I was now referring to as 'my private airport' and still later, Zulu HQ decamped there as well.

It was decided that Task Force Bravo would clear the shanties straddling across much of the approaches to the airport while we would provide covering fire. Alpha would then move forward and clear up the town itself. As I'd expected, there wasn't much resistance as FAPLA had decided it would be prudent to clear out. Thereafter, Bravo marched triumphantly through the shantytown while we headed north to Lobito Bay.

Not everything went according to plan. Erstwhile Portuguese Major Covacha – having been a former member of *Direcção Geral de Segurança* or DGS and hence an enemy of the erstwhile terrorists – was recognised by some locals and immediately attacked and robbed of his rifle.

Recalling a similar incident not long before when Jan was nearly shot by a UNITA soldier, I decided that the problem needed to be immediately sorted out. At the head of a strike force moving into a new region, I had to know exactly 'who was who' in the areas under my control. More to the point, we had to be certain who was on whose side. After all, this was supposed to be a war and issues involving enemies and allies needed to be clear-cut or lives could be lost.

This time I drove into town on my own, spoke to some of the UNITA people that had ensconced themselves in the local police station and was told that the big chap in charge of security in the area was called Valentino. They also volunteered that he was actually attending a meeting at the airport and that I could either wait for him at the cop station or return later. He would no doubt see me then, I was assured. I thanked them politely and returned to the airport.

Until this episode had taken place I had been angry. But when I heard mention of Valentino's name I was furious.

Local gossip had it that he was a fairly powerful heavyweight in this area and what he said, went. Also, it wasn't the first time he'd overstepped the mark because some of the stories doing the rounds made me feel more like shooting the son of a bitch than arguing the pitch with him. No question, he was a brutal and devious bastard, but because I couldn't vouch for the truth, I decided to have a quiet word with him first.

At the airport I went straight to where Colonel Van Heerden had established himself in an office and the conversation went more or less like this.

'Hello, Colonel, was there a guy here by the name of Valentino?'

'Yes, why?' was the reply.

'Where's he now?' I asked.

'I don't know, why do you ask?'

'When did he leave?'

'Some time ago, why?'

'Thanks, Colonel. I'll see you later ...' and I walked out of Van Heerden's office.

'Hey, come back here!' the colonel shouted after me. 'What's with you two? First Jan Breytenbach comes storming in here like a madman, threatening to shoot one of UNITA's senior officers and now you arrive, obviously pissed off about something.'

I stopped in my tracks, turned around and walked slowly towards the colonel. I addressed him directly and with respect: 'Do you mind telling me what has gotten into you people?' I asked him. I ended with the words which went along the lines that if he saw that asshole before I did, 'please tell him that I want my man's rifle back and I want to see him out at my camp because there's a few things he ought to know. More to the point, I want to be the guy who is going to tell him his fortune.'

I saluted smartly, just to maintain good relations with the boss, turned around and walked out of the airport terminal.

When I heard the full story later, I had to find a bit of sympathy for the colonel. Apparently one of Bravos' officers had also fallen foul of a UNITA chap called Lumumba and his henchmen. Jan didn't take kindly to this, so he set out to settle the score. Apparently the colonel had invited these two men to his office, almost in an effort to keep diplomatic relations intact, especially since Jan stormed in and threatened to shoot one of them. I can only imagine what must have gone through the colonel's mind.

I wasted little time and returned to the police station where several uniformed UNITA soldiers were hanging about and obviously trying their best to ignore me. I focused on one of them and though he pretended to be occupied with something, his curiosity eventually got the better of him.

When he looked up with what he must have intended to be a bored expression, and caught my eye, I moved forward and stood directly in front of him. At that point I looked him squarely in the eyes: 'Hey *amigo*, you speak Portuguese, yes?'

He nodded but only slightly.

'Okay, *amigo*, now you listen very carefully, because this is important. You go and find Valentino, *pronto*! You tell him that the commandant of the Flecha Battalion – we are camped just north of Lobito – says he must return the rifle that his people took. If he doesn't do that they'll come down here and fetch it themselves and I'm pretty damn sure you know what that means.' By now I had the full attention of the man because he could see that I meant business.

'*Comprende, amigo*?' I asked in his own language, this time getting the impression that the man I spoke to didn't seem quite as before. That said, he promised to pass on the message and I left.

How Valentino got the message, I don't know, but he did show up shortly afterwards, bringing the rifle with him. He was polite enough, but his approach was distinctly 'mightier than thou'.

I looked him over quickly after he'd driven into the camp and decided that the stories I had heard might very well be true. He asked if I would form up my unit so he could address them. I did so and he addressed them. He apologised for the misunderstanding and promised that in future there would only be the best of relations between us, referring to his forces and ours as 'allies'.

In spite of the performance and the apologies that went with it, I couldn't help but feel that the man was being condescending and said as much.

'I'm sorry, buddy,' I declared forcefully, 'but there's no misunderstanding as far as I'm concerned. We're leaving town soon and I hope my and your people won't run into each other again, but if our paths were ever to cross again, I don't want any misunderstandings like we've experienced here.'

His reply was that my words were harsh, even if he did address me as 'commandant'.

I replied that they were meant to be, 'and I hope your memory is as good as those of the Flechas,' I added. Mentioning my Bushman unit, he knew exactly what I was alluding to: there was no love lost between my by now fairly battle-hardened little combatants and his ragtag UNITA force.

What was meant to be a charming smile went somewhat awry and Valentino left without more ado.

Curiously, I did run into Valentino again long after we had withdrawn from Angola. UNITA was losing the war at that stage and he and his men sat huddled together in the south-east corner of Angola. By that time both Valentino and his men had had all the arrogance and bravado knocked out of them, and at that meeting there was no misunderstanding whatsoever.

That same night I decided that I was going to share a bit of quality time with Staff Sergeant Piet Lubbe. He was a peaceful, no-nonsense sort of guy who was not easily impressed with some of the things that might be important to others.

In turn, some of the things he did in his spare time, like reading the Bible, didn't appeal to others. But I found something in this quiet man that appealed to me, something I couldn't quite put my finger on and that worried me. I wanted to know what made him tick.

A short while later I found him sitting in his sports model Land Cruiser, reading his little pocket edition of the New Testament and Psalms.

'Hey Staff,' I said, 'did you see what we did to those guys at the roadblock last night? Man, we blew their bloody heads off. Why don't you go over and take a look?' Staff Lubbe looked up but said nothing.

So I tried another approach and said that some of the Portuguese chaps were taking the town that night. 'They know their way around, if you know what I mean. Why don't you go with them, one never knows ... you might get lucky ...'

But again, I sensed I was on the wrong track, which was when I suggested that we head off to town and find ourselves a place where we could have dinner. Unit grub had become tiresome and I said that we kind of needed to get away from things for a few hours anyway.

'We could have a nice quiet dinner at the restaurant in town, Staff … they tell me they serve an excellent meal there. He smiled: 'Sure Commandant, I'd like that.'

Since the start of the operation, I'd had my share of worries. Also, I'd been scared a lot by now and had begun to understand the feeling. But that night was different.

When we checked in at the only restaurant in town that was still in business, we were told to leave our weapons at reception. I had anticipated this and had already taken the necessary precaution: my favourite Walther P-38 was nicely tucked away under my armpit, if only because, as they say, you never know …

So I surrendered my Kalashnikov without protest. Piet was unarmed, so they didn't bother him and I went ahead and selected a table towards the back, which I thought was okay. With that we placed our order. We ordered a bottle of wine and were settling down nicely to a very relaxed evening. I was hoping to get to know more about this mysterious man, Piet Lubbe, but it was not to be because a new bunch entered the restaurant and they were trouble from the start.

It is difficult to adequately describe these people, except that they were senior UNITA fighters and they marched into the restaurant almost as if they owned the place. Also, it was obvious that they were rigged for a night on the town. Dressed in olive drab uniforms, every one of them was festooned with military hardware that included side arms, grenades and a lot else besides.

Several had machine-gun belts draped over their shoulders. Others wore leather belts festooned with holsters and pistols that would have made the wildest of the Wild Western cowboys cringe. I looked at Piet, but his eyes said nothing. I knew one thing – this man was not afraid.

For all that, it took courage to stick around, but we did and had a delightful meal, the first since who can remember when. We ignored the thugs, drank the wine and ate the food with gusto. I can't recall any single bit of our conversation, but I thoroughly enjoyed the evening. When the machine-gun-belt-draped monkey festooned with hand grenades brandished his .44 Magnum over our heads, I'd give him a hearty smile and indicate in UNITA fashion that we are all very, very good friends.

In spite of several more close shaves that fringed on violence, the evening ended without mishap. I retrieved my carbine and we left. Piet said thanks, adding that he'd enjoyed the evening. I wasn't sure about that, but what I didn't know then was that I would walk through hell itself with that same Piet Lubbe.

Early the following morning we were again summoned to the airport because, as somebody put it, the 'Top Brass' was due to arrive shortly. That included Brigadier Dawie Schoeman, the man who, until then, had run Operation Savannah. He was accompanied by the officer who was to replace him, Brigadier Johan Potgieter.

For all the fanfare, it was actually a great day in our lives. In almost as many words, we were told how good we were at what we were doing and the rest. Clearly, everybody was delighted and everything seemed to be a great success.

Apart from 'Foxbat', other new names were bandied about, like 'X-Ray', and 'Yankee'. These were additional South African forces that were apparently moving northwards, deep into Angola along routes further to our east. I got the impression that South Africa was really getting into the act.

CHAPTER 16

The Military Approach in Central Angola

Brigadier General Kaas van der Waals wrote in his book *Portugal's War in Angola 1961–1974*: 'The Angolan war has been described as the bloodiest colonial insurgency in the history of Africa south of the Sahara'.[1] He also poignantly commented: 'It was to become a conflict that Portugal would lose not on the battlefield but in the hearts of its own citizens.' It was into this brutal, crazily confused revolutionary melee that the participants of Operation Savannah were thrust.

To really understand conditions in Angola when Operation Savannah was launched, one needs to comprehend the nature of the country that South African forces invaded. It was very different to anything those officers and men had previously encountered. In a sense this was 'raw' Africa coupled to a healthy dollop of European culture.

Angola was a remarkable experience for almost all the young men who went into that country as part of an aggressive mobile force that was intent on trying to counter some of the inroads made by competing guerrilla elements intent on seizing power on 11 November 1975. Some of the youngsters were still in their teens.

'Nothing ... *absolutely nothing* ... prepared us for this ... we had a vision of hell,' one of the youngsters wrote in his diary that he showed me years later.

It was beautiful in places, he conceded. Very beautiful, particularly once his column got into the mountains leading towards the coast. But as another soldier commented on his return home: 'There were a lot of people out there just waiting to strike and what worried us most was that they had stuff that was way ahead of anything we were able to field ... stacks of it: multiple rocket launchers, heavy artillery, rocket propelled grenades and that sort of thing ...'

By today's standards, South African casualties were not dramatic, due largely to poor training and the inability to handle sophisticated weapons on the part of their adversaries, but quite a few of the South

CHAPTER 16: THE MILITARY APPROACH IN CENTRAL ANGOLA   157

African troops took hits. And quite a few more than anticipated were sent home in body bags.

The trouble was, politicians back in Pretoria hadn't actually thought all that through when Op Savannah was launched and, as a consequence, just about everybody paid a price. Even those who weren't hurt ... some of the youngsters had their mind-set changed, like forever ...

Before Commandants Linford and Breytenbach had even left Caprivi at the head of Battle Groups Alpha and Bravo, other developments that had a bearing on the war ahead were taking shape. The objectives of these two fighting groups would be to move quickly across South Angola and take several major towns then controlled by the MPLA. They would then move on to the country's ports of Moçâmedes, Benguela and Lobito. Meanwhile, there were others tackling equally formidable objectives in Angola's central regions.

Long before Operation Savannah was contemplated, in fact, even before Angola thrust off the colonial mantle and became an independent country, Commandant Van der Waals had been seconded to the Department of Foreign Affairs for service as a Vice Consul in the South African Consulate General in Luanda. His duties entailed military liaison with the Portuguese authorities in Angola.

On his return to South Africa and shortly after the Lisbon military putsch, he was ordered by Major General Constand Viljoen, then Director General Operations of the SADF's General Staff, to go back to Angola, this time on a totally different mission.

As this brigadier general stated afterwards, what was not yet known to him was that the government – including the South African Defence Force – was intensely involved in international discussions with regard to the future of the former Portuguese colony of Angola. That included contact with the Central Intelligence Agency as well as the Congolese President Mobutu Sese Seko. Others in that loop were Angola's rebel leaders Holden Roberto as well as Dr Jonas Savimbi who headed UNITA.

The idea, essentially, was to mobilise support for the pro-Western Angolan liberation movements in a bid to counter Cuban and Soviet gains in a country that had been taken over by a seasoned bunch of Moscow-trained socialists and had swung hard to the left.

As he wrote in his subsequent published report, what he did know was that the overall plan, as stated by General Viljoen, was to prevent a Portuguese handover of power on 11 November 1975 to Angola's Pro-Soviet faction that called itself the MPLA (the Popular Movement for the Liberation of Angola).

Brigadier General Van der Waals takes up the story:

The first time we discussed my new role during early September 1975, while I was a lecturer [DS] at the SA Defence College, General Constand Viljoen characteristically played straight cards. He asked me whether I'd personally like to become involved in recovering and maintaining the traditional areas of influence of the two western-oriented movements and, if so, where?

The options were basic: I would either be linked to Holden Roberto's FNLA in the north, where they received most of their support from the Americans through the Congo or, alternatively, in Angola's central regions where UNITA was most active.

As a matter of principle I was almost totally opposed to involvement with the FNLA given their murderous actions of March to May 1961. That, coupled to a dismal insurgency record, weak leadership and their present status being mainly the trumped-up consequences of the CIA-backed American propaganda machine. A week later I would become directly involved in the South African Defence Force's largest military operation since the end of World War II.

To start with, General Viljoen suggested that I make my way to 1 Military Area, the northern border area adjacent to Angola then under the command of Brigadier Dawie Schoeman.

Having made contact, the brigadier informed me that I would have to join him as soon as possible at his headquarters in the Caprivi. It was from there that UNITA would receive the bulk of our support. He emphasised that I would be directly responsible to him and him alone.

1 Military Area with Headquarters in Rundu was divided into three subareas: these were Ovambo, Kavango and the Eastern Caprivi, each under command of a lieutenant colonel or, as it was in those days, a commandant.

His orders issued personally to me at Pretoria's Waterkloof Air Force Base on 19 September 1975 were comprehensive:

1. Stop the MPLA's advance from Lobito to Nova Lisboa.
2. Defend Nova Lisboa as Angola's second city and the centre of gravity of the Central Angolan Highlands at all cost until 11 November 1975 [proposed and accepted independence day for the Angolan nation].
3. Train two brigades of UNITA, one offensive and the other defensive, before 11 November 1975; and in the process, I was to provide Savimbi and his general staff with advice.

My first meeting at Army Headquarters was with the SA Army's Director of Operations, Brigadier Jannie Geldenhuys, my predecessor as Vice Consul in Luanda, who was not overly enthusiastic and left me to my own devices. I had to make my own plans, decide on personnel and armament.

What I quickly discovered was that the first stage of what Brigadier Schoeman had in mind – stopping the MPLA's advance from Lobito to Nova Lisboa in Angola's Central Highlands – was already very much in the hands of the MPLA's enemies. There were regular armed clashes with the political and military opposition taking place, invariably with Cuban and Soviet support. In short, government forces were making good headway.

Except for the operational presence in Central and Eastern Angola, there was already a substantial training task ahead that required a fully fledged South African Army training team. UNITA would provide the recruits and basic weapons and we would offer leadership, instructors and infantry support weapons.

The way I read it, an operation to stop the MPLA advance from Lobito – which included a strong motorised force as well as armoured vehicles – had to be launched without any delay.

On 23 September 1975 I departed for Rundu. In Rundu we were welcomed by Brigadier Schoeman. Our signallers installed our long-range radios at UNITA headquarters in Silva Porto [the old Roads Department complex] and we were installed in a very luxurious house close to the Savimbi residence. Leaving my signallers in this house I once again flew to Rundu to await my training team.

I once again met my ex-colleague Commandant Jan Breytenbach who was then with a small training team training FNLA [mainly ex-MPLA Chipenda members] in Mpupa, an ex-Portuguese military base on the Cuito River.

The fact is, the SADF was in its cross-border actions contravening the Defence Act which obliges government to obtain parliamentary approval for deployment of military personnel outside the frontiers of South Africa. But political sensitivity prevented this.

As with Commandant Delville Linford before me, my two signallers and I were permanently present in Silva Porto from 25 September 1975.

I had three immediate simultaneous and urgent priorities: getting training started; launching an operation to halt the MPLA advance from Lobito and taking stock of the general UNITA and MPLA situation, requiring a fully fledged detailed operational appreciation.

Our training team arrived on 27 September after Savimbi and I had inspected the old prison facilities in Capolo on 26 September.

Capolo, although situated 60 kilometres south of Silva Porto, was ideal from a security point of view, its facilities were good and it also had a disused 700-metre landing strip which could be useful. Recruits, initially 700, varied in age from young boys to old men, many suffering from malnutrition and TB and hardly the kind of tough, determined and malleable fighters that would be required for the task.

We also had language problems as very few of the UNITA personnel understood English and quite a large number among them, not even basic Portuguese. Training nevertheless progressed satisfactorily and by 15 October we had put four companies through their paces, two of them offensive and two defensive, as well as an 81 mm and a 60 mm mortar platoon. There was also a 106 mm recoilless gun crew.

By the time we vacated the training base we had trained three infantry battalions consisting of three companies each, three 81 mm mortar platoons, three 60 mm mortar platoons, three 4,5 inch mortar platoons, three .50 Browning machine gun platoons as well as crews for eleven 106 mm recoilless guns.

We had also trained 60 UNITA soldiers as a leader group and a further 60 as instructors. They would continue with training after our departure.

UNITA's military strength was estimated to be about 10 000 armed, 20 000 mostly unarmed or under training and a further 10 000 ready for training.

CHAPTER 16: THE MILITARY APPROACH IN CENTRAL ANGOLA

Armament was of a diverse nature and included six Panhard armoured cars, three with 90 mm guns and three with a 60 mm mortar, donated by Mobutu or left by the Portuguese Army when they departed. There were also four 120 mm mortars, a dozen 81 mm mortars, some 106 mm recoilless guns, a pair of 75 mm guns, a reasonable number of 7.62 mm light machine guns as well as a variety of 7.62 mm rifles.

Ammunition for all was in short supply and UNITA's main logistic base in Silva Porto was in total disorder. There was virtually no fuel at the base with fuel for day-to-day vehicle use being kept in Savimbi's house's back yard.

As an ally, the FNLA had a rather limited and often disruptive presence in Silva Porto. Regarding Chipenda in Serpa Pinto I shared Savimbi's sentiments and pre-occupation that he could opportunistically revert back to the MPLA and pose a serious threat to what he termed 'UNITA's soft underbelly'.

With regard to the MPLA threat I need to summarise the situation as on 6 October 1975 as follows:

First, the MPLA and their military wing FAPLA threatened the UNITA area of influence almost like a boomerang, doing so from the North and the West. From the East to the Atlantic Ocean FAPLA occupied Cazombo, Teixeira de Sousa, Henrique de Carvalho, Alto Chicapa, Luquembo, Nova Gaia, Malanje, Salazar, Dondo and Luanda. From Luanda southwards FAPLA occupied Porto Amboim, Gabela, Novo Redondo, Vila Nova do Seles, Lobito, Benguela, Norton de Matos, Babaera, Sá da Bandeira, Roçadas, Pereira d' Eca and Evale. Its strength was unknown, but it was known that they had armoured vehicles and Cuban support. Clearly, this was an alarming situation.

Cut off from the sea UNITA could not expect any proper means of provisioning/supplies from the west and this was especially serious from the point of view of fuel. Supplies had to come in by air and this would tax the South African Air Force to the utmost.

FAPLA threatened Nova Lisboa on two fronts, along a southern route from Benguela where an MPLA force of approximately 350 on 30 September 1975 occupied Babaera. A further force of 350 men and three armoured vehicles was positioned at Mariano Machado. This force was checked by two battalions of UNITA which obliged FAPLA to rather also use the northern route from Lobito via Norton de

Matos where the two forces could join. On this route a FAPLA company and one armoured car, supported by a reserve company and three armoured cars, occupied Sousa Lara on 29 September 1975. 150 UNITA soldiers at Monte Belo were the only opposition between FAPLA and Nova Lisboa.

My immediate and priority concern after our arrival at Silva Porto was stopping the FAPLA advance on Nova Lisboa as soon as possible and as far to the west as possible.

This would prevent FAPLA from getting a foothold in the fertile Central Highlands. I had already appointed Major Holtzhausen to lead the force and had arranged for the Panhard armoured cars to be repaired by SA Army technical experts. The ENTAC missile launchers and their crews with 20 missiles had arrived and were ready for deployment on 30 September 1975.

I had also requested crews for a troop of Panhard armoured cars from the RSA and these arrived on 1 October 1975, whereas we did receive some long-wheel-base jeeps from South Africa.

Eight days after our arrival we were ready for action, but we were delayed by Savimbi's absence. We wanted him to be present to prevent friction between our troops and UNITA elements who had been designated to participate in the operation.

Another reason was linked to diplomatic and political considerations because until independence on 11 November, Angola was still nominally Portuguese. Savimbi returned on 2 October and decided to personally accompany the combat team which left for Nova Lisboa on 3 October.

Moving at night via Alto Hama, the combat group reached Luimbale where they were joined by a battalion of UNITA infantry under Major Lumumba – according to Savimbi his most able commander in Central Angola.

Holtzhausen's tourist road map naturally could tell him nothing about the terrain ahead so he hid his column in the bush and went forward with Savimbi to reconnoitre.

About ten clicks south of Norton de Matos they met up with forward UNITA foot patrols who informed them that the FAPLA force was still in the village. They were also informed that a UNITA military element, in a previous contact with FAPLA there had seen a Soviet T-34 tank.

CHAPTER 16: THE MILITARY APPROACH IN CENTRAL ANGOLA

By first light on 5 October the column set off, led by Holtzhausen in his jeep. Between Massano de Amorim and Norton de Matos the column moved through a mountain range with the two Panhards in the lead followed by the mounted UNITA.

Major Holtzhausen and his 19 South Africans returned to Silva Porto the same day having left Major Lumumba and three Panhards (now manned by UNITA crews) in defensive positions east of Norton de Matos.

I had already informed Rundu in no uncertain terms that we were fighting an apparently fairly well-trained enemy supported by Cubans and, what was more, equipped with armoured vehicles including tanks. My advice was to either get in properly or to get out. Half measures would not suffice.

Meantime, Commandant Eddie Webb had also joined us as commander of the training team. On 7 October 1975, in Brigadier Schoeman's absence because of sick leave and in response to my urgent request, we were visited by his second-in-command, Colonel Des Harmse, an experienced and well-balanced professional officer.

We bluntly outlined the situation. More armoured cars were immediately needed: we requested a minimum of six cars, two each for the two western FAPLA advance routes and two for a possible northern route. In the event of a threat on one of the routes the cars could be concentrated to provide a defensive punch.

These cars could unofficially be sold to UNITA whose crews had to man them as no South African forces had to be seen (by the media, especially) as having been deployed in combat.

The ENTACS – French wire-guided anti-tank missiles – were withdrawn to Rundu and we decided to split training between Capolo and the front line with Major Holtzhausen, Captain Holm and three warrant officers forming a team to retrain the UNITA units guarding the approach routes and select and prepare defensive works for them including the placement and setting up of UNITA's support weapons.

It was obvious that in its present state of unpreparedness UNITA was not capable of standing up to FAPLA without substantial help from the South Africans. Savimbi, who attended the discussions with Harmse, had the intellectual courage to acknowledge this. He knew that he needed some convincing early victories, not only to boost his troops' morale but also to lend him the status as a significant player when, later that month, a fact-finding mission from the OAU would visit Angola.

Colonel Harmse returned firmly convinced that Savimbi urgently needed a great deal more assistance than he had had up to now. General Viljoen who visited Silva Porto the next day, agreed.

The prospect of deploying South African armour was initially not considered. However, the higher headquarters also required South African casualties to be avoided and this meant that armoured cars were to be made available urgently.

On 14 October 1975 Task Group Zulu started with an advance from Rundu to clear south-western Angola.

During a short visit to Rundu I had heard that a battle group [Zulu] was being prepared to clear south and south-western Angola up to Lobito. This would enable us in Silva Porto, given reinforcements, the opportunity to launch a 'blitzkrieg' northwards towards the Cuanza River.

There was little or no FAPLA on this route during early October and Zulu and our newly trained UNITA battalions could clear up behind us.

I had also come to the conclusion that 1 Military Area's HQ as a counter-insurgency headquarters was definitely not the ideal HQ for an operation of Savannah's future scope.

Additionally, I was reinforced in this thinking by my frustrating experience with Rundu in just about every respect, from communication with absolutely amateurish codes to lack of understanding of logistic requirements, especially food, transport and fuel – 'Your people must live off the veld' and 'there must be vehicles and fuel in Angola' being typical replies to my urgent requests.

Fortunately, General Viljoen kept his fingers very much on the pulse. To command Operation Savannah, I suggested amongst other proposals that a conventional Brigade HQ be established in Rundu and possibly later in Angola. More frustrating experiences with Rundu were to follow.

With Holtzhausen deployed north-west of Nova Lisboa we gradually began to get a better intelligence picture. The threat against Nova Lisboa still existed and there was talk of a strong FAPLA force moving from Moçâmedes along the Sá da Bandeira–Nova Lisboa route to link up with elements on the Benguela–Nova Lisboa route for a combined attack on the UNITA capital. This was, however, prevented by Zulu's movements later in the month.

By 17 October the first three UNITA companies trained at Capolo were ready for deployment. Two of them were sent to Major Holtzhausen to stabilise the Nova Lisboa front and one to Mussende where FAPLA was applying southward pressure.

Between 17 and 22 October 1975 we received 22 armoured cars, a squadron commanded by Captain G.F. Schoeman. It was a logistic nightmare – no fuel, no ammunition, no rations, no administrative echelon vehicles nor troop carriers to transport the UNITA companies that had to operate with the armoured cars.

The cars were initially hidden at the old Portuguese cavalry school next to the airport from where they were moved at night to Capolo in order to maintain an element of surprise. Through N'Zau Puna's intervention we managed to obtain five heavy trucks to serve as echelon vehicles whereas seven busses were commandeered by UNITA in Silva Porto to take in UNITA infantry.

While Foxbat was being formed – an ancillary force that moved northwards to the east of the two combat groups – and joint training of the armoured cars and UNITA's offensive companies took place at Capolo, UNITA was doing fairly well on its own on the western routes to Nova Lisboa as well as near Mussende and in the Quibala area.

Webb and I could now do some proper operational planning based on the overall appreciation which I'd completed. We planned to act offensively on the Lobito route and to capture Sousa Lara from where we could also attack Quibala. We also considered my blitzkrieg idea from Nova Lisboa to Quibala in order to defend Nova Lisboa in depth.

Rundu poured cold water on our plans and ordered us to concentrate on the direct defence of Nova Lisboa.

We, on the other hand, planned to seize and maintain the initiative by applying an offensive mind-set, thereby placing FAPLA on the defensive and thus preventing them from the opportunity to concentrate their forces on the various routes. But orders were orders and almost as if FAPLA had learned of our plans, they took the initiative and decided to launch another offensive on the central front on 22 October.

As part of this offensive, FAPLA's Lobito force had already reoccupied Norton de Matos, while another FAPLA force with nine armoured cars, according to UNITA *lagartes*, was already in the Santa Comba area.

There was consequently a very distinct danger that the two FAPLA elements could join at Alto Hama just 65 km north of Nova Lisboa from where a combined attack on Nova Lisboa could be launched. Savimbi was on a tour of Europe and N'Zau Puna, in his absence, pleaded with me to let Foxbat loose.

Webb was in Rundu and on 25 October I placed Foxbat on standby to move whereas I also send Holtzhausen and Holm to verify the situation and assess the threat.

Foxbat was no longer the ragtag and bobtail force of earlier. It now consisted of three companies offensively trained UNITA travelling in seven buses; five troops [22] armoured cars; two 106 mm recoilless guns mounted on jeeps; four UNITA-manned 81 mm mortars; three ENTAC teams and four 12,7 mm Browning heavy machine guns.

Also part of Foxbat but not accompanying the combat group were a further ten 106 mm recoilless guns, four Panhard-90 and one Panhard-60 armoured cars, all manned by UNITA.

We also had a twin-engine Beechcraft Baron B55 light aircraft which UNITA had found deserted in Nova Lisboa and which we had collected and flown to Rundu for servicing and fitting of a .30 Browning machine gun. An experienced SAAF pilot, Major Piet Uys, was detached to Rundu to fly the plane and thus provide us with an aerial reconnaissance capability.

On 25 October, while Foxbat was moving to Silva Porto and Webb was on his way back from Rundu, our aircraft, called Dinky Toy, was in the air conducting aerial reconnaissance. It concentrated on all the access routes to Nova Lisboa. Flying on the route Alto Hama, Norton de Matos and Lobito they overflew the FAPLA forward lines and continued until they were over the Atlantic Ocean. Thereafter they flew along the Nova Lisboa–Alto Hama–Quibala route bringing back valuable information of troop dispositions along this route.

At this stage I also had to deal with an untimely and rather silly dispute between UNITA and its official ally FNLA. A whole battalion of FNLA at Santa Comba had fled southwards after a clash with a small FAPLA force and were intercepted and disarmed by N'Zau

Puna. That night the FNLA and UNITA were fighting each other in Nova Lisboa. To prevent similar clashes in Silva Porto we used Foxbat's armoured cars to patrol the streets. The night of 25/26 October Foxbat moved altogether undetected from Silva Porto to a larger area close to Alto Hama.

Various factors inhibited Commandant Webb and Foxbat, unlike Task Force Zulu, to move fast and score successive victories.

One of the main reasons was the fact that it would have to operate along three different approach routes to Nova Lisboa. A further reason of which I was not aware was explicit orders to Webb to prevent loss of South African lives.

To my and later also Rundu's great frustration this led to pinprick operations with great expenditure of ammunition along especially the western routes after which Foxbat fell back to laager areas near Alto Hama and Teixeira da Silva, thus complicating logistics, especially fuel problems and not consolidating operational successes. This series of operations will be dealt with briefly.

On arrival in Alto Hama, Webb learned that Luimbale had the previous day been vanquished by a FAPLA force of 250 men, two tanks and three armoured cars. Three troops of armoured cars and UNITA infantry attacked this force on 26 October, causing ten casualties and destroying the armoured vehicles while capturing ammunition and weapons. The town was left to the UNITA infantry while the rest of the force fell back on its laager area at Alto Hama, thus not pursuing its success.

A combat team consisting of one troop of armoured cars and a company of UNITA was separately deployed on the Santa Comba route to cover Foxbat's northern flank. This force once again returned to the laager area on 27 October.

Massano de Amorim, which FAPLA, unknown to us, had vacated was attacked on 27 October also using 4.2-inch mortars which had joined Foxbat, and was left in the care of two UNITA companies as a holding force, Foxbat once again falling back on its laager area.

After the meeting with the second-in-command of 1 Military Area in Teixeira da Silva on 29 October, Webb was ordered to concentrate on the defence of the Lobito route, and also to deploy a combat team on the Santa Comba route, as well as a further combat team along the

Benguela route where a recent UNITA reverse had led to a threat to the power station between Babaera and Mariano Machado.

A combat team under Major Holtzhausen on 29 October occupied defensive positions along the Queve River 25 kilometres south of Santa Comba and clashed with a lightly armed FAPLA force. On clearing the battle zone after the clash, the uniformed body of a Cuban colonel was discovered.

Thereafter, FAPLA reinforcements were spotted along the Santa Comba route by Dinky Toy, and Holtzhausen's force was strengthened by another UNITA company.

A further combat team with three troops of armoured cars under command of Captain Schoeman on 29 October advanced on the Benguela route, taking Babaera on 31 October. With the UNITA morale along this route reinforced and Task Force Zulu's progress neutralising the threat along this route, Schoeman's combat team returned to Alto Hama.

Having been informed by Dinky Toy that FAPLA had once again occupied Norton de Matos along the Lobito route, Webb once again dispatched a combat team to this location which clashed with FAPLA on 29 October and retook the town. Leaving three companies UNITA as a holding force the combat team returned to Teixeira da Silva. It was during this operation that Dinky Toy crashed and its four-member crew killed.

During the first few days of November, Webb consolidated arrangements logistically and otherwise to once again move in force along the Lobito route, having received information that a strong FAPLA force was present at Monte Belo.

At this stage I planned on moving Foxbat with speed to north of Lobito in order to cut off FAPLA elements fleeing before Task Force Zulu's advance. This required joint planning and coordination as I was also afraid that Zulu and Foxbat could clash. Rundu appears to have vetoed my requests in this regard.

Our course of action was obvious and on 2 November Webb was ordered to once again advance along the Lobito route and not to overnight more than once in the same laager area.

A combat team led by Holtzhausen and consisting of two companies UNITA, three troops of armoured cars under Captain Schoeman, and 106 mm recoilless guns, Browning machine guns, 81 mm

CHAPTER 16: THE MILITARY APPROACH IN CENTRAL ANGOLA

and 107 mm mortars reached Norton de Matos on 3 November and ran into a well-prepared FAPLA defensive position at Caluita 16 kilometres to the west.

After a long and very heavy battle where the armoured cars especially played a critically decisive role, the opposition was overcome. Advancing westward after the battle, light opposition at Monte Belo was overcome and for two days Monte Belo served as the combat team's consolidation and recuperation area.

The advance was continued on 5 November reaching Sousa Lara without any opposition, capturing a large quantity of armament and food. Warned by the local population of the presence of large numbers of landmines, the advance to Lobito [without engineers] was carefully continued on 6 November and the force occupied ambush positions on the main Lobito–Novo Redondo road forty clicks east of Lobito, thus serving as a cut-off force for Zulu where forty plus FAPLA vehicles were destroyed on 6 and 7 November.

Task Force Zulu reached Lobito on 7 November and was visited by Webb and Holtzhausen on 8 November.

It was decided that Foxbat would move back to concentrate on the defence of Nova Lisboa and an advance to Quibala, while also protecting Zulu's right flank as it advanced northwards along the coast.

It should be remembered that the South African contingent had to be out of Angola by 11 November 1975. On 10 November 1975 Foxbat moved to Santa Comba with its excellent airstrip, a move that I had advocated from the beginning.

On 31 October 1975 General Viljoen and a member of the Bureau for State Security had visited Silva Porto and discussed the military and political situation, emphasising the fact that the RSA's military aid would be limited to 11 November 1975.

Phase Three of our involvement, the capture of the Atlantic harbours, was in progress but would not include the capture of Luso. At this meeting I was tasked to draw up withdrawal plans for both Foxbat, the training team and, of course, myself. These plans had already featured in my aforementioned operational appreciation and would generally entail us being flown out by SAAF C130 aircraft with the Foxbat armoured car squadron moving south on its own.

After General Viljoen's departure, a very downhearted Savimbi discussed the military situation with me, emphasising the fact that without our support the military gains of the past five weeks would be lost within weeks.

I sympathised with him but also emphasised that I had to follow orders. He then requested me to arrange for him to speak to Prime Minister John Vorster in order to convince him that we should stay until at least early December when the Organisation of African Union [African Union today] would discuss the Angolan situation. Should his request be refused, he would speak to President Kaunda in order for him to convince Mr Vorster that we should stay.

I promptly submitted his request to Rundu, after which General Viljoen once again visited Silva Porto on 5 November to discuss the request.

Savimbi visited South Africa for a meeting with Mr Vorster on 10 November 1975 and our departure was postponed. It might also be of interest to mention that I was once again visited on 7 November by the local CIA representative to determine whether we would leave Angola by 11 November.

When I confirmed this he asked whether he could leave with us. To which I replied: 'You are welcome – be my guest!' As it was, I would leave Angola on 15 November, mission accomplished, no doubt – but without my knowledge – also due to Delville Linford and his Alpha Bushmen.[2]

---

1 W.S.van der Waals, *Portugal's War in Angola 1961–1974*, Protea Book House, Pretoria, 2011, p. 45.
2 Interview with Kaas van der Waals, Centurion, 17 August 2014.

CHAPTER 17

Ultimate Destination – Luanda?

While Task Force Zulu was going about its business further towards the west, we got on with our side of hostilities at the coast...

I didn't know it yet but it wasn't long after we'd taken Benguela Airport that I started to get the feeling that whatever else was in the way, we were heading straight for Luanda.

In our original briefings back at Rundu, before taking my Task Force Alpha on the long haul into Angola, the idea was that we would try to cover as much ground as we could before that country became independent. The date, following all-party negotiations in the Angolan capital subsequent to the Portuguese Army mutiny, was set for 11 November 1975.

Once we'd reached Benguela, that date lay just a few days ahead and I had been contemplating for a while by then what had become of the plan to withdraw on Independence Day. I didn't dare raise the matter with any of the 'big guys' on the morning they paid us a cursory visit as I was famished. And anyway, Jan and I had planned lunch at the same hotel where Staff Sergeant Lubbe and I had dinner the previous evening.

There was obviously a lot of conjecture between Jan and me about what lay ahead, but what really got my mind going was an off-the-cuff comment made by Brigadier Johan Potgieter that we were to be provided with artillery. Even more surprising, Major Coen Upton would be almost immediately joining Combat Group Alpha as my second-in-command.

Now that was a revelation because I knew Major Upton: he'd already built up a solid reputation as an officer who brooked little resistance and who, given the go-ahead, could achieve solid results. Also, we were all aware that he was a brilliant staff officer and had been involved in orchestrating Operation Savannah from the start.

By all accounts he was an equally steadfast infantryman and to my mind, this was an enormous step forward after all the fumbling and bungling we'd experienced so far: Alpha could certainly do with a bit of professional expertise.

How he was going to accept serving under the command of a gunner was another matter.

My fears were short-lived. It took only days to prove that Coen Upton – for all his other foibles, bless him – was not only the best second-in-command that any field commander could hope for, but also a loyal and trusting friend.

Within hours of Coen's arrival in Benguela, we 'borrowed' the OC's black Mercedes Benz – a fine vehicle abandoned by its original owner and took the town in grand style. Major Toon Slabbert, commander of the Armoured Car Squadron who had joined us at Vila Roçadas went along as well and this pleased me because the force was gradually getting the muscle and brainpower it needed.

It is interesting that Toon had always been a huge and powerful man, even by South African standards, and there had always been some conjecture as to how he actually managed to fit his hulk into the confines of the turret of one of our Eland armoured cars. Somehow he managed, and there were times when we thanked the Good Lord for that because, subsequently, many was the time that the intrepid Toon Slabbert and his 'Eland 90's' saved us from what we believed was certain destruction.

Anyway we had a great meal and lots of wine in Benguela, after which we went our separate ways.

That afternoon I drove my entire unit down to the beach. Considering that these people were from the bush and had never seen the sea, my thoughts were that this was going to be a real treat for everybody. But to my astonishment, they were not the slightest bit interested. Most of the fellows lazed about on what was a delightful tropical beach in the shade of the palms and looked bored. Accepting once more – for the umpteenth time – that I didn't know these people at all, I told them all to return to camp.

When I gave orders to prepare to move the next morning, the sense of relief was almost palpable.

The road we were ordered to take led directly north out of Benguela. Because we'd seen so little of the enemy after taking the airport and its surrounds, I thought our adversaries in the capital might have lost interest, both in the war and our progress towards their seat of power in Luanda.

CHAPTER 17: ULTIMATE DESTINATION – LUANDA?

We spent the night in some remote place along the way and next morning somebody shouted, 'Hey you guys, this is 11 November – aren't we supposed to be going home today?'

Trying to be flippant, I told him to shut up. With that I declared in a loud voice: 'Come on, all of you, let's go ... Luanda here we come!'

But from that day on things started going wrong, beginning with my command vehicle. 'Hurry up, Hendrik, start up, let's go,' I ordered.

'The thing won't start, Sir.'

'What do you mean the thing won't start?'

'I mean the bloody thing won't start, Sir! It just won't go ...'

'Okay,' I replied, 'get my Suzuki ready and let one of the tiffies sort this thing out.'

Within minutes I'd transferred to the little Suzuki jeep we had captured earlier and took off. We hadn't gone far when the armoured commander reported that one of his cars had been hit by a rocket.

From the excitement in his voice I gathered that they had made contact and that the leading car had become a target, though there was no mention of casualties. He went on to explain that they'd obviously run into an ambush and that the rocket was fired from his flank. They were lucky, he told me over the radio: the explosive charge had struck the car exactly where a jerry can of water had been mounted onto the frame of the Eland. Also, the can was full and deflected the blast and caused no real damage.

I warned all the cars to deploy and wait for orders. Meantime, I moved forward in my little jeep across some high ground from where I hoped I could observe the terrain ahead.

I'd gone some distance when I spotted a river running across our intended route. The stream ran east to west, or right to left, and just beyond lay a huge cliff that both overlooked and overhung the bridge which we would need to cross if we were to proceed any further.

There was no question that the combination of the bridge and the towering cliff that dominated its approaches were very well placed for an ambush, but just then I didn't have a clue how else we were going to move ahead if the bridge didn't come into play. Just then, as I contemplated my predicament and searched for answers, the entire mountain ahead erupted in a cloud of black smoke.

It was an awesome sight. Following an initial mighty explosion, huge volumes of smoke and rocks were hurled into the air, almost as if in slow motion. For a few moments the debris remained suspended in the air before tumbling onto the bridge below. Only then was I buffeted by the blast and the sound of the explosion itself. I reckoned afterwards that whoever laid the charges much have used a hefty amount of TNT, probably several hundred kilos.

Still shocked by the sudden turn of events, I quickly turned my binoculars onto the bridge and, to my delight, found it to be intact. 'Okay, chaps,' I called on the radio, 'the bridge is holding, but just watch out for high ground'.

A short while later our armoured cars moved forward. Tentatively they worked their way over and around a rubble of large boulders, rocks and dirt that must have covered an area of several football pitches, which says a lot for the driving ability of the drivers. Having crossed the bridge, the armoured cars secured the terrain on the far bank, standing to while the rest of the unit crossed.

A short while later I gave the order to proceed, which meant getting out of the river valley and moving towards higher ground. Then the fun really started.

Provisionally, I'd signalled the Elands to move forward, telling the drivers to be particularly careful. Obviously, whoever had set the charges that brought half a mountain tumbling into the river were still around, with the result that the men were acutely aware of the potential threat that lay ahead ... they were dealing with professionals. Almost as one, they moved with infinite care and precision.

For a while things went reasonably well. Then once our mortars had been deployed, Major Upton brought up the first company of troops in single file along the road behind the ridge. Meanwhile, we waited with some anticipation for the mortars to start letting rip, hoping that that would soften up the area immediately ahead which, in turn, would allow me to move towards the crest. My intention was to try to get to a position where I could observe enemy movement and adjust our own fire on any targets that might be presented.

But it was not to be. As the first armoured column rounded the ridge, it drew an enormous amount of fire from the high ground beyond the ridge on which we were sitting. I was amazed at the fury of the attack: it was almost as if everything they had was shooting in our direction simultaneously. I didn't know it yet, but the first of our cars had already taken a hit and were out of action.

CHAPTER 17: ULTIMATE DESTINATION – LUANDA?

Just then I had a few other concerns. What worried me most was that the ridge on which we were placed was being targeted with some really accurate mortar and rifle fire. Obviously whoever was doing the directing was good at his job, he was not only observing our progress but was very good at what he was doing. Several mortar bombs landed a lot closer to our position than I would have liked, but fortunately there was a large hole about two metres in diameter alongside the area where I'd halted: it was just waist high on the reverse slope of the ridge and I wasted no time at all in dropping down into it.

The young officer in command of the mortars, Second Lieutenant Aucamp, had meanwhile come forward and joined me and he, too, made for the hole. For the moment we were out of danger.

This was now the second time in a relatively short period that I was lying in a hole waiting for a mortar bomb to fall on my head, something that I just couldn't get accustomed to. There was nothing else to do but stay in the hole.

I did use the opportunity to search the ridge of the high plateau to my right with my binoculars, largely in hopes of spotting a mortar observation post, but all I could see was the dust from the bombs exploding around us. I had been pretty scared before, but this time I was petrified.

To make matters worse a figure appeared out of the dust and smoke ahead. He was tall and lean and sported a beard, walking calmly and unhurried and seemingly without a care. It looked like the picture I had in my Bible of Jesus walking on the water towards the disciples in the boat. This really was it. I was convinced.

A voice out of nowhere called: 'Say, Commandant, you got place in that hole for one more?'

It was Piet Lubbe. Where he'd come from, I'll never know because with all the firing going on, he just appeared. This truly was a remarkable man.

I turned around to see what was going on behind us. Coen was deploying a company of troops on either side of the road and before I could warn him that they were under direct fire from enemy mortars I saw a mortar bomb land directly in the middle of his deployment. To this day I can still see the torso of a soldier somersaulting through the air.

Now I was certain they had an observation post (OP) on the ridge towards our right flank. To stay where we were would have been suicide and I grabbed the radio.

'Coen,' I ordered, 'withdraw the troops immediately!'

Moments later I heard him give the order to withdraw. The platoon commander that had moved up close behind me was ... would you believe it ... Lavado – one of my earlier Bushman recruits out of Angola. He jumped, shouting 'Follow me!' With that he dashed off right into the enemy mortar fire. I could just imagine several dozen of my Bushman troops being slaughtered by mortar fire that was coming down on us in buckets.

'Hey! Stop! Stop!' I called urgently towards the man. 'You are running directly into the fire, come with me ... this way!'

I didn't stop to look who was following, but it seemed that sanity prevailed and when I eventually did look around, the entire platoon was behind me, except Lavado, but just then he was the least of my worries.

I signalled the rest of the Bushman unit to follow me and dashed straight towards the high ground on our right. I was hoping to get the troops out of the mortar fire, and I'm thankful that it worked. But that was not all that happened.

Suddenly the mortars stopped coming at us and for a few moments everything went quiet. I didn't realise why, except that I was just grateful that it did. Only later was I made aware that the OP that had been giving us all the trouble was on the same high ground towards which we were moving, and whoever was making our lives a misery decided to call it a day.

It was already dusk when I eventually left the troops with the company commander and made my way on foot to our mortar position. I was running along the road that we'd followed earlier that afternoon when I heard voices in the dust.

'Hold on my boy, I'll have you at a doctor in no time ... he'll sort you out in no time. Just be strong ...'

I would have recognised that voice anywhere, it was Piet Lubbe and it didn't take me very long to realise that he had a lot of wounded soldiers in his Land Cruiser and was carting them back to safety, irrespective of the fact that he also had a load of explosives on board.

CHAPTER 17: ULTIMATE DESTINATION – LUANDA?

I ran on. Then I heard Coen's voice. 'Hey,' he called to somebody, 'have you seen the commandant anywhere?' I continued forward and in the gathering gloom the Suzuki jeep appeared, and then Lavado, who was hauling the last of the mortars from the ill-fated position onto the road.

'Coen, it's me!' I called loudly.

'Commandant! Thank God, I thought you'd snuffed it. Here, hold onto this troop on the bonnet. If I drive he's going to fall off.'

He had a wounded soldier across the bonnet of the jeep and two more lying in the back of the small vehicle.

We drove off. When we got to the bridge Coen couldn't see the rocks and I had all my work cut out to keep me and my wounded charge from sliding off the hood.

We had just crossed the bridge when we were stopped by somebody in the middle of the road.

'Stop,' he commanded. 'Can you tell us where the OC is?'

'I'm the OC, what the hell do you want?'

'I'm Cap ... I'm in command of the guns ... we have a flat tyre on one of the guns ...'

'Piss off, I'll speak to you in the morning,' was my retort.

It was a slog, but we finally managed to get the wounded soldiers to a first-aid post, a pantechnicon that had been improvised for the purpose and that Commandant Kotzé had acquired from somewhere and turned into a mobile hospital. The medics had spread a tarpaulin alongside the large vehicle and we delivered the wounded soldiers in their care.

By then I was absolutely fatigued. In the final stages of getting our wounded to safety, I'd walked as if in a trance. I was stunned as I looked at my wounded troops lying in neat rows inside and outside the vehicle.

For a little while I felt nothing – only emptiness. As I stood there trying to think what brave and successful commanders would have done in these circumstances, I saw a soldier huddled up in the shadow.

'You okay, boy?' I asked.

'I'm not feeling so good,' he replied wistfully, obviously in pain.

I took a closer look at the youngster. At first glance he seemed fine to me, that is, he wasn't shot to pieces and bleeding.

'Nobody is feeling so good at the moment, son. You just hold tight ... I'm sure you'll be alright.'

I walked on just to get away from those pleading eyes.

As I was to discover only later, he wasn't alright because he was one of the two men who had died in that battle. Eighteen men were wounded that day.

I was up early the following morning and made my way towards high ground on the right of the road. That was some distance before the bridge.

Captain Chris Bouwer, the troop commander of the 25-pounder guns I had so rudely shoved out of the way the day before, was very understanding when he'd heard what had happened. He joined me as I moved ahead, and because this was the first time he would be firing his guns in action, he was pretty wound up.

We started by setting up an OP on the high ground to the right of the road but still a considerable distance short of the bridge. By now the young captain was chomping at the bit.

'Okay, Commandant,' he said, 'where the hell are these chaps?' Moments later he asked whether he should perhaps start softening them up before I sent my men ahead?

'Listen, Chris, I wrote that book you are quoting from,' was my reply. 'What's happened to silent registration?' I asked. Obviously disappointed, he backed down and I couldn't really blame him.

Silent registration was a process whereby the observation officer studies the terrain ahead and marks any outstanding features that can serve as reference points and even likely targets are noted. At Gunnery School this was a rather boring process as everybody knew the shooting ranges like the back of their hands, but here in remote 'Injun Country' in the heart of a hostile Angola it was a very necessary prerequisite.

'Besides,' I added, 'in this kind of half-light we're not likely to observe the fall of shot.'

Gloomily Bouwer set about making marks on his map. I didn't check, because I realised that whatever he was doing was just to please me. The maps we were using were of such a scale that they were virtually of no use at all.

Once the light began to improve and I got a better picture of the terrain ahead, I started to formulate a plan.

CHAPTER 17: ULTIMATE DESTINATION – LUANDA?

Beyond the river lay the ridge behind which we'd got caught napping the day before. 'Ridge One,' I marked the approximate position on my map. Beyond that ran another slightly loftier bit of high ground, but it was not possible to tell the distance between the two as neither were shown on our maps. Anyway, I marked it 'Ridge Two'.

Further towards the horizon I could just make out yet another and taller range of hills: 'Ridge Three'. It looked as if a road disappeared over a crest at that point, but I couldn't be sure because of distance and poor light.

I pointed at the second ridge to the impatient young troop commander: 'Okay, my boy, that seems to be as good a place to start as any. All the positions we had come across to date were open trenches, so if you have airburst, I think this would do just fine.'

'Let 'em go!' I ordered and young Chris did just that.

Meantime, Coen had quietly sneaked up on us and smiled appreciatively, 'Thanks for the demo,' he said breezily.

'You're welcome. Now let's make war. I have eighteen reasons to shoot the living daylights out of those boys on the other side.'

Now that we had definite proof of where the target was on our maps, things started falling into place. A short while later a succession of artillery rounds started falling onto the target that I'd indicated.

We spend the rest of the morning shooting at everything that might have been an enemy position and the enemy didn't waste any time in responding with their guns. Our armoured cars moved forward tentatively, but there was no question, incoming fire was devastating.

As the morning wore on, the enemy bombing started first to vacillate and eventually became less and less. At about midday, it ceased altogether and our Elands were able to move forward. Shortly afterwards they reported heavy movement on the road towards the north. 'Smokey' moved his artillery fire further towards the rear and started concentrating on the road where it dipped over the horizon.

Once the armoured cars had gone far enough forward to make it safe, our infantry was ordered to clear up all former enemy positions. By this time, the enemy had withdrawn and our fellows found only two FAPLA soldiers wandering about the trenches almost in a state of shell-shocked daze. They didn't seem to know what had happened.

Questioned, they told us that a lot of their people had been shot, but they didn't know how many or where the firing had come from.

'The things seemed to be coming from the air,' was one of their comments.

'Yes, old pal, where I come from we call that airburst.'

Meantime, Jan's Combat Group Bravo pulled up, by which time Headquarters had given orders for them to move up and take the town of Novo Redondo. This was a modest-sized former Portuguese administrative centre which lay about a dozen kilometres up the road.

I moved my Alpha Group forward and we pitched camp on an open plain just short of a mountain range running as a crest to the immediate south of the town. There were some buildings there and we made ourselves reasonably comfortable.

Bravo found Novo Redondo deserted by the enemy, but our troops were given a very warm welcome by the inhabitants who had fled to the bush as soon as the shelling started. They all speedily returned to the town when FAPLA left.

Locals also reported that FAPLA must have suffered heavy casualties, which was later confirmed by the horrendous state in which our forces found the local hospital.

CHAPTER 18

North into Angola

Things started to hot up for both sides as we continued with our push northwards and the Angolans had to look at desperate measures in bids to repel them.

After things had more or less settled down in Novo Redondo, Headquarters gave orders for Combat Group Bravo to move north and capture the small harbour town of Porto Amboim. A nondescript fishing village, it lay several hundred kilometres across difficult roads ahead of Lobito.

But it was not to be. FAPLA had blown the bridge over the river, just north of the town and the advance ground to a halt.

Meanwhile, I had been ordered to move inland through the mountains to investigate the possibility of trying to cross the river near a tiny little place called Conda on the road to Gabela on the northern fringe of the Kumbira Forest Reserve. It was a delightful place and in a region where the cotton plantations gave way to mountain upon mountain, each one of them covered with trees and shrubs.

Travelling in my open garry through this delightful country was a treat, the only real problem being that the rainy season was at its peak. At very short notice sometimes, great clusters of white clouds would accumulate in clear blue sky and quite often, even before we were able to find proper cover, we would be soaked.

Because the rain in that area falls from great altitudes, it is still near-frozen by the time it hits the ground. The result was that we would become deep-frozen almost instantly and I still recall how I'd battled to open a can of bully beef with frozen fingers during such a deluge.

Showers would last for approximately thirty minutes or so, then it would stop as suddenly as it had started and around us all the mountains and valleys would bask in glorious sunshine.

Late that afternoon, we approached a village called Vila Nova do Seles. I halted the column on high ground just outside the settlement and surveyed the scene ahead through my glasses.

It was a picturesque little place with tidy, brightly painted bungalows nestling comfortably between rows of large, leafy groves. The streets were lined with beds and shrubs of all description.

I was still sitting there completely taken in by the tranquil scene, when a heavy truck laboured up the hill from the direction of the village. When the driver spotted my vehicle, he slowed down and eventually came to a stop, but still some distance from where we were. There was a driver and a passenger in the cab and several youngsters on the back.

I couldn't spot any weapons but I also wasn't taking any chances. Getting out and standing alongside my garry with my rifle ready, I got the impression none of us knew what to do next. We moved closer.

So, for lack of anything else to do, I raised my rifle, cocked it and removed the safety catch. A silence that was almost deathly fell over virtually the entire area.

I observed a young girl in her teens standing on the back of the truck. She had a pretty friendly face and was leaning over the cab, but from where I stood, I could detect a serious expression. Also, her eyes were troubled.

I guessed that this was a bunch of youngsters that had got wind of our approach, had jumped on the first transport that came along and decided to make a break for it.

So what to do now? The girl looked at the rifle in my hands, and then very slowly raised her eyes and looked me squarely in the eyes. I remember the speech I had given Werner: 'I'm not going to shoot people by the colour of their cravats ...' I'd declared at the time.

The girl kept staring and then my own words echoed back at me once more: 'If I'm going to lose this war, then let me do it my way ...'

It was the girl that eventually caused me to blink first and I indicated to the driver to move on. Everybody took off with loud cheers of 'Viva, Viva ...' Whether they were celebrating their success or my weakness, was anybody's guess. I could only guess it was the latter.

We entered the village cautiously, but there was nobody in sight, not even a dog or a cat. Any sign of FAPLA resistance seemed to have disappeared long before. Then I saw a house with an MPLA flag on the flagpole out front and guessed it to be a local headquarters or barrack building.

CHAPTER 18: NORTH INTO ANGOLA

I made my way over cautiously and found that the place had clearly been recently vacated, possibly an hour or two before we got there, which partially explained the actions of the young people in the truck: they'd probably seen the soldiers flee and decided to take the gap as well.

A gas stove had been turned off, but food in the pot was still simmering. I searched the house for anything of intelligence value but found nothing. Just before leaving, a shiny object on the floor caught my eye. I picked it up gingerly for fear of a booby trap.

It was a crucifix. The wooden cross had been broken, but it was kept more or less intact by the silver body of Christ. I straightened out the cross and walked out onto the broad verandah, typically colonial Portuguese, with a set of steps leading up from the street and stretching all the way around to the back.

Meanwhile, our enthusiastic young mortar platoon commander was in the process of deploying his tubes on the village green in the centre of town. As I stood there I thought how lovely God had made this world, and here we were buggering it all up with a war. I was troubled, but said nothing.

Having taken care of most security issues, it wasn't long in these mountains before a heavy mist had settled in and a foggy screen was slowly rolling in. The entire countryside was slowly being enveloped by an eerie fog. It was weird.

I had just begun to accept our circumstances when, totally unexpectedly, seven black-and-white-clad figures appeared out of the encircling gloom. For a moment or two I nearly freaked, but I could only stand there motionless, watching them approach. They weren't the soldiers I might have expected, but was a tiny set of seven Roman Catholic nuns fully dressed in what I imagined was their ceremonial dress: cloaks, veils, rosaries, the lot.

Almost as if by command they stopped some distance away and one member of the party, obviously the Mother Superior, came forward on her own. She was older, her face serious, but she appeared totally calm, lowering her eyes to the crucifix I still had in my hand.

When she looked up, her blue-grey eyes were brimming with tears and her demeanour distinctly distraught.

'Sir, we have heard all about you and they say you do not take prisoners. They also tell us that your men are not very kind to women. We are not afraid to die, but please …'

This was too much. I raised my hand in a bid for her to let me reply before she said more. Enemy propaganda had painted a grim picture of me and my men, probably of all the soldiers from the south who were heading north.

'I'm sorry, Sister, you are unfortunate, I only shoot people at noon, you'll have to come back tomorrow. Besides I'm rather busy right now, so you will have to excuse me.' I said it all grim-faced and, to her mind, in total earnest. What went through that woman's mind I couldn't tell, but apart from the tears that had disappeared, there was no other visible change in her expression. I saluted curtly and walked away.

I told all my men that not one of them was to make contact with anybody from the village, no matter what the circumstances. But I did instruct my rations master to pack a carton of assorted cans and packets of food and take it over to the nunnery.

We spend an uneventful night in the remote village, and early the next morning while I was shaving, dressed only in my boots and trousers, who would appear again out of the morning mist, but the seven nuns. This time I wasn't awed, but actually quite pleased that they'd returned of their own volition, probably having seen through my charade.

'Well,' I greeted them cheerfully, 'you ladies really are eager, I said noon, not dawn. Only the English shoot people at dawn, but I'm German, I only do what has to be done at midday.'

The Mother Superior didn't think my comment was at all humorous. In fact, she looked at me stern-faced and said something about me joking with them.

'Sir, we spoke to your men last night. It seems we have been very misinformed, I am sorry for the things I said about you yesterday.'

'That's okay, Sister, you should hear what the other people say about us.'

'Sir, you are still joking, but we are quite serious. We have come to apologise and to thank you for the food. You are a kind man.'

By now I'd run out of wise cracks, a situation that seemed to break the ice. The Holy Sisters all smiled and, with hands pressed together as if in prayer, they half-bowed, half-curtsied before turning around and going back to where they'd emerged a short while before. Until then, it never occurred to me that nuns also giggle.

CHAPTER 18: NORTH INTO ANGOLA

Before leaving the village I walked around and found what I was looking for: a small chapel of the kind that characterised every single little Portuguese African village and town. I entered and, as had become my practice, I spent a few minutes on my knees in front of the altar.

On my way out I walked past an open door leading from the vestibule, turned around and went in. I discovered a little room cluttered with robes and other paraphernalia worn by the local priest and other religious functionaries. What then caught my eye was a bunch of beautiful rosaries hanging from hooks against the wall.

In a moment of abject weakness I suppose, I took one, thinking that it would be a nice souvenir for the rest of the journey to the north, but before I'd even reached the door my conscience pricked. I wasted no time in returning the rosary to its hook and walked out into the light feeling a bit stupid.

As we left the village, our group of nuns and various other people in the town who had emerged from nowhere lined the streets and waved us merrily on our way.

Our next stop – the town of Conda – offered no surprises because it was a tiny place. The town comprised a shop, a few houses and, of course, the requisite Portuguese-style café/bar with its back-wall lined with bottles of liquor.

Like Vila Nova, Conda, too, was all but deserted and my first impressions were that it was dull and uninteresting. I passed through to see what lay beyond and left Coen to check out the place.

The country to the north of Conda was equally unimpressive. When I saw high ground loom ahead, I guessed it must be the mountain that overlooked the bridge on the road to Gabela.

We travelled some distance along the bank of the river as it curved slightly to the right around the foot of the high ground. The terrain sloped sharply towards the left of the road and on the right we were virtually hemmed in by a cliff several metres high.

Staff Sergeant Lubbe had been driving ahead and just before he was about to round the bend he pulled up and walked back towards me. Could he use my field-glasses, he asked. He took them and sat at the side of the road with his legs hanging over the edge, and for the umpteenth time I wondered at the nonchalance of the man.

My thoughts and the afternoon silence were rudely interrupted when the world exploded around us. It seemed that every imaginable weapon that FAPLA could muster was brought to bear on us. For a brief moment Piet Lubbe's unruffled demeanour left him, his blue Land Cruiser darted forward and snuggled up against the cliff some distance ahead.

I did likewise with my Land Rover and signalled the four troops in the Land Rover following to my rear to follow suit. They pulled up just as clusters of rockets and mortar bombs started landing on the road a short distance behind us.

Between the side of the road and the cliff face, we quickly found a small gully, and mercifully, this gave us some protection against shrapnel and machine-gun fire. Unless an explosive fell into the ditch where we were, I reckoned that we'd be reasonably safe. And then, almost as if FAPLA was reading my mind, a rocket landed in the road a metre from the rear wheel of the vehicle behind which some of my soldiers had taken cover.

Once the ear-shattering explosion subsided and the dust began to settle, one of the men bounded out of the gully, dashed across the road and scrambled down the slope towards the river. In my mind's eye the youngster had gone a little crazy and for a moment or two I thought that the young fellow had been hit and had bolted in a state of shock. This was all I needed.

The mortar bomb that had maimed eighteen of my soldiers a day or two before was still very fresh in my memory. I could almost picture the boy's bullet-riddled body tumbling down the slope towards the river. In absolute panic I jumped up and dashed after him.

'Hey, come back here, you fool! These bastards will kill you!'

'Bugger them!' he shouted back, 'I'm after my chicken.'

Dumbfounded, I stopped in my tracks. From who knows where on the long trek we had covered since we left Benguela, the man had acquired a chicken, obviously meant for his Christmas lunch. Only afterwards was I told that he had bound the bird's legs with twine and the chicken had been comfortably travelling while secreted between our mortar bombs on the back of their Land Rover.

When the rocket exploded, a piece of splinter severed the twine, and the terrified chicken – now liberated – took off. Not to be outdone, the troopie gave chase, oblivious of the war that raged around him.

CHAPTER 18: NORTH INTO ANGOLA

So what was I to do? I ended up helping the youngster retrieve his Christmas lunch and with it securely tucked in the front of his shirt, we again sought out the safety of our gully in a bid to ride out the attack.

While still lying in the ditch shortly afterwards, I felt like laughing. All I could imagine was the fun the guys would have in the pubs once they got home and this story got out. Still, it was a situation that could have gone badly sour because I again had visions of the sad face of the boy in the first-aid tent the night of the mortar attack.

Caught there in a kind of no-man's-land while the enemy kept firing at us, I wanted to weep instead. Had I only known ... I should have put a comforting hand on the boy's shoulder ... would it have had a different outcome had I whispered something encouraging in his ear? If only ... if only he hadn't died.

During several lulls in the firing, we were able to replace the wheels that had been punctured by the rockets and, one by one we extricated our vehicles.

Once clear of immediate danger, we found the leading platoon sitting snugly behind the high ground. I was annoyed that nobody bothered to check whether we were safe, or even alive. But what the heck, all's well that ends well.

They say that history repeats itself, and you can take my word for it. History has it that the fatal charge of the Light Cavalry Brigade at the Battle of Balaclava happened because of faulty communication.

Apparently a comma had been omitted from the message Lord Cardigan sent to the cavalry commander. That single lapse changed the gist of the message and sent the cavalry right into the teeth of the enemy artillery.

The same thing happened here, but this time it wasn't faulty communications, but no communication at all.

I'd told the company commander to stay put while I made my way up the slope. From there I reckoned I'd be able to get a view of what was going on. What exactly happened while I was making my way up the slope I have never been able to discover, but apparently the first troop carrier driven by the overzealous Lavado, dashed forward and rounded the shoulder of the mountain.

As it reached an open stretch on the river bank, FAPLA opened fire. A bullet passed through the window and lodged itself in the fore-end-stock of Lavado's rifle which was racked right beside his head. Miraculously he was unharmed and to this day, as far as I'm aware, he's the only man known to be able to make a U-turn in a two-lane road with a five-ton truck.

Lavado made it back to our lines with all his bodily parts intact, but the second truck was a lot less fortunate.

A burst of machine-gun fire put that truck out of action and as the troops descended, the driver – De Witt – who was on the enemy-side of the vehicle was hit in the upper thighs of both legs. He managed to take cover beside the road, from where he was later removed to safety by some of the troops that had been with him on the truck.

Things were not going well and I was worried. I was just about to come down from my perch when I heard Coen call out: 'Hey, where's the Commandant?'

'Don't know, up there somewhere …' came the reply.

Figuring 'up there somewhere' to mean 'somewhere ahead on the road' and assuming conditions were safe, he started strolling almost leisurely down the middle of the road.

'Hey Coen, watch out!' I shouted, but it was too late. At that moment a burst of machine-gun fire hit the road just below his feet.

Now, as mentioned earlier, Coen is a big man and also heavily built. In spite of his bulk, he took off vertically, made a complete about-turn in mid-air and landed on all fours facing the direction from which he had just come from.

Another first: To my knowledge Coen Upton is the only man that can 'out-crawl' a volley from a machine gun. He was out of sight before the next burst.

In retrospect, it looked like the whole thing took place in slow motion, and for the second time that afternoon I felt like laughing, but this was serious. Apparently the guys at the river had spotted me hanging precariously on the slope and the next burst of machine-gun fire churned up dust around me only metres away.

I descended from my parlous position at a speed that made Coen look lethargic.

As I was walking back to where I had left my garry, I was pondering all the good and bad fortune that had struck us so far that day and the images presented in my mind were depressing.

CHAPTER 18: NORTH INTO ANGOLA

Being outmatched by a competent enemy was one thing. But nearly getting a platoon of soldiers wiped out was another.

Then something caught my attention and I stopped dead in my tracks. In the road, just ahead of my right boot, and lying in a tiny patch of grass was a rosary like the one I'd seen in the chapel earlier that morning. How it got there I will never know. Although I am not Catholic, I put the rosary around my neck and went on to wear it for the duration of the operation. Not for luck as some people would imagine, but it somehow made me feel good.

That morning, during our advance towards the river – and not very far from where we were – we'd passed what appeared to be a small airstrip of sorts. Coen checked it out and it was just as well he did. We didn't yet know it, but this improvised landing strip – for that was all it was – would come in very useful pretty damn soon.

Under normal circumstances, airlifting a casualty from the battle zone would be a fairly straightforward operation, but what happened here was quite different. Because of the mountain range we'd traversed, we'd lost radio contact with our headquarters.

Coen battled virtually all night trying to make comms and somehow he succeeded in the very early morning. At first light a SAAF Dakota appeared almost like an apparition out of the mist and slithered to a halt on the rain-soaked runway.

The pilot smiled through the small cockpit window and called towards us: 'You guys play rough out here, don't you?'

The story of how Coen had made radio contact halfway around the globe and arranged an aircraft to arrive in the middle of an extremely hostile Angola has never been told. But if ever an officer in the South African Army has deserved the meritorious Southern Cross, it was Upton for that meritorious act.

Who the men were that flew that aircraft, I don't know either. But those pilots should have been accorded recognition, not only for their remarkable flying skills, but also their courage and dedication.

I watched as the medical officer attended to the wounds of the young soldier before loading his stretcher on board.

'Hey Doc, how come no blood?' I asked.

'The bullet only tore through his muscle tissue, but had it been a few inches one way or the other this young fellow would have bled to death.'

'And ...?' The medical officer must have read my mind.

'Don't worry, Commandant, when God made men, he knew exactly what he was doing. By the time that bullet struck him, his testicles were neatly snuggled up beside his tonsils.'

I looked down at the boy lying on the stretcher. He was a strapping youngster with a round, friendly face. In spite of the pain, a shyish half-smile lurked around the corners of his mouth.

I put my hand on his sandy hair. 'Go home now, boy, you have done your share and done it well. Get well quickly, marry a beautiful girl and have lots of fat babies.'

As I spoke, large tears slowly welled up in his blue eyes. This must be what is meant by 'smiling through the tears,' I thought.

I had seen many tears in my life, tears of sorrow, anger, fear, but tears like these – never. They spoke of emotions I could not even begin to describe.

'Have a nice flight, my boy ... and God bless you.'

I jumped from the Dakota and watched as it taxied away and its wheels left the muddy runway, I saluted a handful of the finest and bravest men South Africa has ever produced.

I was proud of having rubbed shoulders with them all.

CHAPTER 19

The Pink House

The next phase of this vast military enterprise was appropriately named 'The Western Front', for that, basically, was what it was: our boys fighting their way up along Angola's west coast towards Luanda. It was a tough and dangerous slog!

While we had been gallivanting around the mountains, Jan's Combat Group Bravo had been keeping itself busy with the frustrating task of trying to get to Porto Amboim. This was no mean task because the River Queve was a rather significant watercourse and the bridge across it – which our people had intended to use to get to the north – had been well and truly destroyed.

I had a rough idea what was going on, but with all the action in my own camp it was difficult to keep up with what was happening elsewhere. I did, however, learn that the other fighting group that was advancing along the main axis from Nova Lisboa to Luanda was running into the same sort of trouble we'd experienced.

What transpired was that there had been an enemy build-up and our commanding general – now repositioned at Cela – decided that Task Force Zulu also had to come and pull their weight to the fracas.

Bravo was the bulk of the force, while Alpha remained a relatively insignificant factor. Whether this was the reason that we were ordered to remain behind to cover the coastal route was difficult to tell, but whatever the reason, I was delighted. The thought of being on my own and away from all the fuss and bother appealed to me.

Besides, I still had a bit of a score to settle with the chaps across the river: they had killed two of my men.

Zulu HQ and Bravo left sometime in mid-November and although I was overjoyed, it wasn't a good thing to take leave of my buddies in Angola, things by then having devolved into a state of full-blown hostilities. In practical terms it also meant the end of Task Force Zulu, the pioneers of Operation Savannah.

We'd had a solid share of successes, and as somebody pointed out earlier, the force under command of Colonel Koos van Heerden, travelling halfway across the subcontinent, had made Rommel's Africa Corps look sluggish by comparison.

Consequently, when Combat Group Bravo moved on, I shifted my headquarters into a building that became colloquially referred to as the 'Pink House'. Indeed, this was quite a house and I never did quite get it figured out. The building looked more like two double-storey houses that had been conjoined at one side, with a large courtyard, or more appropriately, a sort of tropical garden in-between.

The entire structure was furnished in variations of leather, oak, mahogany, velvet and what-have-you. The paintings and rugs which were all part of an elaborate decoration scheme must have been worth an awful lot of money because almost all of it was top drawer.

We never got to meet the owner because he had fled back to Lisbon some time before, but there was no question that he must have been stinking rich. The word out in the street was that he had been some big-shot in politics, owned a fishing fleet, as well as several farms. In fact, somebody mentioned that if a project looked like it had promise and could generate cash, he wanted to be part of it.

On one of the corners of the Pink House was a structure that resembled a tower with glass panels on all sides. From here one had a terrific view of the picturesque village with its tiny fishing harbour on one side and the mountains on the other. Because it dominated the town with its height, we used the tower for our signals centre.

I wasted no time in moving into what must have been the master bedroom, also enormous and complete with a beautiful mahogany four-poster bed, tropical hardwood wardrobe, dresser, as well as bedside cabinet. The bedspread was a snow-white hand-made lace thing that they told me came from Madeira. Although not all to my taste, at least the place was comfortable, but most of all I rather liked the fact that I could see my forward defensive positions from the bedroom window.

Being on the top floor I was also within easy reach of the radio room in the tower. I generally slept peacefully in the big comfortable bed and woke early to the sounds of the surf.

But one night, fairly early on, things didn't go quite so well. I had been fast asleep when I was awakened by a scraping noise. I froze, instantly trying to make out what it was that was causing the sound.

Cmdt Linford and the Scotsman WO2 Jock Irving.

Cmdt 'Punchy' Botha.

Maj. Coen Upton.

Some of the 'characters' of the Bush War. (Photos: Coen Upton collection)

Marksmen and trackers *par excellence* …! (Photos: Coen Upton, Manuel Ferreira)

A relaxed moment at Omega. (Photo: Manuel Ferreira)

One of the Bushman soldiers in a Unimog. (Photo: McGregor Museum)

Bushman schoolboys lined up at Omega for inspection.
(Photo: Coen Upton collection)

José de Oliviera in front of his Soviet Gaz truck. (Photo: Manuel Ferreira)

A welcoming party for Cmdt Linford at Omega's landing strip. (Photo: SANDF)

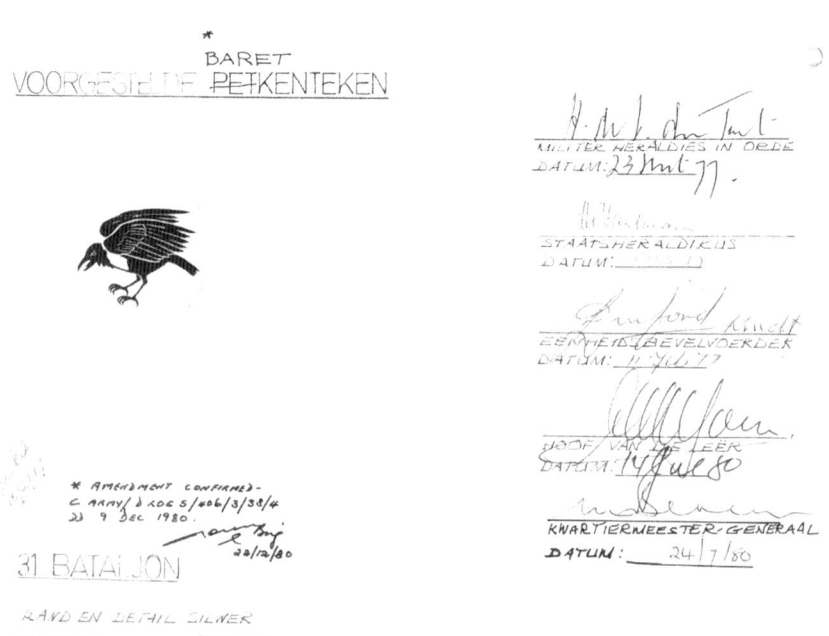

31 Battalion cap badge heraldry approved by Cmdt Linford and Lt Gen. Viljoen as Chief of the Army in 1980. (Photo: SANDF)

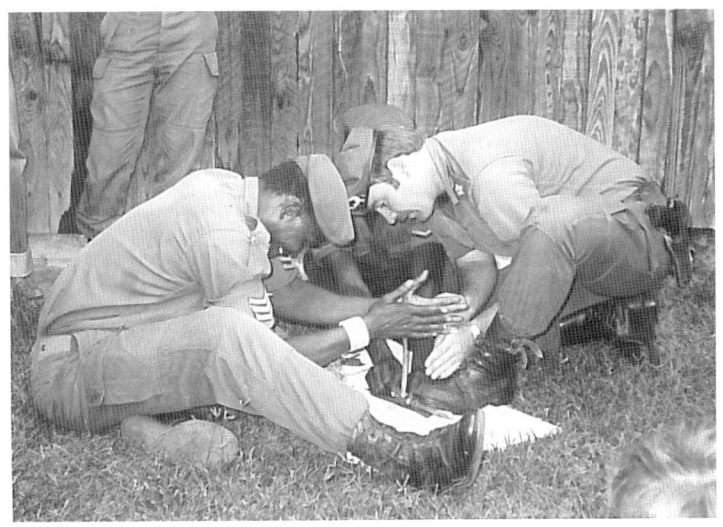

Lt Ben Wolff and Sgt Kamamma Makua, showing traditional fire-making techniques to visitors. (Photo: SANDF)

Early days of a lasting home industry. Leontina Barros (Mama Grande), Marinela Covacha, Conceicão (Cão) Felix and Costodia Covacha at the needlework centre where the distinctive headdress of the battalion was made. (Photo: Linford collection)

One of many civilian visitors to Omega. Bushman leaders from left to right are: Sgts Matoka Mattheus, Kamamma Makua, Murasi Mulasi and Tango Naka. (Photo: SANDF)

Bushman council meeting with Linford. (Photo: SANDF)

A 2,4 km fitness exercise soon became standard practice at Camp Alpha. (Photo: Coen Upton collection)

Linford in the shadow of the Cross at Sá da Bandeira. (Photo: Delville Linford)

Top: Linford with his favourite garry at Sá da Bandeira Airport.
Bottom: Cmdt Linford at the establishment of 41 Battalion in Windhoek, 1978.
(Photo: Delville Linford)

Cmdt Linford with Mama Grande.
(Photo: Manuel Ferreira)

The Bushman school at Omega. (Photo: Danie van den Berg collection)

Gen. Meiring, Mama Grande, Col Linford and Cmdt Van Wyk at the disbanding of 31 SAI on 6 March 1993 at Schmidtsdrift – a very sad day. (Photo: *Volksblad*)

Col Linford with his wife Nelle at the inauguration of the commemorative needle at the Voortrekker Monument in May 2011. (Photo: Ziggy Hentze)

The two legends of Task Force Zulu meeting again after 36 years.
(Photo: Ziggy Hentze)

The three role players who had the 'expertise, experience and guts' during Operation Savannah: Gen. Constand Viljoen, Col Delville Linford and Col Jan Breytenbach. (Photos: Scholtz van Wyk, Ziggy Hentze)

From left to right: Tonie van Niekerk, Gawie Nel, Scholtz van Wyk, Delville Linford, Daan Slabbert and Kamamma Makau at the inauguration of the !Xun and Kwe 31 Battalion Museum at Wildebeestkuil, Kimberley in May 2013.
(Photo: Scholtz van Wyk collection)

Al Venter with Ds Mario Mahango outside Kimberley early in 2015.
(Photo: Caroline Castell)

Dominee Mario Mahango in his office which adjoins his residence in Platfontein.
(Photo: Caroline Castell)

Kamamma Makua was one of the most senior combatants from Angola to form the nucleus of 31 Batallion. Today he is more than 70 years old and still *penorent*.
(Photo: Caroline Castell)

It happened again, and to make matters worse, I started to feel a vibration that seemed linked to the sound.

I listened for a few seconds more, trying to figure out what to do and then I sensed that whatever it was, it was getting very close. With the kind of energy that only fear can generate I bounced out of my mahogany four-poster, grabbed my pistol and flashlight from the bedside table and started to check, but could find nothing.

The noise stopped for a moment and then started again. I listened very carefully and sensed that it was coming from the top end of my bed.

With astonishing logic under these rather austere circumstances, I figured that it could hardly be a human threat: I couldn't quite picture somebody being in that particular spot at that time.

Satisfied that I was not about to stop a hail of bullets, I turned on my flashlight and edged forward carefully.

After much ado I eventually pinned the source down to somewhere between the headboard of the bed and the wall. Shining the light into the dark aperture I was horrified at seeing a large crab-like monster with enormous claws wedged in between the headboard and the wall.

Under the circumstances I wasn't able to make any identification, but for easy reference I referred to it as 'the crab'. The scraping sound made by its claws came from it manoeuvring upwards between the bed and the wall. Where exactly the creature was headed and what it was going to do when it got there, I'll never know. Neither did it concern me much after I'd sorted out the origin of my worries.

Without giving the problem much proper thought, I pulled the bed away from the wall and, as I had expected, the crab fell to the floor. What I hadn't expected was that the bloody thing was going to charge at me with that enormous pincher at the ready position.

It had two great claws, one smaller than the other and therefore didn't count. It was the big one that worried me: an enormous set of pincers that opened and shut as if it was warming things up prior to attack. It sized me up with its tiny crab-like eyes and with one final snap of the claw came at me in full charge. Nobody, except someone that had been chased around his bedroom by an enraged sea crab in the small hours of the morning, would quite understand how it feels.

At some stage during the ensuing chaos I managed to get the light on and this made it easier to get away from the wretched monster.

My eye fell on a long antique musket (the Davy Crockett type), leaning against the wall. I grabbed the weapon by the barrel and now, for the first time, I knew that the odds were more or less even.

I let drive at the crab with a mighty swing of my Davy Crockett club, but not being experienced in this particular type of warfare, destroyed a priceless china vase from a table. The crab, by now accepting that it was at a tactical disadvantage, took temporary refuge in the shadow of the bed.

By now I'd manoeuvred myself into the middle of the room where I could wield my weapon unhindered by antiquarian artefacts, pottery and the like.

Thus deployed I was happy to leave the initiative to my opponent and, fortunately, he fell for it. With his claw raised he charged and I was ready.

I estimated its speed, aimed off the correct distance and at the precise moment I let fly. My aim couldn't have been better. I scored a direct hit right in the centre of the visible mass. The force of impact propelled him into the en-suite bathroom, after which I followed up by making a rapid advance into the bathroom.

There I discovered that I had seriously underestimated my adversary. He must have warded off the blow with that mighty claw and although the sheer force of the blow sent him sliding along the smooth floor, it had no real impact on its operational ability.

This time I wasn't going to make the same mistake again. I realised if I was going to penetrate his defence I would have to make a more direct assault on its vulnerable undercarriage where the armour-plating is less secure. I turned my musket end for end and made ready for a bayonet charge (without a bayonet). The crab must have seen what was coming and realised that he had been outclassed, for the moment at least.

He lowered the mighty claw momentarily (as one would troop the regimental colours at retreat) and then he raised it again, his claw closed as if in surrender.

Now this I could understand. I mean it's not as if I hadn't been in a similar predicament myself, but what on earth do you do with a prisoner-crab in your bathroom at two in the morning. I was temporarily at a loss, and more out of curiosity than much else, I prodded the musket at the crab.

To my astonishment, it opened its claw once more and grabbed the muzzle firmly and held on. I got the message, which led me to carry the crab into the bedroom and hurl it into the void through the open window.

If you could make your way up a double-storey house and halfway up the wall of my bedroom then you can make your way out also.

I heard a commotion in the street below. Thinking that the world was going mad, I looked out, fully expecting to see the crab smashed to bits in the street below. Instead, it was making its way at top speed across the street, a bunch of kids in hot pursuit.

This was crazy, I did not want to kill the thing in my room and now these kids were going to kill it – and just for the fun of it. This wasn't fair in my book.

I snatched my rifle from the foot end of the bed. 'Hey, you bastards!' I shouted, 'leave that crab alone or I'll blow the whole lot of you to hell this minute!'

The kids looked up at my window in disbelief as I cocked my rifle. The next moment they took off down the street.

'Commandant, is something the matter?' It was the signaller who had been on duty in the signals tower, looking at me with a mixture of concern and disbelief on his face.

'No, it's okay now, boy, those savages wanted to kill the crab, but I threatened to shoot them and they took off.'

'Well, okay, Sir. Goodnight, Sir.'

It was only when I was lying in my bed again that I realised what must have gone through the poor guy's head. To be awakened that time of the morning and finally coming to the conclusion that his commander was losing his marbles.

Sometime later I was coming up the stairs to my operations room when I came across a soldier on the steps. He was pretty scruffy, unshaven, shirt unbuttoned and hanging halfway out of his trousers. He had a ridiculous little cap sitting kind of cockeyed on his head.

Though the man looked at me, I got the impression that he didn't actually appear to see me; rather, he looked right through me. My first thoughts were that the fellow was on drugs. That was all I needed in my life at that point in time with the enemy all but banging at our gates.

'Hey,' I said firmly, 'what the hell's wrong with you? This isn't a bloody fancy-dress party.'

He replied in the negative, stating that he'd been told that it was the sick bay.

'Well, they told you wrong, this is my headquarters and if you don't get out of here you're going to need a hospital, not a sick bay. Get out!'

The poor guy looked at me in amazement but turned round and shambled down the steps.

Shortly afterwards I encountered the unit medical officer and told him that there was an apparition wandering about looking for the sick bay, adding that I'd chased him out. 'But I suggest you go and find him and see what his case is. If he's on drugs, I want you to bring him to me personally.'

The MO went in search of the man and I temporarily forgot about the incident. It was only much later that I remembered and asked him about it.

'So, Doc, what happened to your druggy patient? I thought you were supposed to bring him to me?'

The MO looked at me with an expression I hadn't seen before. In a quiet voice he said: 'Commandant, you should really apply your mind to making war, something that you know something about. But please keep away from diagnosing patients – you're not very good at that, I fear.'

'Hey, what's with you?' I replied. 'I'm not the quack around here, you are. I thought the guy is drugged, but what's the big deal?'

'Commandant, that boy was one of those who crewed the armoured car that got shot up the day before we arrived in town. He is not physically wounded, but he is in a state of severe shock … that's why he looks and acts as he does.'

He added that he had put him on a drug, and that if he didn't improve very quickly, he was going to have to evacuate him.

Obviously I'd blundered badly and felt exactly the way the medical officer had intended me to.

'Okay, sorry, Doc, I didn't realise … Sorry about that.'

CHAPTER 19: THE PINK HOUSE

What more can one say when you realise you have behaved in an unforgivable manner, except to say you are sorry?

By the time I eventually did get the opportunity to visit the soldier in the sick bay, he'd been discharged. The MO was pleased with his recovery and let him go.

I felt a lot better, but I was certainly not happy. As days passed, the incident faded and eventually I forgot about it completely.

What I didn't forget and what started to worry some of us a lot, were consistent reports that there were foreign soldiers entrenched with FAPLA troops and that some of them had already seen action against the oncoming South Africans.

The word 'Cuban' was often mentioned in this content and though there were quite a few intelligence reports that the future Angolan leader had met with Fidel Castro and that some of his people might already be in the country, we had seen little evidence of it. I remembered that bearded soldier in the earlier battle, tall and lean and directing his men seemingly without a worry in the world. Could he have been a Cuban officer?

That attack demonstrated a different sort of flair and initiative and my view was that there might have been others involved on the periphery of the fighting who we were still to encounter and with the benefit of hindsight: Cubans possibly?

I wasn't wrong.

CHAPTER 20

The Cuban Role in Angola
Al Venter

Commandant Delville Linford's concerns about the possibility of encountering a Cuban military detachment or two in the slog northwards had already become apparent by the time his and Jan Breytenbach's combat groups had reached Novo Redondo. There had been lots of rumours and some of these became realities a short while later. But one has to look back a little to understand the full implication of this new force rushing to aid Luanda militarily.

Pretoria's decision to go into Angola in force – which was what Operation Savannah was all about – was not done on a whim. By the time that the first troops had headed north from Caprivi onto Angolan soil, there was already a lot of evidence that the Cubans and the Soviets had been actively fomenting their own version of a 'People's Revolution' that was intended to take over the country.

Some of this was only to emerge years later when a batch of Cuban state documents related to Castro's role in the Angolan war was leaked.

Much else emerged in the document, including military training for Angolan cadres in Cuba itself, links to FRELIMO in Angola, the supply of weapons and other materiéls with which to wage war against 'enemies of the people', as well as strong condemnation of the forces of imperialism and capitalism and the rest.

There was a statement that declares that Cuba '… must help [the Angolan people] directly or indirectly to solve this situation, which definitely entails having the people resist against the reactionaries and international imperialists.' Castro's intent to get involved in Angola was clear. In the months following, Cuba went into overdrive to help Neto's MPLA consolidate its position as the dominant force in Luanda and many other cities in the north and along the coast to the south, Benguela and the ports of Lobito and Moçâmedes included.

The CIA knew, of course, because one of the first things Langley did was pass this information on to their South African associates in Pretoria…

By late-1974 sizeable quantities of arms and ammunition had already been shipped from the East to the MPLA, shortly followed by 250 Cuban technicians and advisors who arrived in May 1975, just as the country was in the throes of independence.

Increasingly concerned about the situation on their northern border, Pretoria deployed troops in South West Africa and later posted elements from the 2nd South African Infantry Battalion to the large dam at Ruacana in Angola.

By 1975, when Angola had been assured of full independence later in the year, both Havana and Moscow knew that the first move to achieve the objective of eventually ending up in Cape Town had to be initiated from Luanda. Late in the year, with the Portuguese showing their heels, Neto was urged to act.

FAPLA, the Patriotic Front for the Liberation of Angola which was the military wing of Agostinho Neto's MPLA, secured the harbour so that the first Cuban freighter, *Vietnam Heroica*, could berth there. That vessel would deliver the initial batch of advisors, the *barbudos* (bearded ones, all Cubans) who were to play an increasingly significant role in Angolan military affairs.

Editor, freelance combatant and journalist Yves Debay wrote[1]: 'Soon, thousands upon thousands of tons of Soviet equipment were airlifted into Angola by aircraft flying regular shuttles between Conakry in Guinea and Brazzaville in the Congo.

'Although supported by mercenaries in the field, the pro-western FNLA collapsed. Lightly equipped, Roberto Holden's men were no match for the communists who were lavishly equipped with artillery, particularly 122 mm D-30 and M-46 130 mm pieces.'

It must be mentioned that Cuba's links to the MPLA – and to its revolutionary leader Agostinho Neto – had been consolidated very early on in the 'liberation struggle'.

In fact, almost since the guerrilla war started, that island had hosted fairly large squads of prospective Angolan guerrillas in a variety of training courses that prepared them for war against Lisbon's forces. Obviously all this happened clandestinely and much of it only emerged after the fall of the Berlin Wall, though clearly, there had been whispers within the expatriate Cuban community in Miami from where mercenary pilots, needed to fly fighter aircraft for the Congo's Mobutu, had been recruited some years before, something I deal with in great detail in *Mercenaries*, an earlier book.[2]

A good deal of the Angolan subterfuge was coordinated by Moscow whose commissars divided training and support needs between participating states like Tanzania, Ethiopia, Algeria, Libya, Guinea (Conakry) and several Soviet states that included Bulgaria, Czechoslovakia, Romania and others.

Gradually Cuba came to head the list, underscored by a memorandum from the *Centro de Informacion de la Defensa de las Fuerzoas Armadas Revolucionarias* dated 22 November 1972 (three years before Operation Savannah was launched).

It was written by Major Manuel Piñeiro Lozada to Major Raúl Castro, brother of Fidel, and headed: 'Shipment of Comrades to Angola and Mozambique'. The letter speaks for itself and I quote:

For some time now we have discussed the possibility of entering Angola and Mozambique with the objective of getting to know the revolutionarily movements in those countries. These movements have been a mystery even for those socialist countries that gives them considerable aid. This research would help us give more focused aid to those movements.

I don't consider it necessary to delineate the strategic nature of these countries, it takes only pointing out that a change in the course of events of the wars that are developing in both countries could signify a change in all the forces on the African continent.

For the first time two independent countries in Africa from which the bigger war could be waged would have common borders [with the two countries in the region that has the strongest knot of Imperialist countries in Africa] namely South Africa, Rhodesia, Zaire and the Portuguese colonies.

Our comrades in the MPLA solicited us this May for the following:

a) That we train 10 men in Cuba in guerrilla warfare, taking into account the positive experiences they have had with people trained in Cuba (they are heads of various guerrilla detachments.

b) That we send a crew to fly a DC-3 from Zambia or the Congo [Brazzaville] to Angola transporting equipment for the guerrilla. They explained that because of great distances to the Northern Front and the borders with Zambia and the Congo it is extremely difficult to maintain the supplies by land and it is from that front where they have contacts and are planning urban actions in the capital Luanda, which have military and political importance.

> c) They want to send a high level delegation to Cuba to discuss relations with our Party.
>
> We suggested that we thought it a good idea to send some of our comrades to the interior of Angola to learn about the terrain of battle and to shoot a film, which they agreed to, and they proposed postponing their solicitations until the return of our delegation.
>
> The delegation would be protected by 150 troops directed by one of the commanders trained in Cuba.

It is also worth taking another look at one other event that had a bearing on Cuba's subsequent involvement in the former Portuguese colonial territory.

Late in 1965, a few years after many African countries were handed full independence to run their own affairs by Britain and France (and the Congo, by Belgium), Argentina-born Che Guevara spent time in Africa studying the prospects of revolution.

By then Guevara was a member of Castro's Politburo, the wars in Angola and Mozambique were in full flow and somebody in Havana must have thought that prospects in what he termed in his writings 'The Black Continent' were excellent for expanding the Marxist Credo among the 'uninitiated'.

Guevara spent a lot of time in the eastern reach of Mobutu's Congo, much of it with Laurent Kabila who was eventually to become president of this vast country even though, if we are to judge from his letters sent home, he regarded Kabila as the ultimate nincompoop. Guevara also had dealings with groups of Angolans who were trying to help their co-conspirators oust the Portuguese.

None of it was easy, if we again are to judge by the letter that Che Guevara wrote to Oscar Fernandez Padilla in the Cuban capital. Padilla's code-name was 'Rafael' while Guevara went under the *nom de guerre* 'Tatu', which, interestingly, is the word for 'three' in Swahili.

It read:

> Rafael,
>
> I attach some letters for you from Flavio. Not all is well in terms of organization. Changa insists that he has no money, and that is the reason why he doesn't set up the camp in Kigoma. Now, Olivia has left with Kabila without leaving money. I gave him all my reserve

money, 8,150, which they should reimburse me (5,000) so we can always have money available. The 50,000 came to me like a ring to a finger, since I was out of money and now we have the politics of buying everything, even yucca.

I am completely in agreement in preparing the clandestine base with these characteristics: if possible, buy or make a contract with a warehouse where the principal nutritional products can arrive without bringing much attention, have a ... near the lake and relatively far from Kigoma with a natural loading dock ... [illegible] find one or two boats that can go without being suspicious over there. The best thing would be to have two ... on this side, and cross twice (back and forth) in the night. But that depends on various factors. [Illegible] ...
Tatu

The fact that Che Guevara signed himself as Tatu (Three) suggests that he already saw himself as third in line in the Cuban power hierarchy, directly behind Fidel Castro and his brother Raúl.

The bottom line with regard to all these developments, is that none of it would have happened – *could have happened* – had there not been solid collusion with radical influences at the head of the Portuguese hierarchy, not only in Lisbon but in Angola itself.

What took place was that once the new revolutionary military leadership in Portugal decided that all Metropolitan troops would be withdrawn from Africa, the Portuguese military authorities in Luanda – led by Admiral 'Rosa' Coutinho – declared that the best course of action would be to cooperate fully with Agostinho Neto's Marxist MPLA.

That was the official version. What has since emerged is that Admiral Coutinho had not been dubbed 'Red' – thus 'Rosa' – Coutinho for nothing. He was a full-blown, card-carrying communist and the fact that he had been appointed to the topmost position in Portugal's largest African colony suggests that there were others who thought like he did to have shuffled through what was clearly a highly controversial appointment.

From the start of his tenure, Coutinho maintained close links with Agostinho Neto and other members of his party. They visited regularly, exchanged gifts and as the saying goes, 'covered each other's backs' so that neither UNITA nor Holden Roberto's FNLA could make any headway in the peace process.

Luanda was under full control of the MPLA and it was the admiral's job – and his own volition – to see that it stayed that way.

Other documents that have emerged from Havana's CIDFAR or *Centro de Informacion de la Defensa de las Fuerzas Armadas Revolucionarias* and subsequently in Lisbon, make it clear that Admiral Coutinho was not only aware of Cuban political aspirations in Angola but actually helped make it happen.

For a start, he knew about clandestine parties of Castro's people entering the country and secret arms shipments that were being landed along the coast north of Luanda.

If there was any proof needed of Coutinho's collaboration with his erstwhile 'enemy', it is found in a final personal note that he wrote under the letterhead of his sumptuous Governor General's office in Luanda, dated 22 December 1974.

> *Republica Portugesa*
> *State of Angola*
> *Governor General's Office*
> *LUANDA, 22 December 1974*
>
> *Comrade Agostinho Neto*
>
> *The UNITA and FNLA insist in replacing me for some reactionary guy who may play along with them. If this happens, the whole project we've guised to handle the power solely to the MPLA would crumble apart. Those puppet movements get their support from whites whose sole intention is to perpetuate the heinous Portuguese imperialism and colonialism – the one based on the 'Faith and Empire' motto, that is to say, reeking of moist-smelling churches and of the popish, plutocratic exploitation.*
>
> *Those Imperialist forces intend to counter our Prague secret agreements that comrade Cunhal signed on behalf of the PCP [Portuguese Communist Party] so that, under the aegis of the glorious PC [Communist Party], of the USSR we may extend communism from Tangiers to the Cape and from Lisbon to Washington.*
>
> *Empowering the MPLA in Angola is vital to topple that bastard Mobutu, an imperialist lackey, and secure Zaire as a platform.*
>
> *After the last secret meeting with the PCP comrades, we advise you to immediately start to execute the second phase of the plan.*

> Wasn't it Fanon who said that the inferiority complex can only be overcome by killing the coloniser?
>
> Comrade Agostinho Neto, give your MPLA militants secret instructions to terrorize the whites by every means, either by killing, looting or arson, in order to provoke their flight from Angola. Be cruel especially with children, women and elderly in order to discourage the bravest. Only terror will drive those bloodsucking white dogs out of this land to which they are so attached.
>
> Both the FNLA and UNITA won't be able to count with the white people's support, their finances and military expertise. Uproot them is such a way so that, with the white men's fall, the entire capitalist structure will collapse and a new socialist society may be installed, or at least the former won't be easily rebuilt.
>
> Revolutionary salute,
> The Victory is certain
> Signed António Rosa Coutinho, Vice-Admiral

It is interesting that throughout this missive, the informal 'da' (you) in Portuguese is used in the familiar, amicable way and not in the deferential 'de'. Simply put, this indicates strong, sociable links between the two men that obviously went way back.

Though the 'Red' Admiral might not have been aware of it at the time, his actions as well as those of his communist and socialist *compadres* back home ended up costing more than a million Angolan lives in the 30-something years of horrendous dislocation and civil war that followed the departure of the Portuguese in 1974/75.

Additionally, millions of people had to flee their homes or were displaced by revolutionary violence, one of the reasons why today's slum communities in Luanda are among the largest on the continent of Africa.

---

1 Yves Debay, 'Angola and South West Africa: A Forgotten War (1975–89)', Raids Magazine, No. 44, July 1995.
2 Al J. Venter, *Mercenaries: Putting the World to Rights with Hired Guns*, Casemate Publishers, US and the UK, 2014, Chapter 4 (Cuban Mercenaries in the Central Intelligence Agency's Air War in the Congo), pp. 54–70.

CHAPTER 21

Novo Redondo Adventures

Delville Linford has always been philosophical about the nature of the war in which he had been thrust, especially as each new day presented fresh problems. As he liked to say, 'conflict is a peculiar business and sometimes keeping the peace is more difficult than battling your adversaries'. This, he declared, was one of the conclusions reached when the local population of Novo Redondo fled at their approach. He explains:

I was never certain from whom they were running away: from us or from FAPLA. Jan Breytenbach got the impression that the majority of those we encountered were actually quite pleased at our arrival. I wasn't so sure. Still, I chose to believe that that was the case. However, when the people of the town fled, including the multi-millionaire whose house I'd commandeered, they left everything just like that – pretty well intact.

Imagine what it would be like if overnight the town you live in became a ghost-like backwater and that everything comes to an abrupt halt. The lights go out, and the stove doesn't work. Not only are the houses dark, but so are the streets.

The next morning there's no milk. The shop on the corner is closed. There is nowhere in town where anything can be bought and when the money in your pocket runs out, there is no more cash available because the banks are also closed.

On top of that, the town's water mains have stopped flowing and the toilet isn't working. You want to call for help but there's no phone, and anyway, who would you call? Your child starts to run a fever but there's no doctor.

In an extremely short space of time you start to see all sorts of frightening things happening and though you'd like to call the police, there's nobody in the streets, let alone cops.

Essentially, that was what Novo Redondo was like when we moved into the Pink House. My first – and very important efforts – were to try to get the municipal services going again. This I managed to achieve without too much trouble, in large part because, fortunately or otherwise, everybody had left town in such a rush that nobody had the time to damage or destroy anything.

All we really needed was some fuel and somebody to get the generators and some of the other utilities going once more. Soon we had water running and the lights on. Telephones were not that much of a problem because, simply put, there was nobody to phone, even if the always-erratic phone system – a legacy of the Portuguese colonial period – did work.

Maintaining a good measure of law and order sat at the top of my list of priorities because the locals had started to loot and plunder. It was minimal to begin with, but then more and more reports of lawlessness were coming in. There were those who had also begun to molest some of the local people who had not fled and remained in town.

I walked into my headquarters one morning and, to my surprise, there was a white woman waiting to see me. This was a bit unsettling because I'd been under the impression that all the whites had taken the gap, if only for their own safety and, obviously, this was not so.

Relatively young, late twenties or early thirties, with flowing dark brown hair and grey eyes, she had two children with her, a girl of about nine and a six-year-old boy. There was also an old lady, her mother, who looked really ancient. She was tiny and frail with snow-white hair bunched tightly over her head and tidily caught up in a tight bun in her neck.

When I arrived just about everybody started to speak simultaneously to try and explain the predicament that faced them. Poor Coen looked at me, completely bewildered by this melee before us. It was probably the first time in his life he'd faced something like this, but then Angola is very different compared to where he had hailed from.

'Ah Coen, it didn't take you long,' I said.

'Commandant, you try and sort out this lot, I haven't a clue what it's all about.'

I eventually got the little party – they were obviously refugees – to settle down a little and the children to be quiet. It appeared that they'd been living in town for a very long time and were well acquainted with the owner of the house. In fact my first impressions were that they were probably employed as servants in some capacity or another and were resident in a small house close by.

CHAPTER 21: NOVO REDONDO ADVENTURES

Their problems stemmed from some of the soldiers in town who had not fled when we arrived. Elements of the UNITA force had followed closely in our wake, as they had done in Benguela and Lobito, so an FNLA detachment – also enemies of the ruling force in Luanda – moved with us into Novo Redondo.

Apparently four FNLA troops had sequestrated the house next door to the distressed family and it wasn't long before they started to interfere with the young woman. Though I have always been aware that this is supposed to be common practice in times of war, I was adamant it will not be the case in any conflict in which I am involved.

In the strictly defined disciplinary code of Combat Group Alpha there were three crimes that were punishable by death and rape was one of them.

I turned to Coen and asked him to take matters in hand. I ordered him to walk over to the house in question and tell those guys what this is all about. He nodded and walked out.

The old lady looked about the place with a snort and started tidying up. She sent the children inside and told the young woman to go into the kitchen and wash up the dishes, even though they were no longer working in the Pink House. It seemed that they considered it their duty to keep the place clean, which was why from that moment on we had a cook, housekeeper, and all the local gossip that went with it.

The young woman's name was Cão. The old lady's name I can't remember, simply because her name was never used, but they all seemed likeable, the kids especially, and one couldn't help but respect what they were trying to do under extremely difficult circumstances.

A short while later Coen was back in my makeshift office and said that I should tell 'Grandmother' and 'Sissie' not to worry. 'Those guys aren't going to bother her again,' were his words.

I heard later that he had thrown a hand grenade through the window of the FNLA house and this, of course, I didn't take too seriously. The event was in much the same vein as the one I heard in a pub one evening when somebody told the story about Linford and Upton who went tiger-fishing in the great Zambezi River with live kittens.

Anyway, since the major's command of the Portuguese language was somewhat limited, he translated 'grandmother' as *Mama Grande*.

The young lady blushed slightly at first, but the old woman beamed and the names stuck.

'Coen,' I turned to him. 'I don't want to discourage your enthusiasm about the lingo, but there is something you should understand. In Portuguese, the word *mamas*, means "breasts", and *grande* means "big".' It was a misnomer, but understandable under the circumstances and he just laughed.

'It's not my fault she's flat-chested,' he replied. But the name stuck, for the time being anyway. It changed later for very practical reasons.

Things gradually settled down in town and I had regular patrols doing their rounds to see that things were more or less under control.

I had a very pleasant young Portuguese fellow with me by the name of Trinidade. An efficient young officer, he was a college graduate from somewhere in Mozambique and finished up with Alpha by way of Godfather's ministrations.

I appointed him as public liaison officer, a post in which he excelled. Trinity – as Coen had re-christened him – kept close tabs on things and soon there was nothing that happened in town that we didn't know about.

Still, a few problems did persist and the majority seemed linked to the FNLA troops in town. Effectively they had taken over the town and wanted everybody to be aware of it: they were the 'wheels' as it is phrased in some circles.

One group had acquired a Land Rover and somehow had mounted a machine gun on a tripod on the back. Whether the thing was operational I couldn't tell, but there it was, weapon and ammunition prominently displayed for all to see. Its operator, standing behind the cab, was strapped in with a safety belt to keep him in place as the driver and the rest of the crew careered through town from one drinking hole to another.

The end result came as a bit of an anticlimax for this machine-gunner and in an attempt to display his authority was a rather pathetic illustration of power, or rather a drunk man with an inferiority complex overstepping the mark.

It was reported that the troops had plundered the local bank and made away with several trunk loads full of money. With all this cash in circulation, the economy positively blossomed and there being no

CHAPTER 21: NOVO REDONDO ADVENTURES

other way of earning a living, the ladies of the town followed the line of least resistance.

Drinking holes, or shebeens as we called them, and what went with them, sprung up all over the place and attracted hundreds of soldiers with lots of money and nothing to do with it. They flourished. Very soon this story got around and my own troops got to hear of this exceedingly merry city life.

Camped out on the beach and well away from the flesh pots, it didn't take long for the situation to start to irk some of them. Eventually their dissatisfaction became manifest, but I was sure as fate not going to let my battalion of Bushmen loose in this town, which could only lead to violence. On the other hand, leaving the civilian population at the mercy of a power-drunk bunch of armed FNLA thugs who were almost permanently drunk wasn't in my book either.

I called a meeting with the FNLA Commandant Quiote who also had come to occupy a residence, also deserted, and not all that far from the Pink House. He invited me over. I went alone because what I was going to tell him was not exactly the truth and I didn't want Coen and the other chaps to be privy to a matter that was not quite above board.

He and I sat around the table in his sitting room and one of his wives brought out a bottle of Scotch. Without asking, she half-filled a large water tumbler with about six or seven inches of neat whisky. Thumb inside the glass and totally immersed in grog, she handed the tumbler to me. Commandant Quiote, also primed with liquor, was eager to hear what I had to say.

I spread my map, carefully and elaborately marked with coloured pencils for the occasion and began to explain:

'Commandant, as you know, the main force had withdrawn because we have some reliable information that a major threat was being planned in the east ... in the interior. To coincide with this, your people – the FAPLA – are planning a counter-attack along this stretch of west coast.' I pointed out Novo Redondo, Lobito and Benguela.

I went on to explain – in case he wasn't aware of it, which, as their local unit commander, I hoped he was – that the object of it all was for the enemy to regain the use of the Benguela Railway. They were intending to use it to attack both our South African troops as well as his FNLA units. Effectively they hoped to prevent us from using the rail line to bring in reinforcements and so attack us from the rear.

I paused to let those mouthfuls sink in and I was pleased that the impetus of it all was taking effect. Then I dealt the deathblow:

'We also have information that they are planning a seaborne landing south of here in order to cut off any chance of retreat. You see, they know that the Flechas are holding this town and it is their intention to exterminate the entire battalion.' It was all bullshit of course, but there was good reason for it.

My final words were that I had been given orders to go to Lobito to liaise with his commander and with UNITA to explain the problem, to avoid the Bushmen being trapped, and to offer backup from the rear.

I added: 'We are to withdraw to a position just north of Lobito and you, of course, are to hold Novo Redondo.'

This did it. He took a tremendous gulp of whisky and with large bulging eyes, he spluttered.

'But, Commandant, you really cannot leave us here on our own ... we are not ready ... my men are not trained and they know nothing of the defence.'

He said something innocuous about FNLA soldiers having been trained only to fight in the bush ...

Seeing that my plan was working so nicely, I got completely carried away: 'Don't worry about it, Commandant, my headquarters in Cela has flown in one of the top training officers from the Infantry School in South Africa especially to come and train your men and to help them lay out proper defensive positions north of Novo Redondo. I have also arranged for an excellent interpreter to be at your disposal.'

At that point, the expression on his face brightened noticeably, but at the same time his skin pallor became darker. Where he had been nearly white before, he now became a shade of grey.

'Yes, yes, Commandant, that is excellent,' he declared with a smile. 'When can we start?'

'We have no time to waste. I am leaving for Lobito as soon as I have made final arrangements for your training programme, then the programme can begin.'

'Excellent, my very good friend. I will give the necessary order immediately. Please have another drink.'

'Sorry, Commandant,' I answered in a serious voice. 'It's a bit early for me and also, I've got to get into this planning. But some other time and I'll be really glad to join you for a more social get-together.'

The local FNLA commander was absolutely delighted and I was pleased at the outcome of this little tête-à-tête. We said our goodbyes in good spirit and I left. I didn't feel the slightest bit guilty, because all the things I had said then might as well have been true. Besides, what I did was for a very good cause. I briefed Coen on the discussions I had, leaving out the bits that I had fabricated for Quiote's benefit.

He immediately called the company commanders together and started off with a series of lectures, followed with practical exercises. When the people knew more or less what was expected of them, Coen took them out on the terrain and laid out a battalion defensive position that was 'out of the textbook'.

Our artillery fire power was supplemented by a troop of 5.5-inch (140 mm) guns, which were ordered to be deployed closer behind our infantry position so that we could get maximum range in case it was needed. They registered some targets to tie in with the general defence plan.

The idea worked perfectly. Then came the time for the troops to occupy the position. This they did with mixed feelings, but mostly they thought it was a huge joke. Coen and my officers walked along the defence position pointing out lines of fire, killing grounds and so forth and on the face of it, the entire rigmarole looked like a great success.

That night all the troops, officers included, were back in town. Having been out all day, the revelry reached even greater and noisier proportions.

The next morning I made my complaints very clear to Commander Quiote. He apologised and promised to put the matter right.

This whole business went on until I had enough. This time I had him come to my headquarters and purposely offered no refreshments. I got straight to the point.

'Sir, I'm afraid I have bad news for you. Some senior officers from Cela have been here in order to ascertain the state of readiness of your troops. Unfortunately, I had to report the grave nature of the situation. They expressed their dissatisfaction in no uncertain terms, and the officers concerned got directly in radio contact with Cela and explained the situation. Because of the gravity of what is going on, Cela gave orders to prepare immediately to move to Lobito as planned. I'm sorry, but without your cooperation I'm afraid there is nothing more I can do.'

Quiote looked at me in utter disbelief.

Rather dramatically, I called Trinidade to join us from the adjacent room. I chose not to use the name of 'Trinity' that Coen had given him because I could speak to him in Portuguese for Quiote's benefit.

'Hey, Trinidade,' I said loudly. 'Tell my driver to get my transport ... I'm leaving for Lobito right away. Also get a message to the major to get the battalion ready to move back to Lobito at short notice. I'll get in radio contact as soon as I have tied up with the UNITA people in Lobito.'

Quiote was aghast and went quite pale again. I let him sweat and then got up and held out a hand.

'Okay, Commandant, it's been a great pleasure. If things go as planned I might wait for the unit at Lobito instead of coming all the way back here.'

I thought for a moment that Quiote was going to physically take hold of me to prevent me from leaving.

His response was heartfelt: 'No please, Commandant,' he cried, 'you mustn't go ... you cannot go. It will be a disaster. Think of all the people that will suffer if FAPLA comes back.'

'Yes, I am well aware of that, but I did what I could and your men have embarrassed me in front of my superiors. I'm actually lucky not to have lost my job, so I'm not going to take another chance. Please excuse me, I have to leave.'

'Commandant, I promise you, I will have every soldier in position before dark.'

'Sorry, Commandant, but that won't satisfy my commander. They want your troops to stay in their positions so that the town cannot be taken by surprise. It has become clear to my superiors that you have no control over your soldiers and they are not prepared to risk our soldiers under these circumstances.'

'Yes, yes, I can understand their concern, but I give you my word. My troops will man their positions day and night from now on, I give you my word. We need your assistance and of course your guns. We

CHAPTER 21: NOVO REDONDO ADVENTURES

cannot fight only with rifles when FAPLA are supported by the Cubans and their guns.'

No, you son of a bitch, I thought, you want us to protect your ass while you drink whisky and your troops loot the town and rape the women. He was pleading now and I let him continue. I got the impression that he would burst into tears if he thought it would help at all.

When I considered that I'd adequately made my point, I looked at my watch.

'Tell you what, Quiote,' I deliberately dropped mentioning his rank. 'You get your troops into position. In the meantime I'll contact my headquarters and ask them if I might be able to temporarily postpone the plan. I'll tell them you didn't quite realise the seriousness of the situation, but now that we have discussed it openly you understand it better.

'I will also request that the major be left here permanently so that he can supervise your troops personally, that is if you are satisfied to place them under his command, so to speak.'

He replied in an instant: 'Oh yes, my friend, that is perfectly in order. Your major is a very competent man ... it would be an honour to have him command my troops.'

Ah yes, you old fox, you are so clever, I thought, but we have a beautiful expression – 'bullshit baffles brains'. I replied: 'Very well, we shall see, but I don't promise anything. The whole responsibility now rests on your soldiers for the simple reason that I'm not going to load my officer with the responsibility of keeping your undisciplined troops in their trenches. That, my friend, will still be your job.'

I'm pretty sure that under a different set of circumstances Quiote would not have been happy for me to address him in that fashion. The truth is, he'd painted himself into a corner and he didn't have any options left. In his mind it was as straightforward as 'comply or my men and I are out of here'.

'Okay, Quiote,' and with it I again emphasised the lack of rank, 'you get on with it. Let me know when you're in position, then the major and I will inspect the position and report back to Cela.'

We both realised that the situation had got away from him and that he didn't like it. We also both knew that there was nothing he could do about it. I preferred it that way and I didn't reveal this skull-digging to my second-in-command or any of the other staff. But the plan worked just as well with what information I did give them.

From then on conditions in town became more peaceful. The FNLA commander even went so far as to appoint a squad of so-called 'military police' drawn from his own units to patrol the town. That was largely to ensure that his men did not AWOL from their trenches.

One afternoon shortly afterwards, while returning from an outing with the guns to snipe what we believed was an enemy position, I found three FNLA troops, drunk as lords, having a ball with a woman in an open site next to the wine shop. I called for the MPs and they arrested the culprits. Meantime I'd sent for Quiote. He came screaming around the corner and skidded to a halt, barely inches from where I was standing with his three plastered soldiers. This was adding insult to injury and I even felt a degree of sympathy for the poor old goat.

My words stung: 'I thought you had control of your troops. You also know what our arrangement was.'

'Commandant, excuse me please, just for a minute.' Walking up to the soldiers I thought he was going to assault them, as was their custom. Instead he surprised me by drawing a fancy Luger pistol from his belt and promptly shot the three unsuspecting soldiers dead.

'Now,' he addressed the MP's, 'go and bury them in their trenches.' He turned to me. 'They won't come back again, I promise you.'

'Yes, Quiote, I believe you. They might not fight so well after this, but at least they won't be molesting the women anymore.'

'It won't happen again.'

'I believe you, just be careful you don't exterminate your entire battalion.' He didn't answer, but got into his car and drove off. I got the impression that that was the end of a beautiful friendship.

CHAPTER 22

Personality Clashes with Our So-called 'Allies'

I might have fed Commandant Quiote a load of rubbish about our forces being outflanked, but while I wasn't aware of the threat potential at the time, Luanda was actually planning exactly that kind of strategy. They intended cutting us off and had that happened, we would have faced serious odds.

All I'd told Quiote was not sucked from my thumb. After it had become known that South African troops were heavily involved in Angola's civil war – or in local parlance, the *Guerra civil Angolana* – rumours started to circulate that Luanda's military (FAPLA) had formulated plans to land a major strike force behind our lines in an effort to cut us off and wipe out the entire unit.

In the process it was averred that both FNLA and UNITA elements in the region would be neutralised. Of course, the moving force here would be Fidel Castro's Socialist Cuban Army.

I had already seen Angola's regular army in action. I'd also crossed swords with them a few times and frankly, I was not impressed. Its command structure lacked depth and the Angolan military's operational ability was seriously flawed, in large part because they lacked training.

Still, we were on our own and a long way from home, so one tended to look carefully at one's options once it became known that the Cubans were lending a hand. We were not yet aware of numbers, but some sources suggested that about 20 000 of Castro's elite troops had already been flown into Luanda from Havana in a Soviet-sponsored 'air bridge'.

But just then, down in the south-western quadrant of this recently independent African country, we knew very little about what was going on up north. As a precautionary measure, Headquarters ordered me to visit Lobito and liaise with both the UNITA and FNLA commands in the region and try to establish whether their military viability had improved.

I left Novo Redondo fairly early one morning a few days later and was motoring peacefully along the road adjacent to the coast. It was a lovely, typically African day and the drive coupled to the serenity of the country was a tonic. This was the kind of Africa I'd come to love, though it was a little worrying that there wasn't another soul in sight. There were no sheep or cattle in the field, not a single *mama* working the crops nor any layabouts in the villages I passed sleeping off last night's hangovers. Nothing...

Then I came across a Russian-made Gaz truck by the roadside. I couldn't recall having seen it there on our way north and I could hardly imagine how it had got there. Certainly it wasn't stuck in the mud because there wasn't any: seems the occupants had taken the gap.

A quick survey told me that the thing was almost brand new and in excellent condition. But I was worried about booby traps and didn't think it wise to investigate further. So I made a mental note that I could get our guys to recover the vehicle later: our unit could do with another truck or two.

After motoring for a while longer I saw in the distance a thick cloud of black smoke. I was too far away to even guess what it was, so I motored on and for the first time became aware of the fact that I was totally on my own, armed only with my carbine. Now *that* started to worry me...

I made up my mind to be extra careful so as not to run into unnecessary trouble and was still wondering what to do if I should be faced with problems when over the top of a crest, and just ahead in the middle of the road, appeared two apparitions that kind of resembled the feelers of a giant beetle. When I focused again, I could clearly make out the silhouette of a fighting vehicle.

Before I could even slacken my pace the turret and gun of an Eland armoured car became clearly visible.

Surely, I thought, we were the only nation in that part of the world that possessed Elands. But I couldn't imagine what this one was doing so far beyond our regular lines.

What worried me most was the fact that the hatches on both Elands were clamped shut and I was looking directly down the barrels of two 90 mm guns. Whoever was manning them, obviously meant business.

I stopped my garry and waited, hoping that somebody would open one of the hatches so that we could talk. But nothing happened. So I cautiously emerged from my vehicle and slowly moved away.

It was unnerving that the barrel of the armoured vehicle nearest me tracked me to where I had come to a halt in the middle of the road.

Still I waited, but nothing happened. I got an uncanny feeling that something serious was amiss and not being the bravest of men on the globe, I was now positively alarmed.

What the heck was one to do? Here I was, in the middle of the road in 'Darkest Africa' facing one of the most successful armoured cars in the world. Worse, for me just then, it sported a most devastating anti-tank gun that could hit a penny stamp at 1000 metres, together with a machine gun that could cut a man in half with a single burst. Now that was unnerving!

In contrast, as the saying goes, I was 'armed to the teeth' with a lone 7.62 mm Fabrique Nationale assault rifle. How stupid! Perhaps I should have brought Hendrik along, at which point I chuckled at the thought.

To an onlooker – had there been any – the situation would have been ridiculous. But I wasn't amused. So I put my pride in my pocket, lay my rifle down on the hood of my vehicle and started walking steadily up the road. I strolled along as fast as my shaking knees would allow.

The closer I got to the armoured cars, the more scared I became, because whoever was manning them, didn't make the slightest move one way or the other. They could have been friend or foe.

An evil voice started to whisper in my ear that somehow FAPLA might have got in behind our lines and possibly captured some of our equipment. We'd been worrying that they might do just that. I asked myself whether this might actually have happened. Had they really cut us off? And I was the poor bugger who was going to have to prove that they might have.

I don't know at what stage an individual's nerves shatter, or whether under severe stress you end up wetting your pants, or in a dire emergency just turn around and run, or all of the above, but as scared as I was, sanity told me none of these options was going to do me any good.

In spite of the odds then, my legs kept going and I kept moving towards the pair of Elands.

I didn't exactly lose track of time but just as I was beginning to feel more stupid than scared, the hatch of one of the armoured cars started to edge open, very slowly at first, inch by inch.

I thought it was going to take forever, but eventually it swung all the way and cautiously, little by little, a human head started to appear.

Finally a man appeared and slowly, excruciatingly so, his shoulders followed. I was then close enough to recognise him as one of ours and with a huge shrug of my shoulders I could relax. Dammit! He did give me a scare.

I didn't know the fellow well enough to even be on first-name terms with him, but I recalled that his pals called him Fido. I later learned that this was Fido Smit, but at that moment though, Fido had suddenly become my best and dearest friend.

So I stuck up both my hands and shouted: 'Hello, Fido, old buddy. What the fuck are you doing here in the middle of nowhere?' I hoped my voice wasn't as wobbly as my knees and only then did Fido's face break into a broad grin.

'Shit, Commandant, you scared the hell out of me... I thought you were a Cuban or something and we were about to shoot you.'

'Nice of you chaps not to,' I replied, adding something about us both supposing to be on the same side.

'Yes, I know, Commandant, but how do you expect anybody to recognise you looking like that?'

'Don't be rude, an officer is supposed to be dressed for the occasion. I'm playing war and I'm dressed for the occasion.'

Fido got down from his mobile fortress and we shook hands. I was genuinely pleased to be making proper contact. We spoke for a time and then I discovered that he and the other Eland were part of a troop of armoured cars that was on a deep reconnaissance mission that had taken them quite a distance beyond our recognised defence perimeters.

I mentioned something about there being nothing wrong with patrolling miles and miles behind the front line, but was irked that nobody had taken the trouble to brief him properly. They were in an extremely vulnerable area where it was possible to encounter enemy around every bend in the road, or indeed, behind every ridge.

I put him in the picture about what I was doing, after which we split and went merrily on our respective ways.

Approaching the column of black smoke, I regretted that I hadn't asked Fido what it was. To my surprise I discovered a truck burning

CHAPTER 22: PERSONALITY CLASHES WITH OUR SO-CALLED 'ALLIES'

furiously on the road ahead. It was similar to the one I'd come across earlier that morning, or had been until Fido and his crazy armoured cars used the thing for target practice.

Finding my allies in Lobito was no problem. I motored up to the first hotel on my way in and, sure enough, an FNLA flag fluttered proudly from the roof. I walked up to the front entrance, but for the second time that day was stopped in my tracks.

A little boy of about nine or ten – armed – was lounging in the foyer. Having spotted me, he got out of a chair and stood in front of the door.

The kid was dressed in a miniature combat kit which might have looked cute anywhere else, but just then he was pointing the muzzle of his 9 mm Israeli-built Uzzi submachine gun at my belly button – at which point he cocked his weapon and slipped off the safety catch.

His boyish face and chubby little figure told me he should be playing marbles in the back yard. But at that moment this juvenile little shit looked quite capable of killing somebody. Anyway, what do you do with an officious little bastard who should be sitting at his school desk instead of pointing a loaded machine carbine at your belly button? In truth, you end up being remarkably nice to him.

'Hi, soldier,' I greeted him in as pleasant a voice as I could muster. 'How are you?' I told him that he certainly looked very smart and efficient and then I couldn't think of any more nice things to say.

I caught my breath and went on: 'I'm the commander of one of your friendly units up to the north. I hear you are very good soldiers and I want to come and hear if your commander will lend us a hand.' I followed that by asking whether he was in his office and whether I could speak to him.

The boy turned nonchalantly away, almost as if he was doing me a favour, and spoke to somebody inside the foyer.

'You wait,' he ordered when he turned back towards me. 'The commander is in a meeting and he doesn't want to be disturbed.'

'Yes, I know. As a matter of fact he invited me to come to the meeting, but I had a flat tyre and now I'm late. I know he'll be angry with me, but if he knows I was here all the time he might be angry with you, too. Now we really don't want that to happen, do we?'

He turned again and spoke to somebody I couldn't see. After a while somebody came back with a reply and the little shit told me to wait and that the commander would see me when he had finished what he was doing.

Being terrified by your own men in a couple of Eland armoured cars was one thing, but being scared of a kid with a loaded firearm was something else. What the hell was this war coming to? At this rate I felt that I might develop an inferiority complex. That is if my allies don't shoot me first or beat me to death. I felt that I really needed to get a grip on the situation.

I again started a conversation with the kid and it wasn't difficult. In spite of the cast-iron facade he projected, he was still a child at heart. I spoke to him about the things I thought little boys spoke about and soon we'd struck up a good rapport.

What fascinated him particularly was my pistol. I took it out of my holster, emptied the chamber and showed it to him. He was especially interested when I showed him that it fired the same 9 mm ammunition as his carbine and at one stage I even offered to let him have a few shots.

The only trouble, I said, was that I am a bit short of ammo, adding that 'a man never knows what you can run into on your way home.' He smiled. Also, he appeared to appreciate my problem and didn't hold me to my offer.

Just then a mysterious voice spoke from the foyer and my new little buddy said I could go in.

I explained my story to those present and was offered not only sympathy and understanding but also whatever help I needed. At one point during these discussions I sensed somebody in close proximity to my seat. Looking round, there was a youngster with a shy, boyish smile on his face as he came up and stood quietly alongside me. He was tiny – so small, in fact, that his head barely reached my shoulder.

I returned his smile and gave my full attention to matters in hand. It amused me that nobody else in the room paid any attention to his presence.

After our talks were done the meeting was adjourned. As we started trooping out of the room I felt a little hand touching mine. Looking down the little boy was holding something towards me in his tiny fist. I put out my hand, which was when he opened his and in his sweaty little palm lay four of his Uzzi cartridges.

I'm not one that give in to emotion, but this kind of thing just got to me. Forgetting for a moment where I was and what I was supposed to represent, I bent down and picked up the little bloke and hugged him tightly, tapping him on the shoulder blades as is the Portuguese custom.

The FNLA officers appreciated the gesture, with the result that I was promptly invited to lunch with the commander and his staff and their families. By now I was really famished and I readily accepted.

Mission accomplished, my next step was the local UNITA command. I was aware that the next large hotel was on the far side of town, so I drove there and, sure enough, UNITA's flag was flying as proudly from the roof as the FNLA's had from theirs.

Contrary to my previous unexpected 'welcome' there were a number of soldiers in varying forms of undress hanging around and, as might have been expected, a lot of women, most of them also disreputable. But that was their business, not mine.

As I walked towards the main entrance, I caught sight of a fairly large calibre gun mounted immediately outside the hotel's front door. I thought it looked a bit modern for something ceremonial and in any case, I can't recall ever having seen any monumental weapons in Angola.

As expected, I was stopped at the door and went through more or less the same procedure as before. This time I was invited in and asked to seat myself in a very comfortable plush couch in the centre of what appeared to be at the heart of the UNITA headquarters.

A chap entered the room with a bottle of whisky, an ice bucket together with two glasses and then left again. I was still trying to figure out why there were two glasses when a soldier, accompanied by an attractive young girl, walked in.

'Sir, I'm very sorry you have to be kept waiting but the commander is taking his siesta and will only be able to see you later.' Almost as an aside he added that the lady would keep me company while I waited, 'and if you need anything else she will be able to assist.'

'You really are very nice,' I said, 'but it's a bit early for whisky. Also, I'm afraid ladies are inclined to take a man's mind off one's work.

'So I tell you what. I have other business in town and I'll finish that first. When I'm done and your commander has woken up, I'll return and we'll talk. Otherwise we'll just have to manage the FAPLA sea landing without you chaps.'

The last bit caught the man completely off guard. He asked me to wait a moment and quickly disappeared. Scarcely a minute later he was back.

Almost breathlessly he told me that his commander would see me immediately. 'Just wait a moment, please.'

When the man in charge finally put in an appearance a short while later, the girl promptly disappeared and I was very pleased indeed to discover that the commander in question was my other friend Valentino.

I told him my story and sincerely offered understanding, concern, sympathy and cooperation. I also promised to call on him if we had any further information and he was quite happy. Politely he accompanied me to the front door and walked with me to my vehicle.

As I walked past the gun I noticed that the dial sight and the other instruments were in place. I told Valentino that I had an interest in guns and asked if I could have a closer look. He was quite happy and accompanied me as I walked closer. To my consternation I found that the gun was not only laid on some target or another but was also loaded.

'Commander, but this gun is loaded!' I looked at him questioningly.

'Yes,' he replied.

'But what target on earth could you lay a gun on right in the middle of town?'

'The FNLA headquarters,' came the reply.

I laughed. 'You guys really are nice to have as friends.'

The commander took this as a compliment. 'Oh yes,' he said with a big smile, 'we are great friends with them.' We shook hands and I left.

I still had one call to make before calling it a day. Fido had told me that there was a logistical setup in Lobito and that they had, among other things, to protect a battery of 5.5-inch guns.

I found my way to where these weapons were being held and encountered Felix Hurter, a young gunner major who I had taught in my Gunnery School days.

We spent a happy few minutes chatting and he then explained

that it was apparently the orders from the commander of our logistics setup to destroy all enemy equipment in the area.

I said goodbye to Major Hurter and went in search of the South African Army officer who was in the process of destroying enemy equipment. I found him at his office and it turned out to be a fellow I'd met once or twice at Army Headquarters in Pretoria.

In truth though, I didn't know him well at all, but I did ask him not to go about shooting up the things that we might be able to use at a later date, especially if our own supplies didn't arrive in good time.

First impressions were that he didn't quite understand what I was getting at, so I gave up and left. We did, however, become good friends in later years.

CHAPTER 23

Unconventional Warfare

We have all heard about the *Bridge on the River Kwai*. But few people know about Angola's bridge on the River Queve.

Knowing that FAPLA had learned how to blow up bridges, our venture north had almost become bogged down in the marshy flood plain of the River Queve. Besides being extremely frustrating, it was not in my impatient nature to sit around and do nothing.

Angola's FAPLA forces – together with who knows how many Cubans and Soviets – had ensconced themselves in a strong defensive position north of the river and every time we showed up there, they would let rip with rockets and mortars.

Some distance north of the river was a little harbour town called Porto Amboim. Information had it that FAPLA were having their supplies unshipped there and then conveyed by road and rail to Gabela where their main force was holding up our advance north.

I figured that if we could destroy the loading equipment we were home and dry because this would make re-supply much more difficult – it also meant that we could get in behind their positions at Gabela. It was only much later when I read Jan Breytenbach's book that I discovered that he had had exactly the same plan.

I looked all over town to see if there was anything with which we could cross the river. All I could find in that line were three large wooden barges floating in the small harbour.

If we could get our troops over the river we could kick them out of their positions. Then we could improvise something with the barges to get our transport across.

I decided to have a look at the river myself. I got two armoured cars to come along and we took off to the river. I had scarcely manoeuvred myself into position on the long ridge running parallel to the river when FAPLA started shooting rockets at me.

I then came down from the hills and started to make my way towards the mouth of the river on our left. The terrain was bad and it wasn't long before my garry got stuck in a dry river bed. I got the

CHAPTER 23: UNCONVENTIONAL WARFARE

armoured car to drag me out and I got onto the armoured car. We went along as best we could, but eventually the Eland couldn't get further and we abandoned the plan.

The frustration only made me more determined than ever. I realised that if I was going to get to the river mouth, I was going to have to do it on foot. However, I did give orders to the troop commander of the armoured cars to explore the possibility of going up the narrow flat coastal strip and wait for me at a certain point which I indicated on the map.

I motored along the road to a position where our 5.5-inch guns had been deployed out of sight of the enemy. I found Captain Louis Rheeder sitting in a tree, studying the terrain with his binoculars. 'Louis, do you see those white cliffs there towards the left?' He nodded. 'Well that's where the river flows into the sea. I want to go there.'

'Yeah, Commandant, how you gonna get there?'

'Walk.' He looked at me in disbelief, but said nothing. 'I want you to register that as a target. And if I run into trouble, you must fire. I'll adjust the fire from there. If you give me a radio, that is.'

'You sure that's what you want to do?'

'You got any other ideas?' He just looked at me. His pale blue eyes were noncommittal.

'You going to carry the radio all by yourself?'

'Not if you give me a troopie to help, make certain that he's a volunteer.'

He started ranging in onto the cliffs and when I was happy that he was in fact spot on the target, I said, 'Okay, let's go, where's my radio?'

Two young gunners came forward, one carrying a radio on his back and the other a heavy-barrelled R1 rifle.

We travelled as far as we could and then we set off on foot. We headed towards the sea so that we could meet up with the armoured cars. The going was not all that difficult and we made reasonably good progress, stopping from time to time to change over the radio.

All went well. The cars had made progress and were slightly ahead of us when we reached the sea. It was about that time when the bombing started. Their forward observers must have been sitting on the white cliffs and they had probably spotted the cars, because there was no way they could have seen myself and the two gunners.

We crept forward to where the mortar bombs had landed and as was their custom, the tail fin of the mortar bomb was protruding from the soft sand.

Having commanded an observation battery in the dim and silent past, I had some experience of this sort of thing. I drew a line on the ground, indicating the direction from which the bomb came. The angle at which it protruded from the ground also indicated that it had been fired at a very high elevation. This meant that the mortars were not very far. Probably just north of the river.

I called Louis on the radio and they engaged that area. My guess hadn't been so bad because the bombing stopped and we set off again up the coast.

The troop commander of the armoured cars wasn't at all happy about moving forward and I decided not to press the issue. I told him to wait for us in the cover of the bushes just south of where the mortar bombs had landed.

The two gunners and I set off again and we made it to the foot of the cliffs without further interference. We had to leave the cover of some shrubs and make it the rest of the way in relatively open terrain. Instinctively I hugged the line of the cliffs. I was walking right up against the cliff, the two gunners following. Not expecting any FAPLA on our side of the river, I carried my rifle slung over my shoulder but with the muzzle pointing forward. I had adjusted the sling so that it hung conveniently high. It was also just as well I did, because as I rounded the next bend I looked straight down the barrel of a machine gun not more than fifteen paces in front of me.

Instinctively I fired from the hip and to my surprise the machine gunner jumped and ran. By that time I had gotten my rifle to the shoulder. I fired again but the man kept on running. The gunner came alongside and let fly with a volley from his heavy barrel rifle. The soldier fell and lay face down in the dirt.

If their men had been on our side of the river it meant that their observer must be on the cliffs above us. All I needed now was for those buggers to lob a few hand grenades down on us and that would be the end of our little venture.

Running for it now was going to be suicide because we would be caught in the open by anybody sitting on the cliff above.

'Tell the guns to fire!' I instructed.

CHAPTER 23: UNCONVENTIONAL WARFARE

The FAPLA machine gunner had built himself a neat little shelter of white chalk-like rocks and I made for it.

'Come here and take cover, those guns are going to shoot the hell out of us any minute.'

We lay face down in the sand behind the little shelter and waited. It felt like an eternity and then came the ear-splitting explosions as the 80-pound shells came pouring down onto the cliff above us. Unfortunately, the dispersion of the guns was so that the one gun was firing on the 100-metre strip between us and the water's edge. How long it was going to take for the law of averages to determine that a shell was to fall on top of us, I couldn't tell.

Mercifully Louis had not decided to shoot air busts because then we would have been dead for sure.

Then the shelling stopped as suddenly as it had started. The silence was in shrill contrast to the deafening blast of the exploding shells.

'Listen, you guys crawl on your bellies and stay right up against the cliff, make for the scrubs back there, but don't get up, just in case there are still some people on the cliff. Take the radio off and leave it there, I'll pick it up.'

The troopie looked as if he was going to say something but realised now was no time to get involved in discussions.

'Go!'

Scared and shaken as I was, there was something I just had to find out first. The FAPLA soldier lying some metres away had no bullet holes in his back. What had he died from, or was the son of a bitch playing possum so that he could shoot us as soon as our backs were turned?

Maybe I was getting paranoid, but I wasn't going to take that chance. I crawled quickly to where he was lying and was beginning to doubt my marksmanship. I got to him and prodded him with the muzzle of my rifle. He farted and I got such a fright I nearly jumped out of my skin. I then realised that this must have been a natural discharge of stomach gas, so I rolled him over to see what he had died of.

He was perfectly intact except for a very small hole no thicker than a pencil right between his eyes. The first round I had fired from the hip had caught him between the eyes. It must have been pure reflexive power that had carried him the ten paces to where he fell. His glazed eyes looked at me accusingly. He also was not much more than a kid really. I pushed the lids over the dead eyes.

'Sorry, buddy, but it was you or me.'

I grabbed the radio and crawled hell for leather after the troops. Judging distance lying flat on your belly is not the easiest thing, so there was no way of telling how far we had crawled. I came to the conclusion that we were either out of sight or there was nobody to shoot at us.

'Okay, boys, let's get off here!' We ran zigzag for a hundred yards or so and then took cover in some scrubs. As soon as I caught my breath, I said: 'We can't stay here, if somebody has seen us he can shoot us here … crawl!'

This went on for a long time until I was sure we were safe. Then we got up and started walking. All the time I was wondering what had happened to our armoured cars, they were very conspicuous by their absence. We walked on a little way and then I saw the hulk of an armoured car in the bush ahead. I made for it and was delighted when the car drove up and a youngster popped his head out and shouted.

'Commandant, jump up and hold on, we're going to drive fast just in case they fire those mortars again. You'll get killed on the port side of the car.'

'You're kidding,' I said but smiled and handed him the radio. I got up and pulled the two gunners up.

'Where is the other car?'

'The lieutenant said it was too dangerous, he left.'

'And you? How come you are here?' I looked him squarely in the eyes. He looked away.

'I thought if those people on the cliff didn't kill you, those damned guns will. We just couldn't leave you.'

'Bless the thought, boy. Say, haven't I seen you somewhere before?' He looked away again. 'Yes, Commandant, at your headquarters.'

That was it, he was the chap I chased out of the HQ because I thought he was drugged.

'Sorry, anyone can make a mistake, please forgive me.' He looked away again. 'It's okay, Commandant, I am glad I could help.'

CHAPTER 23: UNCONVENTIONAL WARFARE

I realised that it was possible to cross the river, but with my Bushmen not being the best of swimmers, I decided not to try. But I had received several young national service officers to act as platoon leaders in the place of the Portuguese chaps who were finding it increasingly difficult to cope. Several of these youngsters volunteered to investigate the possibility and eventually I agreed.

They got themselves organised and with a light machine gun, a rocket launcher and a mortar and as much ammunition as we could carry we set off in the pitch-black night.

We made it to the white cliff without incident. I organised myself and my support group in a position where I thought I had the best chance of giving fire support if need be.

The three young subalterns, armed only with ropes, stripped and waded into the water. I had my doubts about the sanity of this operation, but the young officers were so adamant that they could do the job I didn't want to spoil it for them. Besides, with the fire power we had in support I was reasonably sure to get them out should anything go wrong.

Nothing went wrong and much sooner than I had expected I heard the soft sound of splashing water and the three of them appeared out of the black water.

Apart from the mosquitos the operation was a great success, but there was nothing we could do further because the Bushmen were not going to try this at all.

CHAPTER 24

The Grand Plan

It was notable that by the time that the two combat groups had reached the Angolan coast, the South African Navy had also become involved in Operation Savannah. Word came down the grapevine that one of our frigates – the SAS *President Steyn* – had taken up a position off Lobito harbour. In a very short time, the war had escalated ...

During my days at the Gunnery School, I was involved in drafting a pamphlet on naval gunfire support with a naval officer, Carl Paul Weinstein. I consequently was made familiar with procedures that involved directing gunfire from a surface craft onto land targets. I thought this might be a marvellous opportunity to put this bit of expertise to good use. Indeed, we could move the *President Steyn* up the coast to a point directly opposite Porto Amboim.

Somehow, I thought, I could make my way ashore near Porto Amboim and with the ship's guns we could destroy that port's infrastructure without them ever knowing what hit them.

In anticipation, I 'acquired' for our use, one of the fishing boats that had been lying at anchor in the harbour when we got there. Its skipper couldn't complain because he had no fuel, even if he was able to go fishing, which he wasn't. Instead, I offered him some diesel in exchange for the use of his boat and he agreed.

I mounted the 82 mm rocket launcher and a 120 mm anti-aircraft gun on the deck of the fishing craft and with a ragtag crew of excited national servicemen on board, we took to sea. Along the way up the coast, I was able to conduct a reconnaissance and I came to the conclusion that it was quite possible to land near Porto Amboim in a small boat and row ashore.

How the news had reached Cela so fast, I don't know; or whether it was possibly coincidence, but the brigadier decided to pay us a visit.

When I put the idea to him, he turned it down flat. First, he told me the Chief of the Navy refused to get involved and I responded with a request to tell the admiral what he could do with his warship.

I also made the mistake of telling him that I would do the job with my own boat and the 82 mm launcher. He responded by telling me that the Director of Artillery was very concerned about the way in which I was abusing his AA guns. I sent him a similar message as that of the admiral.

'Nobody seems to want to get involved in this war except the poor monkeys that have to do the job. Well that's okay,' I said, 'we'll do the job anyway because neither the fishing boat nor the rocket launchers belonged to either the Navy or the South African Army.'

'Yes,' he replied, 'but the troops are ours and the Chief of the Army is not very keen on the idea either.' Effectively that put paid to my master plan.

'Okay, Brigadier,' I said, 'we'll sit on our asses until somebody decides we can go home ... then we'll all know that we've wasted our time and the taxpayers' money.'

'You don't have to sit on your ass and do nothing, why don't you use the 5.5-inch guns I sent you? All you have to do is shoot a few rounds at these people and they run like rabbits.'

'That's true, but as soon as you stop, they come back again.'

'That's because you can't hit the targets properly,' was his retort.

'Brigadier, this is a heavily wooded terrain and one can't even see where you are yourself, let alone where the targets are.'

'Well, then I'll send you a light aircraft, you can do aerial observation, can't you?' The brigadier and I were both about to lose our patience, but I did my best to try to keep my cool.

'Yes, Brigadier, I can do any amount of aerial observations, but these jungles along the coast are so large and dense and the trees so big that the shells just burst in their branches. It's virtually impossible to see our fall of shot. Besides, in this kind of mountainous terrain, anybody who knows the slightest bit about gunnery will be aware that if you miss a target by 100 metres, the shot could easily end up to a kilometre away. A fat bloody chance you have of seeing that from an aircraft that is moving at 100 knots ...'

'Okay, man, if you have so many problems, I'll find somebody else to do the job.'

'Sure, Brigadier,' I shot back at him, 'that's just fine with me, I'll be ready just as soon as you find that guy ...'

Meantime, I could sense something coming here. The new commander who was taking over from Brigadier Schoeman had been an instructor at the staff college with me. What's more, he was a gunner...

At this point Brigadier Potgieter interceded: 'Hey, cut it out, Dawie ... leave the guy alone. He knows what he's doing and he's quite right. You can't fight a war in this kind of terrain with artillery.'

It was only afterwards that I heard how close I had come to being fired that day and I had Brigadier Potgieter to thank for saving my bacon.

Whether it was Brigadier Potgieter's idea I wouldn't know, but somebody decided to have the operation handled by the reconnaissance guys. A group of recces arrived shortly afterwards in a helicopter, rigged and, as the saying goes, armed to the teeth. They were going to land close to the target by chopper, they said, and then do the rest of the jog on foot.

Well, I thought, at last we were in business, but alas, this was also not to be. They waited for the other helicopter with the rest of the group to arrive and ended up just waiting and waiting some more. Meanwhile, the guys were enjoying what little Novo Redondo had to offer.

Then, after several days, somebody called it quits and they all got back on board their chopper and left. That was the last I heard of them.

Now that my master plan had been thwarted, I started looking around for some other way of getting me and my group to Gabela. I was left with two options.

The first was via Vila Nova do Seles, then on to Conda and over the bridge to Gabela. This route had been tried before and we'd run into an ambush at the bridge immediately to the north of Conda.

The other prospect was shorter and more direct. Jan's Combat Group Bravo had already been sniffing around in that area, but the reports that came back from there said there was no enemy in sight. Which was when I decided to have a look for myself.

I'd thought that by this time Hendrik had had enough excitement to last him a while, so I sent him back to Alpha and before leaving, Jan graciously donated me his driver. He was a huge Portuguese fellow and because his commander couldn't remember his name, everybody called him Sampson.

Now from what I could gather, Jan and Sampson didn't get along all that well and that worried me a little. After all, he was now my

CHAPTER 24: THE GRAND PLAN

driver for the duration of this little escapade to the north. Though he looked like a nice enough kid, I decided not to take any unnecessary chances, which was why I would do the reconnaissance on my own.

When I ordered him to get my vehicle ready he was all agog, but when I told him he wasn't going along, the poor chap was so crestfallen that I took him along anyway.

Together with a bunch of others, including Coen, we set off towards Gabela on a beautiful sunny Sunday morning. It actually felt more like a Sunday morning drive than an assignment to search for the enemy. For part of the way we motored along a reasonably good road with high ground to the south of us set off against a bushy plain sloping gently down to the river.

There wasn't a single foe in sight, and as I was about to turn back I spotted a rather large hill that loomed up on our right. It overlooked the river and the terrain beyond, so I thought I'd take a look anyway. Unfortunately, we had to cross a dry river to get to where I wanted to be, and before I realised what was happening, Sampson had bedded my garry into the loose sand up to the axle.

'That's nice, Sampson,' I said angrily. 'Now you dig!'

I tossed him a shovel I always carry with me in the vehicle. He stripped off his shirt and started digging vigorously. From time to time I heard the shovel hit metal, but thinking it was the shovel butting up against the axle I wasn't particularly concerned. That is, not until Sampson yelled.

'Commandant, come help, quickly.'

I dashed over and to my horror found that he had struck a large gash in the fuel tank. The fuel was gushing out and I could see my hopes of getting home that night drain away into the sand. I rummaged through my tool kit and found nothing. Then, in desperation, I looked in my first-aid kit. I found a cake of soap and with water from my flask I made it into a paste. With my knife blade I managed to bring the lips of the gash together and then smeared the soap paste over the gash. I was relieved to see the fuel-flow diminish and eventually cease completely.

I was starting to see why Jan and Sampson didn't get along.

We stayed the night by the river and left early the next day. The plan was to approach the bridge without revealing our presence. Staff Sergeant Geldenhuys (who had replaced Piet Lubbe) and Coen were to approach the bridge on foot so that Staff could get a good look at the damage to the bridge and appraise its potential for our future use.

Our improvised reconnaissance group comprised a platoon of infantry, a section of armoured cars and, just for good measure, I'd included the mortar platoon.

About halfway towards the bridge the road ended up alongside the river and ran some distance parallel to it. Meanwhile, we moved cautiously and kept a close watch on the opposite bank for any evidence of our adversaries.

At some point, by my reckoning we were getting fairly close to the bridge, second lieutenant Alexander Nicholau – in command of the armoured cars – reported that he had no visibility beyond where the road disappeared around the shoulder of the hill and because I wasn't going to make the same mistake that we had made at Conda, I brought my column to a halt. Alex deployed his cars and again reported no enemy in sight.

I addressed Major Upton: 'Coen, I reckon the bridge must be somewhere just beyond this stretch of high ground. This is your cue. I'll climb the hill, and if you need a hand, I'll position our mortars so they can range along the river and Alex can give us whatever support we need with the cars ... okay?'

A young artillery captain, whose name I can't recall, had earlier shown up at Novo Redondo and asked whether he could come along for the experience.

At this point, having listened to the discussion, he suggested that I let him climb the hill 'so that I can direct the fire and do whatever is necessary?' I agreed and we went into action.

Meanwhile, the mortars had deployed behind the ridge.

And with only the two of them doing the job of reconnoitering the approaches to the bridge, I felt reasonably sure that they could reach the bridge undetected. In any event Coen was an experienced infantry officer and this sort of thing was kind of his meat and potatoes. Whatever happened, I felt that the odds were on our side, so I settled down to wait.

It wasn't very long before the morning's silence was broken by rifle fire from somewhere beyond the hill. Virtually the same moment the radio came to life. It was Alex.

'Contact! Contact! Contact!' he screamed into the radio. There was no mistaking heavy rifle and machine-gun fire from across the

CHAPTER 24: THE GRAND PLAN

river, much of which seemed to be directed at the bridge. The next message was terse: 'We're moving forward to engage, out.'

Obviously the reconnaissance party had been detected and were drawing some solid fire from the positions across the river. I called my observations officer on the hill, but there was no reply. We had considered giving the two officers who had gone forward a radio, but decided against it because I thought it would slow them down.

I called the observation post again. In fact, I called them several times, but to no avail. Then I heard the 90 mm guns and the 60 mm mortars open up, together with some of our machine guns on the armoured cars. The war was on.

Moments later Alex's voice came across on the radio.

'Delta Lima, my number two car has been hit by anti-tank fire. It's out of action but the crew and weapons are okay, and are returning fire.'

I tried again to contact the guys manning the OP but gave up when Alex's car came screaming around the shoulder of the hill. He reported briefly what had happened.

The crew of the car that had been hit – under command of Trooper Janse van Rensburg – had fought back so fervently that they were able to escape. Unfortunately though, the gunner, Trooper Obbes, was hit in the process. With devastating fire from the river and no fire support, the other car was forced to withdraw temporarily to safety.

'How is Obbes?'

Alex replied: 'Can't say. He's lying partially in a ditch with his legs halfway in the road. The fire from the river was extremely heavy so I moved away to draw the fire away from him.'

My reaction was immediate and I said that we would go and see. 'I'll ride with you, get Obbes while you turn around then...'

'No, Sir,' he replied, hands raised. 'You cannot ride on the car ... they'll kill you in seconds. I'll fetch Obbes, but you get our mortars onto the target because they're able to do damage.' I contemplated this for a moment but the determination on the handsome young face told me that he wasn't going to change his mind.

'Okay, Alex, but you bugger this thing up and I'll...'

'I won't bugger it up, Sir. You just don't bugger up with our mortars.' He was already racing off towards his armoured car.

I was about to scramble up the hillside when I realised I'd given my portable radio to the officer who was manning the observation post. There wasn't time to waste, so I drove my garry up the slope in the direction that I thought the bridge was and when I couldn't go any further, I called Alex on our vehicle radio.

'Hallo Alex, how far is the bridge from the mortars?'

'I don't know, maybe a thousand metres ... how is one supposed to know?"

'Never mind, I'm going to fire a round. You tell me where it fell in relation to the target.'

'Roger, out.'

I guessed rather than estimated a bearing and distance and gave the fire order to the mortars. There seemed to be a delay and I was burning up with frustration.

'Hey, what's with you guys?' I yelled at the mortar position. 'Why don't you shoot that blasted thing?'

'It's a misfire, Sir, it'll only take a few seconds.'

I watched two men lift the barrel from its base plate and tilt it forward. A third man with hands outstretched was ready to catch the bomb as it slid from the muzzle. Apparently that was the drill for curing a misfire.

It looked like a pretty crazy thing to me, because what if the guy missed the catch and the bomb fell to the ground. Just then a ball of smoke erupted from the muzzle of the mortar tube, followed by the bomb itself. The third man belched from the smoke and ended up missing the catch – just like I thought might happen.

The mortar bomb took off through his legs and went zigzag through the grass like a cat with a starlight stuck up its bum. The crew stood like statues, mouths wide open, eyes staring. I watched as if this wasn't happening right before me.

The bomb came to rest about a hundred metres away and lay still in the grass.

I called loudly: 'Hey, you guys, stop fooling around with that thing and get on with the job.' The bewildered crew jerked back to life and set about reassembling the weapon. The mortar officer gave the order for the next mortar to fire.

'Hallo, Alex, watch carefully, it's coming.' I waited, but then mortar bombs in flight sometimes seem to take forever to reach target.

CHAPTER 24: THE GRAND PLAN

Eventually I thought I heard a bang: it came from somewhere in the distance.

'Hallo, Alex, did you see where it hit?'

'No,' he answered. 'Where is it?'

'How must I know? It was fired.'

'Yeah, I hear you, but where's it now?'

'How must I know? Watch carefully this time and I'll shoot another.' I gave the mortar squad an order to decrease the distance by about 400 metres and fire another round. When the explosion sounded, it was obviously a lot closer.

'Hallo, Alex,' I called again. 'Did you see it this time?'

'Couldn't miss it, the damned thing nearly fell on top of me.'

'That's nice. Now watch the next one.'

'Yes, yes, but please try and get those bloody bombs away from us.'

'Don't worry, I'm very good at this sort of thing.' I lied. I'd never dreamt of doing anything like this. In fact, I doubt whether anybody else has either.

I visualised his position in relation to the target and gave the order. The next round fell in the bushes just beyond the target and slightly to the left. I gave another correction and then I heard Alex's otherwise serious voice snicker over the air.

'Hey, Commandant, you really are good at it, that round fell right on top of those bastards. Let fly, I'm going in.'

I shouted to the mortar crew, 'Okay, boys, that's target. Now let 'em have it.' They weren't found lacking.

Alex and his crew must have found the wounded man because the next message that came across the ether was straightforward: 'Okay, Delta Lima, I've got him, we're leaving.'

Several minutes later the armoured car came screaming around the bend again. Alex was holding Obbes's body in position on the front of his car.

They laid him on the grass beside the car. He was dead. 'Okay, send him back, he's done his share,' I said hoarsely. I saluted him and turned to go back to my vehicle. 'Now what about the Eland, Alex?'

'What about it, Sir?'

'You must go and get it.'

'Are you mad, Sir? Tonight?'

'Yes, tonight,' I replied sternly because we couldn't have the enemy grabbing one of our armoured cars, damaged or not. 'You can recover what you can and make the weapons unserviceable. Also, bring back all Obbes's stuff.'

'Yes, Sir.' Young Alex saluted grimly and as I watched him walk away, I wondered how I would have reacted under such circumstances when I was his age.

Once again there was silence and then it dawned on me that Coen and the man with him were still somewhere out there. I made one more effort to contact the officer in charge of the observation post, but again, no luck. I gave up and decided to send a patrol out along the tracks taken by the reconnaissance party.

While I was briefing the troops they heard someone scrambling through the bushes. It was Coen and he presented a rather sorry sight. His face was burnt from the sun and his skin and clothing seriously scratched by branches and thorns. Also, the guy was so exhausted he could hardly speak. He explained bit by bit what had happened while trying to catch his breath.

When they arrived at the bridge, Staff Sergeant Geldenhuys was about to begin his survey of the area ahead when the enemy opened fire. Geldenhuys was hit in the chest by the first volley. Coen retaliated by emptying his rifle magazine in the general direction of the bridge. Then he grabbed the wounded man and half-dragged, half-carried him to safety in some bushes further back.

A brief examination of Geldenhuys told him that because he was on his own, he wouldn't be able to haul him all the way back. Making the wounded man comfortable in the shade of a tree, he hotfooted it back as fast as he could.

Following that, I gave him a quick run-down of what had taken place with our group, told him to rest up, and as soon as he was up to it, he was to take a stretcher-bearer team together with a fighting patrol and bring Staff Sergeant Geldenhuys back to our lines.

I left the platoon of troops and took the rest of our contingent back to our temporary base. Having got here, I told the chef to prepare sandwiches and get a case of cool drinks. I also summoned the medical officer and briefed him on the situation. He was to get ready to accompany me, I said.

By this time it was just getting dark and because I didn't want to risk being spotted by the other side, I told the MO not to use his ve-

CHAPTER 24: THE GRAND PLAN

hicle lights, which meant that he would have to stay right behind me, at least within visual distance for the duration of the journey.

We motored on cautiously. It had been a heavy day and the action was beginning to have its effect. I must have lost concentration for a time, because when I looked around again I found that the white Kombi we were using as an ambulance was no longer following. What the hell now?

I stopped, waited a moment or two and then charged back along the road. When I saw the white shape of the vehicle ahead in the dark I pulled up and ran forward. The MO was nowhere in sight.

I walked around the vehicle, which looked as if the left front wheel was hanging over the edge of a sheer drop on the left of the road. Then I saw my medical officer standing precariously on the edge of the road holding onto his vehicle, hard.

'Doc, what on earth are you doing? Get away from there or you'll fall into the bloody river.'

'I can't let go, Sir ... the Kombi is going to fall over the edge.'

'Then let it be, what's wrong with you?'

'No, my medical kit is in there. Everything.'

'Okay, then hang on!'

With my garry and tow rope, we spent the next half hour dragging the Kombi back onto the road. When we'd finished I handed him a cool drink from the bag. 'Have a drink, Doc ... this has been a helluva day.'

We sat down and he sipped the drink in silence. I sensed that he wasn't in the best of moods so I let it ride. Eventually he broke the silence.

'I'm really sorry, Commandant.' He said in a limp voice.

'What happened?' I asked. 'You fall asleep?' I tried to make light of it but that didn't help either.

'Commandant, this isn't funny.' He had another power failure.

'Okay,' I replied. 'Who said it was funny?'

Then the truth emerged. He told me that he was night blind and that he couldn't see a bloody thing in the dark.

'When I lost you driving ahead, I didn't know where I was and just ran off the road.' He shrugged his shoulders in despair.

'Then why didn't you tell me?' I asked, adding that he could have got himself killed.

'I was too embarrassed. You people chase around here at night as if it were the most natural thing in the world to do. Meantime, I'm too scared to put my foot outside because I'm afraid I'll trip over something.'

I chuckled at the thought and he looked up sharply. 'You mustn't laugh at me, Commandant. It isn't easy to be like this.'

'I'm not laughing at you, Doc. Here, let me tell you a little secret. As you are night blind, so I have no sense of direction. As you can't see at night, I just cannot tell which way I'm going. If I can't see the sun or the stars, I haven't the vaguest idea in which direction I'm going. But then this, of course, is just between you and me.' The MO looked at me, astonished.

'I don't believe it, how do you make your way around at night?'

'I travel by the stars and, if it's cloudy, I get somebody to tell me the direction.' This explanation seemed to relax him a bit and then almost out of the blue, his face broke into a broad smile.

'Well, I'll be damned!' And he burst out laughing.

'Now don't you laugh at me, Doc. You have your problems, but it isn't easy to be like this ... but still, we make a good team ... you tell me which way to go and I'll see to it that you don't fall over things.' All the tension had disappeared. We finished our cool drinks and took off again, only this time I made very sure the Kombi was right on my tail.

We reached the rendezvous and there was nothing to do but wait. The medical officer settled down in his ambulance and I tried to get some sleep on the seat of my garry.

Only later that night I heard the approach of our patrol returning. I woke the MO and he attended to the casualty. We got him into the ambulance and I ordered two troops to accompany him. I also told the medical officer to use his lights this time because they were headed away from the enemy and make the best speed possible.

Driving with lights was no problem and he took off at a stiff clip. He was his old self again, in full control.

Coen and the patrol enjoyed their refreshments and we eventually followed the ambulance back to base at a more leisurely pace. Benguela Bridge, like Conda Bridge before, we all agreed, turned into a very different kind of experience.

Nasty, some would call it ...

CHAPTER 25

The Lord Takes Care of His Own

Now that it had become evident that we were not going to get across the river at any of the bridges, there was nothing we could do but mark time until headquarters at Cela decided what they wanted to do. However, sitting around doing nothing didn't appeal to me either...

One of the consequences of this kind of inactivity was that each day, at the crack of dawn, I'd take some of our heavier weapons and we'd head out from base and strike at enemy positions wherever we found them. Or we would target the other side of the river. We might have caused a lot of damage, but artillery always seemed to wrong-foot Luanda's forces.

It wasn't a one-way street. What did catch my attention was that we would hardly be in position before the enemy would either mortar or rocket our position. It was strange. I asked myself how it was possible that they could have been aware of our movements. Moreover, they were pretty accurate in tracking us and that puzzled me.

Until one morning when I took more notice than I'd done in the past of a column of white smoke that rose vertically from some high ground that overlooked our guns.

Finally it dawned on me: I'd seen similar smoke signals earlier in this ongoing operation and when I remarked about it, somebody suggested that it was the local population burning debris in their land. He might have been right, of course, because this was typical African custom almost everywhere on the continent and usually done before replanting the next crop.

Initially I accepted the explanation, but then it struck me: Hey, who cultivates anything on a mountaintop? Clearly, those were smoke signals. So the next time it happened, I directed my gunners to aim at the position from where the smoke was coming from. They were delighted, of course, because now they could engage a target with direct fire.

They were even more pleased when the smoke signals stopped as abruptly as they'd first appeared. But over the next few days someone persisted and we'd see smoke again. After several more of our gunnery exercises, all efforts at signalling by smoke were halted and we were left in peace to do our business without any harassment from the enemy.

It was difficult to tell how successful our sniping actually was, but it did keep the guys busy and I was content with the idea that the chaps across the river weren't getting much rest during daylight hours. Later we started doing the same thing after dark, but trying to get some sleep through barrages of accurately aimed 80-pound shells can take some getting used to.

At about this time, company commander Covacha received news that his father, mother and little sister, who had been farming in the vicinity of Vila Nova do Seles – not far from where we were then operating – had been burned out by the enemy. I told him to take a patrol and investigate.

On his return, Covacha reported that government forces were building a military-style Bailey Bridge over the river. Reports also came in that FAPLA vehicles were regularly spotted in the area of Conda, indeed, many more than before. This might have accounted for the reason his family had been targeted.

To our collective minds, all these events suggested that we should retaliate and, as a result, a lot of fighting talk resulted. This was when I decided to have a look at what those chaps across the river were actually up to.

Commandant Quiote – always fascinated by our guns – had been nagging me for a long time to take him along on one of my jaunts. While I wasn't very keen on the idea, he was so persistent that we finally decided to take him with us to Conda. Almost schoolboy-like, he was overwhelmed by excitement.

With a company of my men, I told Quiote to muster a company of his own soldiers, and with a troop of guns in support, we set out.

Reaching our final forward position, I deployed the guns behind some high ground that overlooked the bridge. With Sampson in support, we climbed the mountain and established an observation position on the forward slope so as to be able to observe what the enemy was doing below. Naturally our movements were cautious so as not to be detected, and we weren't. Not yet, anyway.

Using my radio, I ranged our guns directly onto enemy positions on the northern bank of the river, at which point our infantry started to move forward. Halting all movement, I gave orders for everybody to remain under cover and not become involved until I was able to establish the situation. Our guns firing volleys into FAPLA position, I hoped, would reveal all.

I engaged the positions with our artillery and, surprisingly, each time a volley of shells landed in their vicinity the Angolan soldiers would fire their rifles and machine guns. I couldn't understand what they were shooting at because there were none of our troops anywhere nearby. And certainly nothing visible from the other side of the river.

We carried on like this for a while and I was beginning to wonder who would run out of ammunition first: them or us?

Sampson was lying prone in the knee-high grass a short distance behind me with his radio. But then, quite suddenly, I got the feeling that we were no longer alone. I wasn't really sure what it was, but I sensed rather than saw movement in the grass ahead of me.

I signalled to Sampson to pass me my rifle, and looking through the sights at the direction of the unexpected movement, I slowly let off my safety catch. On the point of opening up with a burst of automatic fire, I was caught short with the appearance of a bunch of tail feathers of a guinea fowl. I hesitated for a moment and it was just as well that I did, because below the bundle of feathers appeared the floppy blue corduroy hat of Commandant Quiote.

His face was as white as a black face could ever be under the circumstances.

'Hey, Quiote, where have you been?' I asked in surprise.

'I was down by the bridge,' he replied hoarsely.

'You bloody fool. I've been shooting at the bridge for about half an hour.'

'Yes, I know, I've just come from there.' Shelling the enemy position didn't seem to be getting us anywhere so I had decided to try and knock out the bridge. I could only smile at this bloody fool.

There is no question that our 5.5-inch guns were extremely accurate. Manned by well-trained South African Army gunners their 80-pound shells could cause enormous damage in a direct hit. Also, our procedures were straightforward and, as expected, things went according to plan until Alex – who had a direct view of the bridge – screamed with delight into his radio.

'Hey, Commandant, you've hit the bridge. Dead centre ... the whole thing seems to be buggered and bent.'

I turned to the African officer who by now had taken up a position alongside me: 'That's it, Quiote! We've done our job for the day. Let's go home.'

When we arrived back at Novo Redondo I was surprised to see two Portuguese fellows waiting at the Pink House. They were strangers and I'd never seen them before. Their spokesmen explained that they were former Portuguese intelligence operatives with the old colonial security forces who had been sent to join Combat Group Alpha at Novo Redondo.

What surprised me was that they said they were there to help 'liberate Angola', something they declared with considerable enthusiasm.

There were thirteen of them in all and when I enquired what their background was, they assured me that they were very competent 'freedom fighters'.

'Very well,' I said, 'you all get yourselves ready. When we next go on patrol, you come along.' I wasn't at all excited about the prospect of having a bunch of hangers-on with my troops, but then I was willing to try everything because our resources were thin on the ground.

I did recall my previous experience with their likes. They behaved in exactly the same way. Also a largish group, they moved into the local hotel, opened the restaurant, got the local women to provide for all their needs, acquired what serviceable transport was available and promptly charged through town from shebeen to shebeen. They soon became known as the 'Dirty Dozen'.

I had rid the town of a crowd of FNLA ruffians and now I had this. Worse, I just didn't seem to be able to get rid of these guys. One particular incident is worth mentioning.

One afternoon, shortly after arriving back at the Pink House, the signals officer collared me and said that my presence was required at the village square. There was to be a public execution, he told me, something that I had no prior knowledge of.

Now, for a quiet country boy like me, I had adapted fairly well to the many and various surprises war had to offer, but this?

I'd already had a particularly heavy day and wasn't exactly in the

CHAPTER 25: THE LORD TAKES CARE OF HIS OWN

best of moods. 'What the hell are you talking about, man?' I asked the signals officer.

'Sir,' he answered, 'Quiote was here a while ago and he said he was going to execute one of the Dirty Dozen in public today at 1700 hours at the town square …' Those were his orders, he declared.

I didn't waste any time setting out for the square and sure enough, the entire FNLA battalion had been formed up. At the head was Quiote, together with a member of the Dirty Dozen squad up front.

The FNLA commander had worked himself up into quite a state by now, obviously high. Judging by the way he brandished his Luger pistol, I was wary of getting any closer. If he was going to shoot this guy, there was no telling who else was going to get hit. I stopped some distance off and listened as Quiote explained at length how this man had been a member of his unit and had not only deserted, but also committed a number of offenses punishable by death.

He declared to the gathering that he was now about to pass the death sentence and execute the man who had been charged, all in one go.

Being excitable as he was, as well as having a reputation for possessing a very itchy trigger finger, I couldn't predict exactly when he was going to shoot. But I knew that somehow I had to intervene. I walked closer with my hands in the air and my hair on end.

'Commandant, excuse me,' I was hugely deferential in my approach so as not to annoy the self-appointed executioner.

He didn't stop my approach, so I went on. 'I don't wish to interfere with your proceedings, but these people have been assigned to me to fight against FAPLA. If you now shoot one, you are depleting my fighting strength and I don't think my headquarters will take kindly to that. I will have to check with them, anyway, but in the meantime, hand the man over to me and if he gives me any trouble I will shoot him myself and save you the trouble.'

Quiote contemplated my offer for a short while and finally nodded, 'Okay, Commandant, it's a deal. But you can have him tomorrow. Tonight he must stay at the quartel.'

The next morning they delivered the unfortunate man to his buddies who took him to the sickbay for treatment because he was in very bad shape. I actually wasn't sure that I'd done him any favours by saving his life and, in retrospect, I should perhaps have let Quiote shoot him. He would have been a lot better off, poor chap.

The so-called Dirty Dozen took off quietly during the night. Where they went and what became of them, no one knows. I doubt if anyone really cared.

I was shaving early one morning when I became aware of the droning of an aircraft somewhere in the distance. This worried me because I wasn't partial to aircraft – any aircraft – just then because the previous day I had had a rather embarrassing encounter with one of our planes.

I'd sent out another patrol to the Gabela Bridge, and while they were out doing their job, I climbed the high ground that faced the river in a bid to retrieve the set of field-glasses and radio my so-called observers had abandoned the previous time.

I was about halfway up the hill when the sound of a low-flying aircraft drew my attention. Seconds later a small blue and white Cherokee came cruising merrily along the river at a very low level that kept it just above the water.

I looked back in the direction of my garry which I'd parked at the foot of the hill, and was close enough to see the little pink doll that some of my troops had tied onto the radiator grill: it was waving cheerfully at me in the breeze. With her bright red tartan skirt she stood out against the green background for the entire world to see.

The pilot had obviously also seen the doll because he pulled away from the river and started circling my vehicle. I was in the open and the only form of cover was a solitary tree about a hundred metres up the slope.

The pilot couldn't help but observe my movement and almost immediately swung his plane in my direction. I read his mind, and made for the tree. More to the point, I beat him to it by several metres and was just in time to dodge behind the trunk when somebody sitting in the co-pilot seat let rip with a burst of rifle fire through the open cockpit window.

I threw my arms around the trunk and moved around the trunk as the Cherokee roared past, making sure to keep the tree between myself and the guy on board that was trying to kill me. For how long this little drama went on, I'm not sure.

The idiot would fire shots in my direction each time the plane made a pass, but the chances of him hitting me was not very great. I actually got the impression that these guys were having a lot of fun at my expense. Besides, I could only imagine what the troops would think when they came back from their patrol to find me embracing a tree trunk.

This prospect actually bugged me a lot more than the possibility of me being shot. So the next time the plane made a pass, I dropped down onto one knee and emptied the magazine at it, which finally put an end to this silly game.

I don't suppose I had much chance of hitting the Cherokee, but the upshot was that the pilot wasn't eager to take any more chances. He dipped the left wing of the little craft and went back to zigzagging along the river bed.

I abandoned the search for my radio and returned to the vehicle. The little pink doll welcomed me with her pretty pink doll smile. I considered removing it, but changed my mind. Instead, I stroked her blond little plaits and whispered in her ear: 'That's okay, my little baby, they didn't scare us, did they?'

My thoughts drifted back to the present. I could still hear the aircraft flying about in our area and then its antics again surprised me because it was now circling our gun position.

Over the radio I shouted at the bombardier who was in command of the anti-aircraft guns: 'What's with you people? Why don't you shoot at that damned thing?'

'We don't know who it is, Sir. We thought maybe it was one of our people inspecting our position.'

'Well, don't think, shoot the thing!' I was shouting so loud that the pilot might have heard it. Moments later he made off in a northerly direction.

Later, back at base, I was having tea on the terrace when the radio operator stuck his head out of the tower and shouted: 'Sir, there's a Queen Air five minutes out … it's approaching from the south …'

His voice was drowned by the harsh bark of our 20 mm anti-aircraft gun and my blood ran cold. I had repeatedly warned Headquarters about arriving unheralded out of the blue without any warning.

'Stop! Stop!' I shouted. 'That's one of ours … don't shoot.'

'But its blue and white,' was the reply.

'Never mind what colour it is, just don't shoot!'

'But you said we must …'

'Never mind what I said,' I replied harshly. Then I realised how stupid this must have sounded to the bombardier, which was when I dropped the matter. I ordered Sampson to take my vehicle to the airstrip and bring whoever was on board the plane to the base.

When I had the chance to regain composure I spoke to the bombardier again. They'd seen the aircraft approaching and, bearing in mind what I had said earlier, he ordered the gun crew to open fire. As fate would have it, the camouflage net that covered the gun position caught the barrel of the gun just as the firing lever was pulled. The gun was slightly dislodged off its line of fire and a burst of anti-aircraft shells missed the tail of the plane by metres.

'Don't worry, buddy,' I said to the bombardier, 'you'll get your chance yet.'

A short while later my vehicle returned from the airstrip and I went downstairs to meet whoever it was that was bulletproof. Two guys came up the stairs, ahead of Sampson. They wore faded blue-grey SAAF flying overalls, but no badges of rank or other insignia. Both wore the traditional gold-rimmed dark glasses.

'Who's in command here?' barked the one with the more-expensive-looking glasses.

'Me!' I barked back.

'What's wrong with you people?' he demanded to know. His demeanour suggested that he was somebody who didn't have much regard for protocol.

'What's wrong with *us people*?' I retaliated.

'Why do you shoot at your own aircraft?'

'We don't – not if we know they are ours.'

'We told you we were coming.'

'Maybe you did, but that doesn't mean we heard you.'

'We called your operator when we were five minutes out and he acknowledged our call.'

'That's true,' I replied. 'But by that time you were already thirty seconds over our positions … and let me tell you something else. You have just flown over a section of the most potent anti-aircraft guns in the world and it's only by God's grace that you are alive to tell the story.'

The senior man removed his glasses. He then ogled me with some hostility, his flashing blue eyes like proverbial ice chips. At that point I thought I'd said enough and offered the newcomer my hand.

CHAPTER 25: THE LORD TAKES CARE OF HIS OWN

'Look,' I said, 'we don't usually welcome our guests like this. My name is Delville Linford and I command Combat Group Alpha.' The aviator grudgingly took my hand.

'I'm Commandant Julius Kriel, from the air component at Lobito Bay, this is my OPS officer. We're here on a liaison visit and to inspect the runway.'

'Well, gentlemen, come inside and let me offer you some tea.' I asked Mama Grande to pour for them. I then told them about what had happened before.

'Gentlemen, let me tell you what led up to this unfortunate incident.' I related the story of being strafed by the Cherokee and ended with my usual spiel about the dangers of pitching up unannounced. Curiously, I got the impression that neither of them was particularly interested.

When I got to the part of the camouflage net, the air force commandant looked at his OPS officer and raised his brows ever so slightly but said nothing. The other guy just sat there with a poker face, which, in my mind, suggested something.

They finished their tea and as soon as it was polite they excused themselves and left. What their inspection of the runway was like I wasn't told, but the liaison part of the visit was a complete disaster.

Some years later I was introduced to a very distinguished-looking gentleman in an Officers Mess back home.

The introduction was quite formal: 'Colonel Linford, this is Colonel Julius Kriel.' I gulped and then I recognised the man.

'Yes, I know,' I said, adding that each time I heard that name my blood ran cold.

'And every time I hear the name Delville Linford I get cold shivers up and down my spine,' was his retort.

'Well, at least we have something in common, and a lot to talk about, so let's have a drink.' We did, and went on to become very good friends.

Some folks believe in luck and nail a horseshoe on their door. Others call it good fortune. But call it what you will, to me Julius Kriel will always be a living reminder that the Good Lord has his very own way of taking care of his own.

It was a few days before Christmas and we were still at the Pink House when a Portuguese family arrived with a very sick baby. The medical officer examined the infant carefully and with great concern in his voice, he diagnosed leukaemia.

'If this child doesn't get expert medical care very quickly it will surely die.'

'Where is that likely to happen?' I asked.

'The only place I know of, Sir, is Pretoria.'

'And how are we supposed to achieve that from the middle of an Angola at war?'

'Search me,' came the disjointed reply.

Then it struck me that one of our air force planes was on its way in our direction to pick up some or other VIP chap that had to get to Cela.

I explained this rather complex situation to the family and they decided that there was no option but for the mother to go with the child to Cela. From there they believed they were sure to be able to evacuate both of them to Pretoria.

Reluctantly and with great emotional upheaval, the father and his young son took leave of the mother and baby girl. I thought it prudent to go along with them to possibly help things along, if I could.

Arriving at Cela, we were met by a car at the airport and hurried to the hospital in the village that was manned by the South African Medical Corps, as it was known at the time.

The hospital OC, Commandant Tony Dippenaar, confirmed the diagnosis. As fate would have it, the Minister of Defence, P.W. Botha, and his entourage of top brass were visiting the troops. Commandant Dippenaar explained the situation and the minister kindly consented for the woman and child to fly with them that afternoon.

I was promptly formed up to listen to General Malan's Christmas speech to the troops and subsequently invited to lunch. Apart from the food and the distinguished company of Ministers Botha and Chris Heunis, I was relieved that there was hope for the baby.

It just wasn't so easy after we'd returned to the Pink House to explain to the father and his little boy when his mother and little sister would be coming home.

What happened afterwards, I never did discover. I could only pray that somehow this tragic story would have a happy ending, but the devil kept telling me that this was one prayer that was going to remain unanswered.

CHAPTER 26

From Alpha to Omega

Christmas 1975 arrived soon enough. I spent the morning visiting the troops and wished them the compliments of the season.

Mama Grande, her daughter, and Mrs Covacha were busy with preparations for Christmas lunch. How Coen had managed to organise a supply of fresh fish from Cape Town, which the ladies prepared in traditional Portuguese 'codfish' style, is anybody's guess. It was delicious!

After that delightful lunch, we spent the rest of the day quietly. This was now my third Christmas in the bush and I could hardly remember how Christmas was spent in the 'States'. In the aftermath, I could see that each one of us was quietly busy with our own thoughts, memories and longings…

My thoughts turned towards the future. We'd already been given our marching orders, and any time now Operation Savannah would be another piece of history; for us anyway. We also arranged that Coen would take the unit back while I stayed on to hand over to my successor.

Apart from Mama Grande and her family, we'd picked up another family from their remote farm, the Covachas, packed them all into a three-ton truck and sent them off with the unit. The driver was a Portuguese volunteer who had joined the outfit somewhere along the line and he was given instructions to branch off before they reached the South West African frontier to make his way to the refugee camp in Katwitwi.

Commandant Myburgh, the OC of the relief battalion, was allocated a light aircraft of his own and we spent several days traversing the area so that he could become acquainted with the terrain and the enemy positions.

When that had been done I made my way to our headquarters at Cela. There I met an old friend, Paul Lombard, and Brigadier Johan Potgieter.

Lombard had been acting as Dr Savimbi's personal adjutant, and was now also on his way home. Brigadier Potgieter had already taken over command of the operation from Brigadier Dawie Schoeman who had gone back to this farm.

We spent a pleasant evening swapping stories and drinking whisky, possibly a fraction too much and that, unfortunately, was the last time I saw Johan. He was tragically killed in a helicopter accident shortly afterwards. The next day I made my way to Rundu where I ran into General Magnus Malan.

I wasn't shy to ask for a lift to Waterkloof Air Base in his private jet, after all, the plane was half-empty. It was actually quite a lot of fun to see how the other half lived.

So ended the year of our Lord 1975. I was glad to have been a part of such a remarkable and exhilarating adventure and was more than happy that the Good Lord had thought it fit to bring me out of the whole thing unscathed. I was also enormously pleased that I was able to play my small part in the history of the Bushman people and 31 Battalion.

A lot of stories are told of these people, some true, others apocryphal. The fact is that while an awful lot happened to the Bushman unit in a very short space of time, not everything happened as some said it did. It fact, quite a few whoppers emerged that are quite embarrassing. At the same time, there are several events that took place that are well worth recounting because, collectively, they put matters into proper perspective.

Indeed, the real Bushman story for the history books is their loyalty, their uncanny skills and their remarkable ability to rise to the occasion when called upon. This is truly a society apart and for those of us who were involved with them, an experience of which to be proud.

After we'd returned from Operation Savannah, we were incorporated into the South West African Defence Force. Among other things, this meant that our name – the unit to which we belonged – was altered, for reasons only known to those 'Desk Jonnies' responsible for such things way back in Pretoria.

We ended up becoming 31 Battalion, while Bravo was renamed 32 Battalion. In turn, both now became what was termed Border Units, like some of the others in 1 Military Area.

CHAPTER 26: FROM ALPHA TO OMEGA

The names of the bases were also changed, and not always for the better, I fear. Bravo promptly altered its name to *Pick-a-Pow* (woodpecker in the Bushman language), but we had great difficulty in finding a suitable title to replace the well-known and dearly beloved Alpha. That was a place that had become so deeply engraved in the hearts of so many of our people.

One day Coen and I were summoned to the regional headquarters at Rundu. We were speculating morosely on a new name for the base, but when we turned off the highway into the base at Rundu, we still hadn't figured out a replacement.

I turned to him and said: 'Coen, this has been a great time in my life but it all appears to be coming to an end. We might as well call the place Omega.' The inference was alpha and omega – the beginning and the end. And so the camp became Omega.

It took a while for the name to take hold and to be frank, with some of the old timers it never really did. In their hearts, Alpha will always be Alpha and we could never forget the good and the bad of that beautiful place in the heart of the western Caprivi.

With the integration of Group Alpha into the SADF, we also had to produce a unit emblem. There were some lengthy discussions in the mess and we finally settled on using the ubiquitous Caprivi black crow as our unit motif. And again, there are numerous stories told about the reason this crow was chosen, but none are true.

The real reason is as follows: With the arrival of the group of FNLA soldiers in Alpha, Godfather, who was running our operation from Defence Headquarters in Pretoria, got me on the Flossie – one of the regular flights to the border, usually a C-130 or French-built C-160 – to discuss the matter. During our initial talks it was suggested that because of the clandestine nature of South Africa's involvement that was developing in Angola and our 'secret' role in that civil war, those involved – the Bushman unit in particular – had to be given a code name.

'I think we should call them *mossies* or canaries, or something like that,' he said, *mossies* being the Afrikaans word for sparrows.

I replied flippantly: 'They look more like crows to me than sparrows.'

'Okay,' he replied, 'then we'll call them *kraaie* (crows)'.

The name stuck and although the Flechas were not strictly black Africans like the majority of FNLA troops – in fact the skins of some of these little people had a distinctly yellowish tinge – the combat unit went on to inherit that name.

While in Pretoria, I paid a visit to one of the heraldry artists and asked that a picture of a crow be drawn for me. Unfortunately, I wasn't able to answer the kind of questions that the dear ladies wanted to know about unit origins and so forth, so they told me to buzz off.

Fortunately, I had a friend in the office next door by the name of Chris Wehrmann. He'd overheard the conversation, and once we got together, I explained the situation. A short while later I received the most beautiful drawing of a black crow from what I supposed was the 'heraldry department'.

Unfortunately, the graphics involved didn't make it suitable for a cap badge. So, with a black fibre-tip pen, I sketched a black crow against the backdrop of a white cloth and one of the Portuguese ladies sewed it onto my beret. Later the heraldry ladies sewed black crow badges for the troops and the badge had come to stay.

Another bunch of women working in the clothing factory excelled in producing the regimental flag. It consisted of a black linen material with a white circle in the middle and a black crow at the heart of a white circle.

To get this flag approved by the so-called 'powers that be' back home was another matter. Fortuitously, this was solved during one of the cursory visits by Defence Minister P.W. Botha.

After his aircraft had landed and we walked together from the airport to our headquarters, a fresh breeze suddenly caught our flag on a flagpole at the entrance to our headquarters. Almost ceremoniously it billowed open, as if I had ordered it to do so by some hidden signal.

'Ah,' said the minister appreciatively, 'now *that* is a really nice flag'.

'Thank you, Sir!'

With that ministerial 'approval' our crow had come to stay.

The other issue that caused quite a lot of trouble was our headgear. The standard army bush hat worn by South African forces on the border had a fairly broad rim, the intent being to protect our men from the sun, which, for many months of the year could be blistering.

The Bushmen got theirs but then they would tuck the hat rim under the hat on either side, leaving only the front and rear ends sticking out. When I asked them why they did this, they said the normal extended brim tended to make it difficult for them to hear properly in the bush.

'Come now, Luinna,' I declared to one of my men with a disbelieving smile, 'you guys are taking this thing too far. The white soldiers can hear perfectly without any of them tucking in the brims.'

The reply to this comment was salient: 'Commandant, the problem with you white people is that you don't know that you *cannot* hear.'

I recall an incident early one morning during one of our operations. We had made plans to attack a village in the interior because the intelligence guys had said it accommodated terrorists. But for a short while before we set out, we were stymied because our guide that had been designated to lead us to the village didn't pitch as he should have. Undeterred, I decided to give it a go anyway. We set our compasses at the bearing I judged the village to be and we set off.

After blundering through the bush for what felt like hours, one of our Flecha combatants pulled me by the shirt. 'Commandant,' he pointed, 'we have to go this way.' He indicated a direction to the left of where we were headed, but I told him to beat it, and carried on.

A little while later the man approached me once more.

'Commandant, we are going the wrong way, we must go this way.' He pointed again. This time I listened. I told him to point in the direction that he thought the village lay and I took a bearing over his arm. I told our platoon leaders to swing their compasses 15 degrees to the left. After a bit more bundu-bashing we walked straight into the village.

When it was all over I asked the Flecha how he knew where the village was and his reply was succinct: 'I could hear the roosters crowing.'

In any event, our Bushman troops continued with the tucked-in headgear, but so did the grumbling. Eventually I was forced to do something about it.

The Portuguese uniform that I had been wearing had a Glengarry type of cap, but with a peak at the front and a hang-over stretch of cloth behind. This combination irritated me and I tore them off, leaving only what appeared to resemble a traditional Glengarry. Because I wasn't 'officially' associated with the South African Army at that stage – we operated kind of semi-autonomous, though obviously our orders still came from the same headquarters as before – nobody gave much attention to whatever gear my guys had on, head coverings included.

The cap I wore was very comfortable and I asked the ladies from the dress shop to make another similar batch from the same brown army material worn by our regular forces. This was a great success and that was the origin of the 'keppie' that became part of 31 Battalion tradition.

But the battle wasn't over yet because army dress regulations once again caused a bit of a furore. It took a visit by the then Chief of the Army, General Magnus Malan, to sort out this business.

From stores, I drew an army hat with a particularly broad rim, and during my briefing – which took place under some large mopani trees – I kept my hat on and I would peer at the general from under the rim, obviously looking a bit like the village idiot, which was my intention. This went on a while, at least until General Malan couldn't take it anymore.

'Linford, now take off that bloody hat,' he ordered.

'Sorry, Sir.' I removed the hat, and later, while walking through the camp, I donned one of our khaki 31 Battalion 'keppies'. Whether the general noticed it or not, I'll never know, but he said nothing.

Later when the matter was raised at Rundu, I said that the 'keppie' had been personally approved by General Malan and this kind of brought the matter to a close.

And so the 'keppie' became official headgear for 31 Battalion.

CHAPTER 27

Life After Savannah

By the time Operation Savannah had officially ended and we returned from Angola, the population at our original base camp had grown substantially. In fact, Alpha was battling to contain so many people, and they seemed to have come from just about everywhere.

'Godfather' General Fritz Loots, the man who had originally founded South Africa's Special Forces, was adamant that the new camp must be built of mopani trees – which are common to this northern region. They were to be thatched with buffalo grass. But it took almost 300 hundred young mopani trees to build a single hut and I pointed out that if we had to build the entire camp using mopani, we'd exterminate the species in the process in that region.

The alternative was split poles holding up corrugated iron roofs. The idea was approved and with the help of Commandant Steve Cope (an architect from the office of the Quartermaster General) we laid out the camp. By May 1975 Second Lieutenant Da Silva from 5 Military Works Unit started to build the first log cabins. These all took a long time to erect – too long, in fact – and the idea was scotched in favour of pre-fabricated wooden huts imported from what was then still Rhodesia.

So did the new camp, a couple of kilometres north of Alpha, come into being, and in record time. By February 1976 we were able to move in and this camp was not renamed Omega as suggested by some of us. The camp remained Alpha for a long time after I'd left and the name Omega was only coined much later.

What was a quiet little community in the old camp soon evolved into a throbbing village. While the soldiers were kept busy with border operations, women and children of all ages were roaming around the base with nothing to do. Still worse, they had all day to do it. The girls did not present much of a problem to start with, but that was not the case with the boys.

For almost forever, these youngsters had been accustomed to roaming the bush with their fathers. It was part of tribal lore and tradition: it was what the Bushman people had always done. But now their fathers were otherwise employed and these juveniles had nothing to do except get up to mischief. One day, one of them shattered the windscreen of one of my former Portuguese Army Unimogs with a catapult and that was the final straw.

I mustered every national serviceman available in the immediate area and told them to round up all the boys in the camp. We herded them together in the open clearing in the centre of the camp, lined them up in single file, the tallest on the right and the shortest on the left.

Then I divided them into five equal lots and assigned a young soldier to each group. They listened attentively while I addressed the group:

'Okay, now we have a school. You lot,' and I pointed towards the smallest of the assemblage (some were little more than toddlers), 'you will be "Class One". And you,' I said, pointing to the second group, 'you are "Class Two",' and so on until we had five classes in all, each one of them with his teacher, which would be one of the national servicemen who would 'volunteer' for the task, though they didn't yet know it.

The Bushman youngsters thought it was a huge joke. Some started giggling, others laughed out loud. They'd never heard anything like it. School! Forget it! was the message imparted.

'You mustn't laugh,' I said, stressing that this was a serious business. 'You are making history, because this is the very first Bushman school in the world and it must also be the best in the world. So you'd better get your backsides into it and I don't want any nonsense.'

One of the troopies involved piped up: 'Commandant, what are we to teach these kids? I've never taught anybody anything in my life, let alone these little savages who most times can't understand a word I'm saying.'

Another added seriously: 'Me too, Commandant ... doesn't work for me either.'

I told all the national service troops present that they were not to worry. 'You'll learn fast,' I said. Then I added: 'You can count, can't you – we'll teach them that, and to speak Afrikaans ... you know, things like that. And keep the little buggers out of trouble ...'

I turned to Bokvoet, my translator. 'You tell them they are to stay with their teachers and not to leave them under any circumstances. If I find one of them roaming around I'll tie him to a tree ... or something.'

The whole business was actually quite foreign to us all and I wasn't sure of the ground we were covering in such rapid strides or even if it would work. But I left them to it and for the rest of the morning went about my business of running a camp and trying to fight a war.

I had all but forgotten the whole thing until lunch time, when an irate young soldier stormed into the dining room.

'Sir, you had better come and sort out this damned school of yours, I've got two dozen brats in my cabin and they won't leave because you told them to stay with me.'

We sorted out the teething problems as they arose and the school got under way. I was pleased that after the first difficult week, it had gathered momentum all on its own. Also, I was always amazed and often amused at the initiative displayed by some of the youthful 'teachers', quite a few still in their teens. I even got the impression they were beginning to enjoy their new role.

Walking between the classes one morning, I found to my surprise that the 'Baby Class' – as it had been dubbed – had all the children sitting flat on the ground and in a straight row. Each child had his legs around the child in front of him and the one in front was holding the ankles of the one behind him. I watched in fascination.

'Corporal, what on earth are you doing?' I asked, perplexed. This was not what I'd imagined they'd be doing.

'Feeding the kids, Sir, why?'

'Yes, but isn't this a rather unusual way of doing it?'

'Well, I suppose it is, but then everything is a bit unusual here, Sir, isn't it?'

'Well, yes, but just as a matter of curiosity, why do you feed the one at the back and not start at the front of the line?'

'Tried that, Sir, but it's impossible to get these little buggers to keep still for long enough to feed any of them. I'd worked out that the front kid holds the feet of the one behind him so he can't snatch anything and the other one can't run around. The one who has his hands free is the rear one, so I feed him ... seems to work quite well.'

'Okay, then, if it works it must be right.'

I strolled towards the next class, the so-called 'Senior Class'. The teacher had them all neatly lined up in three ranks, standing at ease. As I arrived, the troopie called them all to attention and saluted. They too all saluted, then cheered and finally clapped their hands in glee.

One of the other classes I visited was busy with a drawing lesson. One of the children had drawn a street, something he'd never experienced for real because none of them had ever been beyond the bush.

'Corporal, surely these kids haven't been out of this bush, how do they know what a street in the city looks like?'

He answered that he'd asked the boy about it and he had said that he remembered the stories Kambinda had told them when he returned from his visit to the doctor in Pretoria.'

One lives and learns, it seems.

It wasn't long before most of the young girls at the base also wanted to join the school. I had my doubts, but I felt that since I was in for a penny, it might as well be in for a pound.

We incorporated them all and things went from strength to strength.

Some of the girls were already teenagers and I didn't think it was a good thing for them to attend class in boob tubes and mini-skirts. So I discussed this with some of the Portuguese ladies and they ended up deciding to make them all proper school uniforms. Once we bought some white linen material the ladies got stuck in.

This was something totally new and obviously the girls were thrilled with their white wrap-around school dresses. But then, shortly afterwards, the teachers started complaining that the boys looked shabby in their everyday clothes and that the girls were getting preferential treatment. They suggested that the boys also be issued with uniforms. We got in touch with our contacts in Pretoria and soon the boys were marching around proudly in grey shirts and trousers.

In fact, everybody at Alpha was marching: boys and girls alike, big and small. Everybody marched.

I returned from an operation by aircraft one morning and as we circled the airfield to get downwind, I was surprised to see hundreds of children in their ranks all marching in the direction of the airfield. By the time I'd deplaned, the whole school was formed up and started to sing.

It was the finest welcome I'd ever experienced.

However, what had been worrying me for quite some time was the fact that the Bushman boys were no longer exposed to the vagaries of the bush as their fathers had been. One could hardly expect their tracking skills and bush craft to last if they were not exposed to the kind of conditions in which their fathers and forefathers had grown up in and were given solid opportunities to practise these arcane skills.

We decided to send the boys in the Senior Class into the wilds for bush training over weekends. We picked three of the top sergeants and divided the class into three groups and they were given a small group each.

The boys were handed a water bottle each and went off with their sergeants, with the strict instruction that they were to learn how to survive in the bush.

The sergeants were allowed to take their rifles but with strict orders to use them in emergencies only.

This series of exercises turned out to be an enormous success, so much so that we had difficulty in keeping the little ones from sneaking off after the others. In fact it wasn't long before the girls complained that the boys were being given preferential treatment and that they were being neglected.

I wondered what we could do about this. Coen didn't have any bright ideas either, so I discussed it with the village elders. They suggested we allocate a piece of ground for the girls and teach them to make and keep a garden.

'But surely that's a boy's task,' I remonstrated.

'Not at all,' they assured me. 'It was the man's task to hunt but the women had to provide the rest.' As food wasn't the problem, I suggested that each class be allocated several of the large trees in the base. The girls were to make and keep flower beds around the trees and this would keep them busy and the trees would be regularly watered: a win-win situation for all.

I told them when I laid out my plans that the exercise would serve to beautify the base. The scheme was accepted with great enthusiasm and it worked really well.

However, real problems with the school started when the Department of Education in South Africa somehow heard of our goings-on in the bush.

One day, from nowhere, a stranger arrived. He introduced himself as Inspector somebody-or-other and told me that he had arrived to see how his department could, as he put it, 'get involved'.

I gave him a briefing of sorts and hoped that he would take the next transport back home. I'd already stressed that I was extremely busy with a very delicate operation in the bush. But as I might have expected, this was not to be.

The fellow made his inspection and then, like a good teacher, he made us sit around a table to discuss the matter. Coen would have nothing to do with it so he left me alone with the inspector.

The man spun the little wheels of the locks on his black fibreglass briefcase and produced a number of books and these he placed – almost ceremoniously – before me on the table.

'These, Commandant, are the syllabi for the different classes as prescribed by the Department of Education. They are for you to implement as soon as possible. I will forward more copies if needed and if you would let me have a list of stationery and other requirements, I'll see what can be done ...'

He was still droning on when I lifted the cover of the book on top and with one finger, flicked the pages. I didn't really take an interest in the contents but I was shaken rigidly to attention when my eye fell on a heading that read something like 'The arrival of Jan van Riebeeck at the Cape in 1652'.

I was astonished. Effectively, the piece suggested that the entire African continent only had its real start when the first of the Dutch settlers arrived at the Cape, which he and I both knew was rubbish.

'But surely you can't be serious about this,' I said. 'These people have a perfect understanding of time and space but they are not able to express the concept in understandable terms because of their lack of understanding of the elements of arithmetic or science. Yet you want me to teach them about a person that is of absolutely no concern to anybody except to historians and school teachers.' The man's face fell. He pulled himself together and then addressed me with grave concern.

'I beg your pardon, Commandant. I cannot agree with you. But that is neither here nor there, because we are here to see that the education policy that has been laid out for your unit is complied with.'

He stopped for a moment to see whether he was making any progress. I suspected that he could see I viewed his approach with skepticism.

Then he went on. 'And while we are on that subject of policy, I notice that you are using the girls to do the gardening while the boys are roaming about in the bush. I wish to point out that it is completely wrong.'

Mmm ... I thought. I had suspicions of my own that he would touch on that without regard for reasons why these programmes were initiated in the first place.

'I appreciate that you are planting flowers to beautify the place, but would it not be more beneficial if you get the boys to do this instead of the girls? And to teach them to plant vegetables, instead of flowers?'

With that little verbal broadside, the official from the Department of Education sat back in his chair and waited for me to respond.

'And what would you suggest we do with the girls?' I asked. 'Let them roam around the bush?'

'No, get them involved in needlework, what else?'

'I see, and where do we get the needles?'

'We will supply a number of sewing machines and the necessary additional material so you can get sewing classes going for the girls.'

'That'll be nice, just make sure there are sufficient *Teach Yourself Sewing* books so that my men and I can get the hang of the thing first.'

'Very well then, Commandant, that is all from me. Carry on with the good work and we'll be in touch from time to time to see how you are getting along.' He then asked for transport because he said he had 'other business' to discuss at Katima Mulilo.

With time, some of the boys started to outgrow the base school and we decided to establish a cadet platoon.

The youngsters were issued with cadet uniforms obtained from back home and United States M-1 carbines. They were taught the drills and other basic military subjects in preparation for their absorption into the army, while school subjects like reading, writing and arithmetic continued.

The boys assumed their new role with so much enthusiasm that we entered them for a drill competition in Rundu where they walked away with flying colours.

From then on every schoolboy on our base had just one ambition and that was to become a cadet.

As was my custom I got up one night in the small hours and walked around the base and eventually ended up at the sick bay. The place was generally in darkness, but a dim light was on in one of the wards. I made my way there. The scene that confronted me was almost crazy.

One of the national service medical orderlies was sitting on a bed. He was a huge boy, built like Apollo. He was stripped to the waist with muscles bulging all over his sun-tanned torso. In one enormous hand he held a feeding bottle while stretched out comfortably in the palm of the other hand was a little Bushman baby, sucking noisily at the teat.

The troopie looked up with a rather sheepish expression because I was chuckling quietly to myself. 'What are you laughing at, Commandant? You think I like feeding pocket-size Bushman babies in the middle of the night?'

'I know, my boy ... just stick out the rigmarole for now. We will get to training their own people as nurses. Meantime, I think you're doing a great job.'

Following this and some other incidents, we decided to train some of the young girls as nurses. The project was undertaken with solid dollops of enthusiasm but, ultimately, the girls never really became nurses in the true sense of the word.

The problem stemmed from the reality that they were being asked to enter a different kind of world, far and away from the tribal mores and traditions of their society in general. Working professionally at a job like nursing was totally alien to them, with the result that the exercise never really got off the ground.

For the duration, any real nursing at the base still had to be handled by our medics.

CHAPTER 28

Post-Savannah Tracker Operations

Because the Bushmen had established a solid record as reliable combatants against what had become a resilient and determined SWAPO enemy, a lot more demands were made on their services. They were involved in numerous operations throughout Ovambo, and while I had no problem with this, problems started to surface when South African commanders started commandeering Bushman soldiers in bids to utilise them as trackers.

This brought us face to face with the problem they had had in earlier days with the SA Army. The Bushmen were sent ahead of the troops and if the enemy had planted an ambush, the leading Bushmen would be the first to be killed. The troops would then launch an attack and disperse the enemy.

I was not taken with this idea and this led to serious clashes with some gentlemen from the 'States'.

I remember one particular incident during an operation. The commanding officer of an infantry battalion was briefing the young company commander of a Bushman company on a pending operation. The company commander in question was known for his lack of tact, so I sneaked into the tent where they were talking. Neither of them knew I was there.

It became immediately clear that the officer was trying to split the Bushman unit that had been allocated to him into little groups and attach them to his platoons as trackers. My company commander objected, quite strongly, as it turned out, and it wasn't long before the discussion developed into a fairly heated argument.

The unit commander took offence to the junior officer's lack of respect and told him so in no uncertain terms. When translated the conversation went like this:

'I don't mean to be rude, Sir, but you're talking crap.'

I simply couldn't let this conversation go on.

'Sorry, Commandant,' I started, 'I don't mean to interrupt.'

'Who the hell are you?'

'I am the commanding officer of this young man, and seeing that you are so direct, I'm afraid I have to agree with him. I can put it more politely – but I also think you are talking crap.'

I told him in almost as many words that the young man he'd been addressing had an awful lot of experience with these people and that he'd be well advised to listen to him.

I wasn't able to finish. The commandant stormed out of the tent mumbling what we could do with our 'bloody savages'.

The consequence of this little incident was that the Bushmen were effectively, to use the appropriate military phrase, 'left out of battle'. But the word had got out and the next day, while we were hanging around, waiting for something to happen, I was told that General Constand Viljoen who had flown in by helicopter, wanted to see me. Expecting the worst I reported to our headquarters.

'Morning,' the general greeted me curtly and we shook hands. Without further formality, he posed the question: 'Can these Bushmen of yours track from the air?'

'I don't know, General, they can't even fly.'

'Listen,' he said, 'an infantry unit has been chasing a set of tracks now for days and each time they get within reach, night falls. As a result the terrorists are able to slip away as soon as it gets dark.'

I nodded, expecting more and he didn't hesitate: 'I want you to put one of your Bushman trackers in my helicopter, the pilot will take him to the troops in the field and let's see whether he can get these people before dark.'

This I had to see, I thought as I climbed into the chopper with Pedro, one of my most experienced trackers. I told him what we were going to do and he thought it would be great fun, particularly since he had never been up 'in one of these things' before.

The pilot flew us directly to the point where the infantry troops were following tracks. Still in the air and flying just ahead of the pursuers on the ground below, he had no difficulty in picking up tracks and from his seat behind the pilot he steered him left or right by pulling on one of the epaulettes on the aviator's shoulders. I was amazed.

It wasn't long before we followed the tracks into a native village. Pedro signalled for the pilot to circle the village and, sure enough, he was onto the tracks again where they left the village on the other side.

CHAPTER 28: POST-SAVANNAH TRACKER OPERATIONS

I was beginning to get the hang of the thing and at one stage I said to Pedro, 'Hey, Pedro, these are not the tracks we have been following, these are different.'

'Sure, they're different, but they are the same people ... because we are getting very close now they have taken off their boots and are running ... these people are worried.'

Just as I was beginning to wonder what we were going to do when we found the buggers we were looking for, Pedro grabbed the pilot's shoulders with both hands and nearly pulled him out of his seat. He was aware, he said afterwards, that the plane was being shot at.

'Commandant,' he shouted, 'we must get away fast, we are directly over them, they have scattered!' A moment later, even more urgently, he called out: 'Pilot, let's get out of here, they're below us!' Because we were flying so low, Pedro feared that we would come under more enemy fire at any moment.

The chopper pilot wasted no time. He pulled his machine up and away from there so fast it made my head spin.

After we'd landed the pilot did an all-round inspection in his helicopter and found a bullet hole in one of the rotor blades. I didn't realise the full significance of this until I looked at the pilot's face – we were pretty lucky that we didn't take more serious knocks, any one of which could have gone into our hydraulics and crippled the chopper. By then General Viljoen had joined our little group at the improvised helicopter pad.

'Well,' he asked, 'what happened?'

I turned to him and replied: 'General, I have just done two chopper recces'.

'When was the other time?'

'Today. The first and the last, General.' With that, I told him what had taken place while we were aloft.

'Well, at least now we know,' he replied after I'd finished my report and judging by the smile he was left with, the good man was obviously amused by my reaction.

'Yes indeed, Sir. Now we know ...'

Several other incidents also took place that involved my Bushmen. By now these little people had been involved in numerous operations and had achieved an astonishing success rate. With it, my unit had gained an enviable reputation: the Bushmen were excellent trackers.

But there was also the problem that once they'd achieved their measure of success in the field and knew where the enemy was, how many of them there were, where they were headed, and so on, they simply didn't know what to do with all that information. Obviously there were many opinions.

It was argued that if three Bushman trackers were seconded to a team with two national servicemen, my guys could pass on what they knew to the servicemen and they 'being more intelligent' could make the necessary deductions. Of course I didn't agree, but the order came through that I had to send a dozen of my best trackers to Grootfontein for a course. There they would marry up with a group of national servicemen, and a tracking instructor detached from the School of Infantry in South Africa would train them and form them into what was hoped would be several expert tracking teams.

I selected a dozen of my young Barakwenas and briefed them. When I told them that they were going on a course to Grootfontein, they were about as excited as I'd ever seen these folk. Now *this* would be an adventure, they told one another. What it all meant to them was difficult to fathom, but in their minds, all this rigmarole clearly had a monumental effect on their lives. Sadly, it was ephemeral.

I wasn't able to go along, but according to the officer that accompanied them the episode was a disaster from the start.

At Infantry School it was common practise to shout in a very loud voice when the troops get to the parade ground: 'Form up!', and if the soldiers supposedly didn't act sharply enough, the standard drill was: 'Come on, you idle lot, you see that tree way up on the hill, bring me a leaf!'

The young servicemen, freshly out of basic training, were already accustomed to this kind of drill which is standard fare in most armies and they would set off at a stiff gallop for the lone tree perhaps a kilometre away. Everybody, that is, except the Bushmen.

Naturally the instructor was infuriated and he would turn to them: 'Come on, you idiots, don't stand there like fools. Go and get me a leaf … all of you!'

The Bushmen looked puzzled. Then one of them would amble over to a shrub nearby and from it, he'd pick a leaf and give it to the instructor.

Annoyed, the instructor would bellow that he didn't want that bloody leaf: 'I want one from that tree,' he'd declare pointing.

CHAPTER 28: POST-SAVANNAH TRACKER OPERATIONS

Which, more often than not would result in the question: 'What do you want with that leaf? It is good for nothing, but this leaf is good, you can use it for heeling sores and it also keeps the mosquitoes away if you rub it into the skin. Look!' the tracker enthusiastically demonstrated as he rubbed the leaf on his arm.

In exasperation the instructor then turned to the officer. 'Sir, please explain to these savages what this is all about.' But it never was and by the time the *dienspligtiges* (soldiers) had returned from the designated tree on the hill, the matter had been dropped.

Though things went reasonably well for a while and the Bushman candidates were making the most of playing the role of ignorant students, they enjoyed these little charades immensely. Whenever the instructor said something that did make sense to them, they'd nudge each other and vociferously agree.

When something emerged that they either thought was plain stupid or didn't agree with, they'd discuss it amongst themselves. Then they would explain to the instructor where he'd gone wrong.

One way or another, things got to the point where they were told that they were going to display their acumen and do a practical tracking exercise. All the students were told to cover their eyes while an assistant instructor laid a track. He walked in a wide semi-circle and hid behind a small bush some distance behind the group.

A bright young serviceman was first to try, but he hadn't gone far when he lost the track and stood staring vacantly at the ground. This resulted in guffaws of laughter from the Bushmen.

'Okay, wise guy, it's your turn now,' he said, pointing at one of the Bushmen. These youngsters jumped up enthusiastically and immediately headed off in the opposite direction to where the track had been laid.

'No, you fool, this way!' shouted the instructor. 'You're supposed to be so smart, but you can't even *see* the track, let alone follow it.'

'Here, let me show you,' and the NCO pointed at the ground. 'There it is,' he said in a loud voice, at which point the Bushman tracker turned around and pointed directly at the bush.

'But there is the man behind that bush,' the little Bushman tracker firmly declared. He'd obviously been onto this little ruse from the start.

That, unfortunately, or perhaps fortuitously, was the end of what seemed to be a good idea but went on to become an absolute farce.

The exercise in forming tracker teams having failed and tracking by chopper being too risky, we now had to devise other ways to speed up our tracking techniques.

Because of their outstanding eyesight and their already proved ability to read tracks from a distance, we started working on having our Bushman trackers working from moving vehicles. The idea was immediately successful: trackers on vehicles could move a lot faster than the enemy on foot and they invariably caught up with them.

It didn't take long for the routines they followed to become standard practice within the various Ovamboland operational areas. Once our trackers were within striking distance of the enemy, troops following up in Buffels or Casspirs would disembark and the results were inevitable.

Once again 31 Battalion was on track.

We got Warrant Officer Koos Moorcroft and Staff Sergeant Dewald de Beer – two of the top instructors from the Reconnaissance Regiment – to spend some time with us. They trained our men in some of the esoterics of scouting and other related skills such as first aid, support, back-up and so on.

One fine Saturday afternoon, while the troops were busy with their training, Koos and I were relaxing in the shade of the tree beside the mess. We'd taken a bit of time off and were enjoying a glass of beer.

'Koos,' I said, 'you guys with all your experience, tell me what you'd do if a clutch of mortar bombs were suddenly to start falling all around us ... what do you reckon we'd do?'

'I don't know, Commandant, I think we'd grab another beer and lie low.'

During the final months of Portugal's presence in Angola (and Lisbon's other African possessions) Pretoria made whatever contacts it could with those members of the Portuguese security forces who were still trying to 'hold the fort'.

It was a futile effort of course. After five centuries in Africa, this colonial power had run its course. In brief, it lacked the will to continue fighting which resulted in all its troops being pulled back to the European metropolis.

Some of the old guard – quite a few of them with strong South

Africans contacts – remained at their posts and many of them helped ease the transition as best they could. Among these was an old bush veteran and former security force commander, Oscar Cardoso, who had made a name for himself combating insurgent forces in South Angola. It was he who actually brought Angolan Bushmen into the war, training and arming them to fight the rebels who for so many years had persecuted them, most times with unconscionable brutality.

Years after Delville Linford and his men had returned to South African soil after Operation Savannah and Cardoso had returned to live in a mountain village north of Oporto, this former Portuguese commander paid a belated tribute to the unit which he had originally founded under the green and red Portuguese banner.

He wrote:

> *Colonel Delville Linford,*
>
> *The first time I saw the !Xun people was in 'The Land of the End of the Earth', in Angola in 1966. I was really impressed by the ability of these people with bow and arrow, by their extraordinary tracking capabilities and their special hunting skills. At the same time, they were really tough and frugal.*
>
> *These people, known ethnologically as 'Bushmen', were, in the distant past, the dominant race in Africa. After successive and massive invasions by other races which outnumbered them, they had to withdraw, always fighting, to the most desolate regions of the Black Continent where they struggled to survive and to resist the humiliations inflicted by the invaders.*
>
> *We [the Portuguese people] gave them freedom to live, human being status and a fatherland to worship. We formed with them highly mobile units of counter-guerrilla warfare [the Flechas] to defend the Christian civilisation and the principles on which we believed and they also.*
>
> *As retribution they fought on our side and some fell with us in a war which we won in the battlefields but which were, ultimately, lost by the treachery of our politicians in Lisbon.*
>
> *The character of the !Xun people fitted perfectly in the very ancient principles of the guerrilla defined by Sun Tzu: 'Faster than the wind and as mysterious as the bush. Destroyers like the fire and as*

silent as the mountains. As impenetrable as the night and as furious as the thunder ...'

I had the honour of being their first commander and instructor and had the privilege of learning with them.

Today we gathered to pay homage to the veterans of the 31 Battalion, and to you for the way you led them, understood them, dignified and protected their families. A military unit is the reflection of its commander. You managed to achieve their esteem, loyalty and dedication. You have made history in southern Africa.

In my name and in the name of all who are attending this ceremony, I want to express our admiration for you as a soldier, and as a man for the results achieved and for having given them a uniform of the prestigious SADF, which I also had the honour and privilege of serving.

Finally, I ask you to tell your brave men that they were the most gratifying experience of my life. The Flechas still remain in my heart and will always be in my prayers. To those who paid the highest price in battle, my profound respect and saudade.

To Colonel Delville Linford and his men, I wish all the very best. God shall bless you, your families, your children and the generations to come.

To South Africa: Alles van die beste.

Signed: **Oscar Cardoso, September 2011**

CHAPTER 29

Exit Alpha

All good things come to an end, and so did Delville Linford's adventures at the head of Combat Group Alpha.

It did not take long before Pretoria decided that Operation Savannah had served its purpose and that the majority of South African troops – including the Bushman fighters attached to 31 Battalion – should come home.

There were some extremely valuable lessons taught while the fighting went on, the most important being that well-trained and reasonably equipped South Africans were more than a match for both the Angolan Army and many of the Cubans who were shoved into the front line in a bid to counter their advance.

Another surprise to emerge from Operation Savannah was that the ragtag group of Bushman fighters that Delville Linford knocked into shape at Omega did not take long to prove themselves extremely capable under some of the most difficult conditions yet encountered under fire. They were not to know it yet, but more hostilities followed and today, when we speak to veterans who served in the unit, those involved have nothing but praise for their old *compadres*.

There is no question, the business of making an efficient fighting unit out of refugees and what some people like to call 'primitives' was hard work, Delville recollected years later: 'I learned the hard way, but I'm thankful for the experience ...' True to the character of the man, his final thoughts are poignant:

'The task would never have been either possible or as successful as it became had it not been for that bunch of efficient and dedicated men that served with me in the unit.

I wish to mention the six young national servicemen that helped me chop open the bush where the Omega Base was finally established. They were Wouter du Plooy, Phil Erasmus, Chris Kies, Anthony Lloyd, Vaatjie van Heerden and Lance [surname unknown].

I wish to pay a special tribute to the men whose names are carved on the Roll of Honour. They paid a high price so that the people of

South West Africa – Namibia today – could be spared the horrors of war.

My time at Alpha came to an end late in 1977 and I was transferred to Windhoek where I had orders to initiate a similar operation with the people of South West Africa. It also meant that I left my Bushman *compadres* with a heavy heart. What I'd learned from those people cannot be bought with money. It was a once-in-a-lifetime experience and I am enormously pleased that I was the individual who can relate many of the things that took place. It was history in the making and I am grateful for having been a part of it.'

With United Nations Resolution 435, Namibia became an internationally recognised independent state in 1989. A few of the changes that followed had drastic results for some of the people involved in the 21-year long Border War, particularly for the Bushman communities that had given us such solid support, even if it was because their very survival depended on it.

One of the immediate implications, among others, was that 31 Battalion was disbanded. The Bushman troops involved were given the option of moving themselves and their families to a designated area within the frontiers of South Africa or remain within the confines of the Caprivi.

As we all know by now, the Bushman community had vivid memories of what had happened to their people in Angola when that country became independent. Consequently, a total of 372 Flechas decided to move south. They were settled at a military base at Schmidtsdrift then under the command of Commandant Scholtz van Wyk.

Omega was left vacant for a while, but was later occupied by the Namibian Army. It kept its name, but everything else at the original Omega base would never be the same again...

CHAPTER 30

Back to the Future
Al Venter

Recently, almost 40 years after Operation Savannah was launched, I again made contact with some of my old friends in what was once 31 Battalion (it subsequently became 201 Battalion Omega). I visited the village near Kimberley where the survivors and their families live today, not exactly a pretty picture but, compared to what is going on in Angola today, it could be a lot worse.

The place is listed as Platfontein on the map of the North Cape and is a short drive out of Kimberley on the road west to Schmidtsdrift.

Those who visit the settlement will find a number of surprises, including the fact that Platfontein is home to 7000 people, the majority descendants of the original Bushman fighters who served in the original combat unit.

There is also a bank, clinic, post office and significantly, a fairly new structure that houses an SABC unit that broadcasts programmes in both Khoikhoi dialects, !Xun and Khwe, still referred to as Barakwena and Vasekela by some old-timers.

Most striking was the 31/201 Battalions obelisk erected on a modest little stand in 2012: hallowed ground to those who fought in the war...

According to Moshe Maghundu, librarian and archivist at SABC Platfontein, the ceremony was broadcast live, details of which are held in the local SABC Media Library, the local information hub for audio and printed material related to both !Xun and Khwe communities. Obviously, somebody in government has taken notice of the needs of this tiny community because almost everybody living there survives on monthly pension payments.

First impressions of Platfontein are instructive. Though clearly economically depressed, the place is a lot tidier than some Cape Flats settlements. Also noteworthy are the number of South African army tents to be seen in many back yards and gardens: relics of a time gone by and quite a few of them obviously quite useful adjuncts where space is clearly at a premium.

My first objective on arrival at Platfontein was to make contact with the religious leader of the community, *Dominee* Mario Mahongo, whom I had met when I first started work on the book with Delville at a safari camp on the main coast road leading north out of Cape Town. This was under the auspices of Scholtz van Wyk, who had arranged for a group of these former Bushman combatants to drive to Cape Town, and we all had breakfast together in the camp dining room. Apart from Ds Mario there was also Kamamma Makua who, like his former Angolan colleague, had fought against insurgents while serving in the Portuguese Army.

Once Lisbon's forces had returned to Europe, he joined the National Front for the Liberation of Angola (FNLA), a political grouping that strongly opposed Luanda's Moscow-supported 'Popular Movement' or MPLA.

It was only after elements of the FNLA broke with the main political grouping and headed southwards into South West Africa that this Bushman force was gathered together and formed into a fighting group under Commandant Delville Linford.

I visited *Dominee* Mario Mahango at his modest home on the far side of Platfontein and his recollections of that period remain vivid. He was quite animated while talking about his personal history and, of course, the unit featured prominently.

Invited into his small office, which is set apart from the main house, we entered a room clustered with files and books that lined some of the walls. A brilliant red and green Portuguese flag adorned one of the walls, set off against a decorated ostrich shell on a shelf. A Bible lay open on the small table which was surrounded by comfortable wooden chairs. He indicated with a wave of his arm that we should be seated.

After a few preliminaries about family and friends coupled to questions about how Colonel Linford was getting on and what we'd last heard about the man, he sat down and we started to talk. It was then that he suggested we accept that while still in Angola, the Bushman people were quite a large force. He reckoned there must have been between 2000 and 3000 Bushman fighters spread about in eight separate military units in the southern province of Angola, which, he underscored, was a very large area.

'But then all of Angola is a very large area ... and when Lisbon still ruled, it was a very large war, which many people do not realise. It went on for about a dozen years,' he quietly stressed.

Ds Mahongo went on: 'The Portuguese Army wasted little time in getting us involved in the war and because we had been so badly persecuted by the black tribes – something that had gone on as long as anybody could remember – we were very willing participants.'

Animatedly, he emphasised that for many generations the Bushman people had been subjugated, often brutally, by African people: 'We were little more than slaves to them, doing their bidding ... if we protested we were slaughtered. It was as simple as that ...'

According to the *Dominee*, the Bushman fighters were paid monthly by the Portuguese, but it was minimal.

'I was working out of the Serpa Pinto headquarters at the time and somehow we managed, because we had no option. Remember, even Portuguese conscripts were paid subsistence wages ... but it wasn't all that tough because in those days five rands could buy you a shirt or a pair of trousers.'

As he recalled, he earned something like 1500 Angolan Escudos a month, at a time when there were 40 Escudos to the Rand: or by today's standards, less than R5000 a year. Also, he was married and already had a small family ... 'so things were, as they say, pretty well stretched ...'

His very early years started in the Cuito Cuanavale region of South Angola – he was born there in January 1952 – and that was where he learned many of his bushcraft tricks from his father. This included gathering honey and selling some of the skins of animals they had hunted. But though his dad died comparatively young, there were others who stepped into the role of traditional mentor.

'I also spent two years working in the coffee plantations in the north of the country near São Salvador, which is close to the Congo. That was where the first attacks took place from UPA terrorists who had crossed the frontier from the Congo and murdered tens of thousands of people. Which is why I decided to return home to my family, almost all of whom had remained in the south.

'At the same time the skills I'd been taught by my father and others who took over my upbringing stood me in very good stead. I'd already mastered many of the fundamental bush and tracking skills and could very effectively hunt with bow and arrow.

'It might not sound like much, but as youngsters, we were able to creep up to many of the animals in the bush – including eland and buffalo – and shoot them. It wasn't our arrows that killed these creatures of the wild, but the poison with which we tipped them. Once hit, the animal would run a short distance and drop. Then we would move in, disembowel and skin it and call for others from the village to come and remove the meat to safety.'

He recalls, too, how they had to guard their kills against predators like lion or hyena. If they failed to take these measures they could easily lose everything.

'But we were very good at all that ... very good indeed, which is why we were so valuable to the Portuguese.' Mario admits that there came a time when the Bushman fighters ranged against the insurgents were so effective that they were much feared.

'On our bellies, we could creep right up to their lines in the dark without their sentries being aware that we were there. Then, when morning came, the camp would rise and find that all the guards posted had been killed, every one of them with their throats cut ... obviously they had a good respect for our ability as bush fighters.'

As he recalls, it was a conflict where it wasn't always necessary to fight with a gun, though they were all issued with firearms by the Portuguese Army, the standard G3 rifle. 'Sometimes in the dark, a sharp blade is just as effective.'

Once Mario Mahongo and his tribal group had been moved across the border from an embattled Angola into the Caprivi region of South West Africa, a totally new phase began. For a start, they fell under the command of Commandant Delville Linford.

'It was very different working with the commandant when you compare it to what we went through in Angola. We had to completely readjust our lives, even though domestically, we still had our families with us and lived our lives very much as we did before.

'While our Portuguese commanders were fairly easy-going once we were operational – they expected results and we gave them the best of our ability – this South African officer was very strict and soldier-like, the truly professional military man, as we've all since come to realise.

'At the same time, he had spent quite a time in Lisbon's war and could speak good Portuguese, so we had no difficulties in communications. It was, as they say in Afrikaans *'oop kanale met hom'* (open channels with him).

'He was a man who we found it easy to talk to and we were able to quickly get his interest if something bothered us or we thought that a decision was wrong. Looking back on those early days, I think you can confidently say that he was a very good listener…'

According to Ds Mario, Linford was also quick to spot both the good and the bad, in all its guises…

'There were a few of us who were obviously listened to by our people and who could see what some people like to refer to as the 'bigger picture'. He put a few of us in charge of the unit – which is why I became a sergeant, and afterwards a staff sergeant.

'But he didn't tolerate slackness of any sort … he was very strict on discipline, even though Bushman discipline was often very different from the kind meted out to South African troopies who had been naughty.'

One of the questions I did ask this respected Bushman leader was whether his people ever had a name of their own for their commandant? He first looked away and then he smiled.

'Yes,' he said in his usual quiet voice, 'we did indeed have a name for that man, but I confess that it would be disrespectful of me if I were to disclose it.' I left it at that, though someone else said something about Delville Linford being called something along the lines of 'he who growls'.

I could never get confirmation, either from Mario or from his compatriot Kamamma Makua who is also an elder within the Platfontein community.

In an interview with General Jannie Geldenhuys, the former chief of the South African Defence Force (1985–90), Mario admitted in the general's book *We Were There* – his classic account of the SA Border War and the SADF's victory over Cuba – that this was an enormously emotional event.

The two men got together at Platfontein and spoke under a thorn tree in the *dominee*'s garden. Mario admitted to him that it was a sad time for him and his people after the Border War ended. The Bushman community faced almost naked aggression – *vyandigheid* was the word he used – from the newly elected black political order in the so-called Rainbow Nation. The ANC was also quite public about it.

'As they have been saying these past 40 years, we, the Bushman people, fought against black people [in Angola].' And that, he added, was demonstrably a vicious, hurtful lie (*'n eenvoudig kwaadwillige leuenagtige beswaddering*).

'Let's be honest. When we became members of the South African Defence Force and South West African ground forces, the various Angolan political and military groupings – and that includes the MPLA, FNLA as well as UNITA – were already all fighting against one another. And they were 99,9 per cent black. We became part of a conflict where it was overwhelmingly black against black. And now this [South African] government says to us that we don't like you because you fought against blacks ...'

His time with 31 Battalion, he explains, was very well spent, having served as a platoon sergeant for two or three years. Previously, while with Chipa Esquadrão, the FNLA offshoot that eventually turned to Pretoria for help, he'd held a fairly senior commissioned rank. From Omega, his first bush operations were in the Luiana area, south-east of Cuito and not far from the Zambian border.

In his interview with General Geldenhuys he also explains how in 1977 he was taken under the wing of Gert Theron, a military chaplain with the SADF. Though he did manage to complete his theological studies, he was never formally recognised as a chaplain while in the army. That came afterwards in 1986 once the Bushman community had been relocated.

Also at Platfontein, I was able to visit another of the stalwarts of the old battalion: Kamamma Makua, now in his seventies but still as strong and forthright as ever. Always a big man, well-built and as straight as a ramrod, old age had hardly withered him, though characteristically he was hugely emotional and on meeting again, it was big hugs and a few tears all round.

It had been Coen Upton who had originally introduced these Bushman leaders to Delville when he first arrived in Caprivi from Pretoria. Among them were Mario, José Pereira, Costa Diaz and, of course, the incorrigible Padua. Ostensibly, the leader of the group was Kamamma.

These Portuguese-speaking leaders were each in command of a group of Flechas, exactly as they had been grouped by Lisbon's commanders when they served militarily in Angola. Pereira was the senior man, in command of the !Xun with Lucas Strongo as their leader. Costa Diaz headed the Khwe group with Kamamma as their leader. Padua was not in a command position and immediate impressions suggested that he was the original 'odd jobs' man. It was Kamamma, though, who commanded the respect of all and his orders were always promptly carried out.

In summary, these leaders have walked the road with Delville through the past quarter of a century from the time they left Angola, through the Caprivi, and Schmidtsdrift to Platfontein. As Delville put it during one of our exchanges: 'The circle has been completed. This book is in remembrance of the humane, sometimes amusing, sometimes tragic stories that have been part of the lives of the Bushman fighters of 31 Battalion.'

It was possibly to be expected that something a little more melancholy would emerge and though it took a little time, the unit composed its own 'battle hymn', a fitting tribute and legacy to glories past and friends departed …

The War Song of the Alphans
We heed not the time of the day or night
We fear not a man or a beast
We be not on the pale bosoms of women
That whisper and sigh
We die not in the arms of mothers
That moan and weep
But we sleep 'neath the stars
And we march by the moon and the sun.

We have claimed for our own
This land that we love
From the still waters of the Cuando
To the rapids of Bagani
So we ask of you all
To leave us alone –
There is naught for you here
But death and despair.

Our arms are strong
And our eyes are true
Black Angel of Satan beware
For the Alphans have cured
Not a few of their evil ambition
With a medicine bitter and strong
And sent not a few to their doom
With a sword that is whet and keen.

Take heed black Serpent of Doom
Though you sneak in the grass
And leave not a trace
Our arrows will find you
And like many before
Your journey will end
In a heap of sand.

Epilogue

Schmidtsdrift, 75 kilometres west of Kimberley in the Northern Cape was a military training area with a notoriously harsh climate and terrain which was not kind to life and limb. On a frosty July 1990 morning, I was sitting in my office at the headquarters of 31 Battalion, contemplating the future of the almost 4000 Bushmen who had a short while before been relocated from Namibia. I had just finished reading a letter from Colonel Delville Linford. He had responded to my questions and suggestions about the continuation of the traditions of the battalion which he had founded 16 years earlier in the western Caprivi. The origin of the distinctive head dress – the Bonnie – was explained in great detail and he elaborated on the virtues of the men who proudly wore the Crow. In closing, he thanked me for asking his opinion … something which according to him, 'is not given freely'!

As the weeks became months, we had embarked with youthful enthusiasm on the re-establishment of 31 Battalion and the Bushman community. It gave me a glimpse of what the pioneers of the unit had to endure, and although we had different odds stacked against us, their efforts filled me with respect and awe. I realised that Delville Linford had laid the foundation of a unique military unit in a special way. Not only did he manage to endear the Bushman community to himself, but he also commanded respect from his soldiers and superiors. The commanders at all levels – officers, warrant officers, non-commissioned officers and men who succeeded him – had done a sterling job in establishing 31/201 Battalion as a formidable combat unit and home to the Bushmen. This would also not have been possible without the efforts of hundreds of national servicemen who passed through the gates of Omega. I recognised that we would never be able to emulate that, not in the unforgiving Northern Cape environment, nor against the fierce opposition from local groups to the permanent location of the battalion and the Bushman community. We nevertheless persevered, drawing strength from small victories over adversity and ever mindful of the enormity of the task at hand!

Enthusiasm very soon made way for cynicism and a feeling of hopelessness – even anger – when 31 Battalion, the home of the !Xun and Khwe, was prematurely and without consultation disbanded in March 1993 ... for reasons to this day yet to be revealed. Dreams of continuing the legacy of Delville Linford and all those who contributed to the wellbeing of these people were swept aside by the stroke of a pen. Hopes of a bright future in the New South Africa were sacrificed on the negotiating tables of political masters!

Delville and Nelle at his side made a last effort from 1996 to 1997 to guide and assist the Bushman community through this very difficult period. They returned to Schmidtsdrift and camped on the base. He was 'home' again and walking tall amongst his erstwhile comrades, albeit to assist in agricultural projects, youth development and missionary projects. The ever industrious Nelle continued with the home economics projects and ran the bakery, all the while spreading the Word.

In 2013 Delville and I met again when we travelled to Kimberley for the inauguration of the !Xun and Khwe: Angola to Platfontein Museum where the story of 31 Battalion and its brave soldiers will continue to live on. After spending 20 hours on the road listening to the legend sitting next to me sharing his memories and wisdom, sometimes interrupting him with questions and together enjoying long stretches of Karoo silence, I began making sense of my role at the battalion and its Bushman community.

For now though, let us celebrate life and the future of the !Xun and Khwe on their own land and toast those friends and comrades departed with a bottle of 'Old Crow Red Reserve', a blend of Ruby Cabernet and Merlot, combining the smokiness of a thousand Omega fires with the sweet smell of Bushmanland grass after a Namibian thunderstorm.

Salute!

Lieutenant Colonel Scholtz van Wyk

Acknowledgements

The scale and timeframe of this book is vast – it stretches over decades, though the period we are most focused on, Operation Savannah, late in 1975 lasted only a few short months.

The original plan was for me to cover the entire history of 31 Battalion (which eventually became 201 Battalion), but all things considered, that would have become a pretty voluminous volume, probably twice the length of this work. We finally decided on the tried and trusted maxim that less is more. So it is too, because we've managed to encapsulate some of the most interesting developments in the period immediately before – and for a while after – the formation of this remarkable fighting group.

Obviously, nothing would have happened without the generous support of the man himself, Colonel Delville Linford, and his lovely wife Nelle. Their contributions were seminal throughout and included not only person-to-person exchanges, notes, observations, photos and the rest, but also the series of manuscripts that this enterprising military man had written down in long-hand many years ago. It was left to Nelle to type it all out…

In truth, while my name appears on the cover of this book as co-author, almost all of that which is substantive came from Delville himself.

In producing this book, my role was simply to string it all together and add a few observations of my own that resulted from experiences on the periphery of what was going on further north in Angola at the time. It was simply good luck that I was in both Luanda and Nova Lisboa (Lubango today) at the time.

Several other individuals need to be recognised. The most important is certainly Scholtz van Wyk, the last serving commander of 31 Battalion before it was shafted sideways into obscurity by South Africa's new political dispensation. Scholtz showed great patience in waiting for completion and for this I am grateful. The bottom line, basically, is that had Scholtz not been at the helm, this book, simply put, would not have realised.

I am grateful, too, for the help given to me by my old friend Jan Breytenbach. I went to see him and his delightful wife Ros at Sedgefield and he came up with a lot of new data. Both powerful forces within themselves, Jan fondly remembers that 'Delville never followed the rules in a strictly military way and was always looking for ways to exploit the unexpected. I think that is why we got on so well. With his sense of humour he could make light of the worst combat situations until you thought it was all a big joke.' Jan also gave us permission to use one of the chapters involving that crazy battle around the airport at Benguela on Angola's western seaboard. That came from one of his best books – *Forged in Battle* – while in command of Combat Group Bravo.

During the course of gathering material for this work, one of the few surviving Bushman members of 31 Battalion, *Dominee* Mario Mahongo, who worked closely with then Commandant Linford in the early days, told me when I visited him at the new home of this Bushman community at Platfontein outside Kimberley that his recollections of this 'truly professional military man' were 'as clear as day'. He was humoristic and deeply human, as the colonel himself confessed after spending a few minutes on his knees in front of the altar in a Vila Nova do Seles chapel deep inside an extremely hostile Angola.

Interestingly, also at Platfontein with Ds Mario Mahongo was another Bushman leader, Kamamma Makua, also a former member of the original Portuguese Army Bushman unit.

A common friend of all these men was Inspector Oscar Cardoso, still alive, well and thriving in northern Portugal. He was one of two men who originally founded the Flechas. Cardoso's view was always that a military unit 'is the reflection of its commander and in this 31 Battalion was no exception'.

Brigadier General Kaas van der Waals (who, too, was involved in Operation Savannah) agrees. Given the manuscript to read prior to publication, he declared: 'I fully concur with this sentiment. 31/201 Battalion was a super unit and I only realised at a later stage – confirmed by Delville's book – that Combat Group Alpha, Delville's Bushmen, also substantially contributed to my and Combat Group Foxbat's successful completion of a virtually impossible mission.'

A few of the other names that come to mind while I worked on the book include Les Rudman, Koos Stadler, Dries Velthuizen, Bertus Steenkamp, Gawie Nel, Danie van den Berg, as well as many more. It would need another page to record them all, so I hope I am forgiven for not going into too much detail on that score.

Photographs were kindly obtained from the collections of McGregor Museum, SANDF Documentation Centre, Wouter du Plooy, Manuel Ferreira, Danie van den Berg, Petrus Roux, Coen Upton, Ziggy Hentze and Scholtz van Wyk.

I would be remiss if I did not mention the efforts and contribution of a young corporal who served under Colonel Linford in 41 Battalion at Luiperdsvlei, Windhoek in 1980: Tonie van Niekerk. It was Tonie who provided the wherewithal to get this book into print.

Tonie – who today lives in Limpopo – went on to become a very successful businessman, something he ascribes to the groundwork he assimilated under the guidance of the good colonel, backed by the kind of solid military training that the majority of young men who had been called up were given.

Production-wise, I would like to thank my long-suffering editor and co-conspirator Danél Hanekom, who once again kept things together.

Al. J. Venter
31 July 2015

Bibliography

Breytenbach, Jan, *Forged in Battle*, Protea Book House, Pretoria, 2014.
Debay, Yves, 'Angola and South West Africa: A Forgotten War (1975–89)', *Raids Magazine*, No. 44, July 1995.
Den Hertog, T.N., 'Diversity behind constructed unity: the resettlement process of the !Xun and Khwe communities in South Africa', Special Issue: Old Land, New Practices: The changing face of land and conservation in post-colonial Africa, *Journal of Contemporary African Studies*, Vol. 31, Issue 3, pp. 345–360, 2013.
Geldenhuys, Jannie (Gen.), *We Were There: Winning the War for Southern Africa*, Kraal Publishers, Pretoria, 2012.
Spies, F.J. Du T. & Du Preez, S.J., 'Operasie Savannah, Angola 1975–1976'; Pretoria, 1989.
Uys, Ian, *Bushmen Soldiers*, Helion and Company, UK, 2014.
Van der Waals, W. S., *Portugal's War in Angola 1961–1974*, Protea Book House, Pretoria, 2011.
Venter, Al J., *Mercenaries: Putting the World to Rights with Hired Guns*, Casemate Publishers, US & UK, 2014.

Interviews
Former members of 31 Battalion
Dominee Mario Mahongo, Platfontein, 2015
Brigadier General (Ret) W.S. (Kaas) van der Waals, Centurion, 2014
Colonel (Ret) Jan Breytenbach, Sedgefield, 2014
Lieutenant Colonel (Ret) Scholtz van Wyk, Cape Town, 2013–2015

Other sources
Manuscript by Delville Linford – "My Bushman Experience"
Manuscript by Delville Linford – "As the Crow Flies"
SANDF Documentation Centre, Pretoria
McGregor Museum, Kimberley